THE
BAREFOOT
SHOEMAKER

THE BAREFOOT SHOEMAKER

*Capitalizing on
the New Russia*

Vladimir Kvint

in collaboration with

Natalia Darialova

ARCADE PUBLISHING · NEW YORK

First Edition

Design and maps by GDS \ Jeffrey L. Ward

Library of Congress Cataloging-in-Publication Data

Kvint, V. L. (Vladimir L'vovich)
    The barefoot shoemaker : capitalizing on the new Russia / by
Vladimir Kvint in collaboration with Natalia Darialova. — 1st ed.
        p.   cm.
    Includes index.
    ISBN 1-55970-182-X
    1. Investments, American—Russia (Federation)   2. Investments,
Foreign—Russia (Federation)   3. Business enterprises, Foreign—
Russia (Federation)   4. Investments, American—Former Soviet
republics.   5. Investments, Foreign—Former Soviet republics.
6. Business enterprises, Foreign—Former Soviet republics.
I. Dar'ialova, Natal'ia.   II. Title.
HG5572.K85   1993
332.6′73′0947—dc20   91–44911

Published in the United States by Arcade Publishing, Inc., New York
Distributed by Little, Brown and Company

10   9   8   7   6   5   4   3   2   1

BP

Printed in the United States of America

To Liza and Valery Kvint—with love

Лизе и Валерии Квинт с любовью

"We all live under the same sky.
We just don't all have the same horizon."
—Konrad Adenauer

Contents

INTRODUCTION   1

CHAPTER 1 Stepping into the Ring   6

CHAPTER 2 Forging Ahead   25

CHAPTER 3 Dead Souls Awaken: The Russian Worker   43

CHAPTER 4 Inside a Soviet Enterprise: SibAuto   63

CHAPTER 5 The SibAuto Saga, Part II   88

CHAPTER 6 SibAuto, Part III: Things Turn Around   100

CHAPTER 7 Finding the Right Key   114

CHAPTER 8 In the Land of the Free Economic Zones   141

CHAPTER 9 The Free Economic Zones, Part II: Making
            Inroads Northeast   167

CHAPTER 10 Look Before You Venture   181

CHAPTER 11 The Beginning of a Beautiful Friendship   201

APPENDIX   213

INDEX   223

Acknowledgments

I wish to begin by thanking my parents, whose love and managerial skills started me out on the right path. There are many people who helped me with this book years before I began to write it. Vladimir Daryelsky, my first professor and one of the founders of the Norilsk Concern; Dr. Abel Aganbegian and Dr. Vasily Ivanchenko, whose approaches to the realities of the Soviet economy deeply influenced my thinking; and my good friend Dr. Alexander Granberg, now State advisor to President Yeltsin.

The Russian workers and engineers with whom I was associated over the years I thank, for they taught me how to live under inhuman conditions and maintain humanity.

The writer Natalia Darialova's gifts and enthusiasm helped bring this manuscript to light, and I am grateful to her.

Many of the ideas in this book first found expression in the pages of *Forbes* magazine and the *New York Times*, and I am also grateful to their editorial staffs. There are many others who deserve recognition: Barbara du Pont and Karl Hampe read an early version of the work and didn't laugh out loud; Evelyn and Arthur Rosenbloom; and Ann and Kenneth Bialkin.

I am especially pleased to thank my colleagues and friends at

Fordham University's Graduate School of Business Administration; my former colleagues at Babson College; and my new colleagues at Arthur Andersen.

I must single out my literary agent and friend Vicki Weiner, and Ron Weiner, whose invaluable support and belief in what I have to say forced me to put my thoughts to paper. I have sorely tried the patience and good nature of my publishers and editors at Arcade— Dick Seaver, Jeannette Seaver, and Tim Bent—and benefited from their skills. I am grateful to Tim for making my peculiar dialect readable, and for letting it keep my accent. Whatever awkwardness remains is my responsibility alone—as usual.

Lastly, it is impossible to list everyone who deserves mention here, but I want them to know that I am grateful to them for what is of greatest value in any part of the world, East or West: friendship.

THE
BAREFOOT
SHOEMAKER

Introduction

This book was written to help outsiders understand Russian business. It began as a guide to investment in the former Soviet Union, designed to show foreign businesses where to find the ravenous consumer markets and abundant resources in that vast and complex country, and how to make the most of them. But my experience with both the Russian and Western financial communities has taught me that simply showing where to find the free economic zones, oil fields, diamond mines, and coal deposits, or spewing out the latest unemployment and inflation figures, important though they might be, does not tell enough of the story. To consider long-term investment in Russia—the only type of investment really worth pursuing—outsiders will need to know *why* Russians do business the way they do.

Not every headache in Russian business can be attributed to our communist past. The dynamic between entrepreneurial initiative on the one hand, and repressive and autocratic ruling systems on the other, between the individual and the state, goes much further back. The recent years of explosive change stem from ethnic, social, political, and, most of all, economic struggles that have been waged for centuries. I therefore decided that any guide to investment in Russia needed to widen its horizon, so that it could include larger perspectives, not just recent statistics.

My own perspective on the business culture in the former Soviet Union is somewhat unique. Twenty-five years of experience, first as a simple laborer and then as deputy general director of a Siberian industrial company, combined with a professorship in Moscow, meant that when I came to the West for the first time in 1989, I knew what was really going on in my country. I take great pride in having predicted the collapse of the Soviet Union years before it seemed imaginable to the rest of the world—but I had only half the picture. Lively discussions with Henry Kissinger, Zbigniew Brzezinski, Inge and Arthur Miller, Gail Sheehy, and Vasily Leontev, among others, helped me understand what outsiders needed to know about Russia and gave me the other half, as did my consulting work with European and North American companies. Taken together, my experiences in the East and West have given me a clear view of how they might help each other—and profit from the experience.

I have long felt frustrated that trade agreements and economic cooperation between the Soviet Union and the outside world did not go far enough. In 1990, during interviews with the *Chicago Tribune*, I argued that the situation in the Middle East and the emergence of a strong Russian government created fertile soil for growing cooperation between the United States and its former antagonist. My reasoning was simple: the United States is the world's largest oil consumer; the former Soviet Union is its leading oil producer. Shipping oil from the Ob-Yenisey region to the States would cost approximately one-third less than shipping it from Saudi Arabia. America is the world's largest automobile manufacturer; Russia is potentially one of the world's largest auto markets, once the move to a market economy has been made. (It still takes ten years' pay for the average Russian to come up with the money to buy a car.)

Now, Russia is opening for business. Boris Yeltsin and the progressive wing of the Russian Parliament have pushed through an enormous amount of legislation in the last few years, especially in recent months, and it is beginning to alter the investment picture radically. Whoever survives the power struggles, the process Yeltsin has helped set in motion is unstoppable, in my opinion, even if the pace is uneven. Each month, foreign investors create nearly a hundred new joint ventures, 12 percent involving American money. Privatization is on the fast track. By January 1993, the Russian government had privatized forty-six thousand enterprises, 25 percent of which were retail stores, 10 percent restaurants and cafeterias, 15 percent in services, 5 percent in construction, 3 percent in transportation, and 2 percent in heavy industry. Those percentages say a great deal about where the government recognizes a need for immediate change (consumer products and services), and which sectors are changing more slowly (heavy industry and the infrastructure). They also should tell foreign investors where to look. Recently enacted laws governing private businesses and land ownership, spearheaded by Boris Yeltsin, are specifically designed to attract foreign businesses, and offer them very attractive conditions, such as tax holidays and other forms of subsidy.

Foreign businesses in Russia will not be strangers in a strange land. Along with the other changes going on in the former Soviet Union, traditional capitalist institutions are developing. There are now more than twenty-five hundred private banks, four hundred and fifty commodity exchanges, two stock exchanges, and several thousand brokerage houses. More will come. The best news recently is that Russia has become part of the International Monetary Fund.

But doing business in Russia means understanding differences, not just opportunities. These differences can be basic. A simple example: asking a Russian "What can I do for you?"—merely a polite and fairly noncommittal formulation to an American—is to pose a very serious question. He might very well startle you by making a specific request. He might also come right out and ask you how much money you make, and then be confused when his question is taken for rudeness. He would be surprised if anyone took offense at a filthy joke. He will be offended if his new business partner doesn't join him in polishing off a bottle of vodka.

My point is that business in Russia is not just business as usual; it is deeply personal and idiosyncratic. There is, strictly speaking, no "Western logic" to business calculations. Russians are unabashedly moved by their emotions and motivated by their immediate reactions to personalities and situations. Money still talks in Russia, as in the West, but it doesn't always use the same dialect. This is why—though I tout the infinite opportunities (the untapped resources crying out for attention in Siberia and the Russian Far East, for example)—I will be candid about the problems foreigners might have in taking advantage of them. I know from experience that they might make all the right moves and still not succeed.

Rather than a dry catalog of do's and don'ts, this book provides examples and anecdotes I have culled from my years in mines, factories, Kremlin corridors, and on board research expedition ships. It will introduce readers to some of my more memorable contacts, high and low, from government ministers to truck drivers. They will illustrate not only the character of the Russian worker in all of his true glory, but the nature of the system that for so long kept him from achieving all that he might.

I believe very strongly that one can do business with Russians only if one understands how, over the years, they have survived despotism, whether at the hands of czars and or at the hands of the Politburo. Tyranny has created paradoxes of every nature in my country: labor shortages and high unemployment, heartbreaking poverty and fabulous natural wealth, entrepreneurial ingenuity and bureaucratic lumpishness. We became a nation of barefoot shoemakers. Either we had the productive capacity but not the raw materials, or the raw materials but not the productive capacity. Things are changing, slowly. A second requirement for doing business with Russians is understanding how they are adjusting to new business freedoms, and the responsibilities that come with them.

Teaching at Fordham University's Graduate School of Business Administration and acting as a consultant to Western companies considering joint ventures have also made me aware of what expectations foreigners, particularly Americans, bring when they sit down to negotiate with Russians. It is therefore easier for me to locate the pitfalls—and there are pitfalls.

The republics have gone through so many changes so rapidly over the last few years that it is sometimes difficult to say where old habits leave off and new ones begin. Outsiders can take precious little for granted. The Soviet command economy contorted commercial transactions to such a degree that although Russians might be very sophisticated about some aspects of business operations, basic concepts—involving accounting, for example—escape them. There is no traditional business culture. The capitalist institutions previously mentioned are new and sometimes function erratically. The banking, legal, and taxation systems are evolving by trial and error. Interest rates are scandalously low; inflation is disastrously high. Yeltsin's fiscal policies, though infinitely more innovative than Gorbachev's, have not always been sound. He has tended to solve serious economic problems by printing more money. Last, although there is no danger of another coup, in my opinion, political stability—as anyone who reads a newspaper or watches CNN can see—is not a given. Democratic institutions in Russia are as new as free-market institutions.

They are linked. Democratic and capitalist traditions can survive individually only if they *both* survive. That is why I hope this book will speed the flow of intelligently invested foreign capital: so that both democracy and capitalism will be strengthened. Like so many others whose work I admire and follow, inside and outside Russia, my vision of the future sees a blurring of the distinction between East and West. Even now, if Russians and Westerners look far enough, they will see they share the same horizon.

CHAPTER 1

Stepping into the Ring

When I was five I almost drowned in a barrel of transformer oil at a Siberian construction site. It was my baptism into the oil business. I recalled this little misadventure one afternoon not too long ago while looking out of the fortieth-floor window of a Manhattan skyscraper. I was listening to representatives from an American consulting company (ACC, as I'll call it) as they tried, as it were, to pump oil out of the Russian Minister of Geology's pockets. ACC was hoping to negotiate the right to develop a region of eastern Siberia with the richest oil, gas, diamond, copper, nickel, and cobalt deposits in the former Soviet Union. I knew that handled carefully the project could mean hundreds of millions of dollars in profits; I also knew it would involve a sophisticated interplay of political forces, business interests, and big money.

The Russian minister—Minister H., I will call him—had just arrived in New York and was suffering from serious jet lag. He had come directly from a session of the Russian Parliament, where historic legislation permitting ownership of private property had just been enacted (I will discuss that legislation later). Jet-lagged or not, Minister H.'s presence at the New York meeting was yet another sign that the gulf between Russia and America was closing rapidly. This convergence was possible, ironically, only because the Soviet Union was coming apart at the seams.

I take some credit for having predicted the breakup long before most people did; not because of some grand revelation, but simply by looking at the numbers and assessing their political significance. In 1978, I began writing a twenty-year forecast of Soviet economic development. By the time I had finished the paper in 1981, the future collapse of the Soviet Union was clear to me. I knew the real—not the official—figures and the true condition of the Soviet economy, from the deepest mines to the towering tops of Kremlin offices. The economic basis of tyranny had been deteriorating since 1970. Over the next fifteen years, the gross national product's rate of growth declined two-thirds. This mounting economic crisis forced the communist leadership to swap guns for butter, and to open up a quarter of the earth as a new market for the rest of the world.

Contrary to the common belief in the West, Gorbachev did not invent perestroika (literally, "reconstruction"). Perestroika's basic concepts date back to 1979, when national income (again, using actual rather than official figures) grew by a mere 2 percent. For a population increasing two million a year, that actually meant 0-percent growth. Preparation for economic reforms became more active under Andropov and continued under Chernenko, though not because either of these two Party bosses were in favor of it; neither Soviet leader viewed reform as a mechanism for democratic change. In the West, many called Gorbachev the Great Liberator, but he, like his predecessors, was motivated by his insider's knowledge that the economy was galloping at breakneck speed toward collapse—a collapse that would threaten the Communist Party's absolute power.

Gorbachev does deserve credit for continuing reforms and for glasnost—that precious ration card of freedom. However, even the vaunted glasnost did not permit anyone to criticize the president. In 1991, Gorbachev insisted that a resolution be passed by the Soviet Parliament warning newspapers and periodicals that under no circumstances would they be permitted to write negative things about him. He got his resolution, but Soviet journalists, who were beginning to flex their editorial muscles, were little pleased, to say the least. Gorbachev might have tried to rebuild the economy using Stalinesque methods, but didn't (the world had evolved beyond the point where such despotism would have been acceptable). However, his more liberal methods didn't prevent him from trying to assume dictatorial power, as he did in January of 1991, when he sent tanks into Lithuania. By that point, thankfully, the hour for tyranny had passed and he was rebuffed.

By 1989, it had become clear to me that Russia would soon become independent from the Soviet Union, and that it would begin more aggressively to invite foreign investment. In February of 1990, *Forbes* magazine made my article "Russia Should Quit the Soviet Union" its cover story for that issue. Almost two years later, in December of 1991, Russia declared its independence. Boris Yeltsin, leader of the movement toward freedom and a market economy, became the first democratically elected president in Russia's thousand-year history.

The open warfare between Gorbachev and Yeltsin that began in the fall of 1990 helped open Soviet doors to foreign investment even further. The Russian Parliament, led by Yeltsin, moved toward a free market by adopting progressive legislation. Overnight, Yeltsin released all Russian banks from the Soviet banking system and broke the central government's monopoly over foreign trade and currency transactions.

In spite of the political disarray, American corporations almost immediately showed a keen interest in doing business with Russia (though, as I will show, they lagged for a time behind Japan and the Europeans). By January of 1993, total American investment had exceeded the $3-billion mark. Pepsico signed a $3-billion, multiyear trade pact, and McDonald's invested $50 million in a food processing plant. General Electric chairman John F. Welch has proven especially adept at doing business in Eastern Europe. The corporate leadership of GE scrupulously monitors political and economic trends in Russia and, as a result, has built a core of expertise in technology transfer, export control regulations, and in dealing with regional governments. Some 280 to 300 major projects of natural resource development and industrial construction involving foreign companies are currently under way.

You don't have to be a GE or some other anointed member of the *Fortune* 500 to do business in Russia and succeed. Many smaller companies, unknown in their own countries, are rising to prominence in Russia—establishing boards of trade, television stations, fashionable restaurants, consulting groups, and even large industrial co-ventures. Thousands of small and medium-size deals and ventures are also starting up. In Russia, foreign businessmen these days enjoy something akin to celebrity status. Most Russians now understand that integration with the outside world, and in particular with the

West, is the only way of salvaging the economy. Chancellor Bismarck once quipped, "It takes the Russians a long time to harness, but once they do they ride quickly."

Meanwhile, back on the fortieth floor of the Manhattan skyscraper, the negotiations between ACC and Minister H. were interrupted by a sudden thunderstorm. The leaden sky over Manhattan rumbled, and gusting winds made the windows shudder. As for the climate inside the room, it was equally unsettled.

One of ACC's directors had arrived late, apologetically explaining that the storm was the cause. Minister H. smiled, and I understood why. A Russian boss would never have apologized. A Russian boss is never late; he has merely been delayed.

Despite the glorious opportunities for profitable East-West cooperation, the differences—here personified by the ACC director and Minister H.—can be daunting. The basic Russian management structure is a source of confusion to foreign companies. Which authorities should they contact? Which level of management is responsible for what type of decision? Or, as Frank Stenkard, vice president of Chase Manhattan Bank, put it so bluntly: "Who the hell are you supposed to negotiate with?"

Doing business in Russia is very often a matter of manipulating those who hold power—once you have located them. In fact, it is important to recognize that, unlike in the West, decisions are *not* based *primarily* on economic considerations. Instead, the players who dance among the overlapping rings of power evaluate a deal by how much it will add to or subtract from their personal clout. The entire Soviet structure, and the bureaucratic structures that have taken its place in the various republics, are geared not to profit, but to power and privilege, and it will take a long time for that mentality to change. To deal with Russians successfully, you must go through two or three opposing parties and find a way to make them work together.

Because politics and ideology still govern business decisions, commerce in my country is inordinately complicated, and many outsiders are too discouraged to get involved. "I wouldn't invest a nickel in that mess," I often hear Americans say. "Too confusing; more trouble than it's worth." Yet a study I did (featured in the March 31, 1992, edition of the *Christian Science Monitor*) shows not only a marked rise in foreign business, but a success ratio higher there than it is in many Western countries. Those who throw in the towel too soon will miss out. Foreign discouragement stems from a lack of understanding of how things work. Russian business methods might indeed be at times complex and Byzantine, but the rate of success is considerably higher in the former Soviet Union (about 33 percent by my estimate) than it is in Manhattan or Zurich.

ACC, though a novice in Russian business, had taken a very promising first step. From the beginning, they had focused on the major Siberian oil fields and the plentiful natural resources that vast part of the world offers for potential development.

How did they find out about them? I had advised ACC to make contact directly with a Russian enterprise when they needed reliable information. Had they gone first to the Ministry of Geology or some other government agency, they would have been fed false information and gotten nowhere. Foreign businesses should be skeptical about all figures and data offered by government officials. They are masters of the "double lie squared." Any information channeled to them has already been doctored by the so-called First Department, which operates within every State-owned enterprise (and many private ones). The Central Statistical Bureau contained its very own distortion division, and employees there were proud of their creativity. Most would have made first-rate writers of science fiction. According to an old saying, there are small lies, bigger lies, whopping lies, and statistics. This is especially true in Russia.

Decades of Soviet paranoia about any sort of open disclosure made matters even worse. A prodigious amount of humdrum information was given the same classification as figures dealing with the nuclear arsenal. This is why foreigners are more likely to receive accurate information from the managers of enterprises at the grassroots level than from any official source. I was recently invited to join the advisory board for the *Russian Oil and Gas Sourcebook*, which would provide figures to potential investors. When I discovered, however, that not one of the other members of the board actually worked in the industry, I knew it would be a waste of time and declined the invitation. My advice to foreign businesses is that they gain access to several sources so that they can compare and contrast information. Not only does this make financial good sense, but provides highly comical reading.

Unlike the typical Soviet bureaucrat, the general director of the Siberian geophysical company ACC approached immediately showed them the best oil field in his region. It also happened to be one of the best in the entire country. He was eager to do business with the West, and he and the ACC manager hit it off from the start. American executives often find Russian managers eager to open dialogue with them. Russian managers are "among the most brilliant and well-educated people compared to their colleagues worldwide," said Motorola's senior vice president David Bartram. Admittedly, they have much to learn about the free market, but as Ronald Weiner, president of Weiner Associates, a New York-based accounting company, says, "You don't have to be that smart to do business. You just have to do it often."

In fact, ACC and the Siberian general director got along so well they got carried away by their initial success. They forgot about the ministry, Big Brother, who was represented at that Manhattan meeting by Minister H.—and he looked none too pleased. The general director had overestimated the extent of his powers. For openers, he had no hard currency to pay for consulting services. (In this case, a moot point because ACC expected to be paid by foreign oil and gas developers it would bring to the region.) Next, although he was in a position to sign an agreement with a foreign consulting company, and to search for Western investors, he was not empowered to authorize a foreign company to produce and export oil.

Because of its inexperience with the Russian system, ACC didn't know about such basic limitations. Matters weren't helped when the director displayed a typically unrealistic Russian optimism that his deal with ACC would pass unnoticed by Minister H. and other bureaucrats.

Regrettably, I entered the picture after the mistake had been made; otherwise, I would have informed ACC that any Russian company wanting to deal internationally in the areas of natural resources and high technology must first get permission from the appropriate ministry. Exporting natural resources from the former Soviet Union requires a license and later an export quota. Before negotiating, potential investors should find out whether a given company is allowed to conduct international business; and if so, whether it has done all of the paperwork. No deal should be finalized without it.

ACC might have been smart to go directly to the Russian company, but they should have verified that the director had obtained permission from the Ministry of Geology *prior* to negotiations. Had the ministry been consulted earlier, it most likely would have cooperated with ACC. Because the director consulted the ministry after the fact, however, it responded negatively. The Russian director had thus encroached on the ministry's monopoly on making these decisions. Bureaucrats are enamored of their right of refusal. (One Ukrainian official I knew liked to respond to requests by saying he was "satisfying the request by way of refusal.") Under the gray Manhattan sky, Minister H. was exercising his government-given right.

The ministry also hadn't misled anyone. The consulting agreement arrived at between ACC and the Russian firm didn't commit the ministry to saying yes automatically. It had given the Russian director advance warning, rather than saying to him (as it easily could have) "Sure, go ahead and consult!" and only afterward informing whomever he contracted with that the ministry opposed the project.

My advice to ACC was to not give up. A no from the bureaucratic mandarins doesn't necessarily mean defeat. Soviet bosses, and now their successors, are commonly referred to as "lumps," because innovation or change is not in their nature; it threatens them. They are also mortally afraid of going too far in any direction—being either too conservative or too progressive. If you can convince them that what you propose is the safest and most sensible course, they might go along. Like the lumps, the very ministries that are supposed to increase free-market activity sometimes impede progress by passing restrictive regulations, such as the ones they placed on intermediary companies in 1989 in an effort to retain a monopoly on export trade. (These regulations were done away with by Yeltsin in 1991.) However, in that no governing body in the former Soviet Union is united in any sort of agreement, there is always room for maneuvering. A company preparing to do business in Russia should remember a central tenet of the Russian mentality: They are right who take more rights.

During the negotiations between ACC and the Russian company, I realized that the director's negligence was only one of the reasons for the negative response from the ministry. Political events of the time, and in particular the power struggle between Gorbachev and Yeltsin, had played their part. Two colossal scandals in recent history obviously influenced Minister H.'s decision: the Chevron-Tengiz scandal and the Case of the 140 Billion, which was fabricated to destroy Yeltsin before the 1991 presidential election. The story behind both bears retelling.

Yeltsin became president of Russia in June of 1991—a development that hit Gorbachev, who was on his way to Canada and the United States, with the impact of a surface-to-air missile. His standing at home was deteriorating. (According to a Russian joke at the time, one morning Gorbachev was talking to his portrait in his office.

"Well, old chum," he said, "soon they'll be taking us down." "You are a fool, Misha," replied the portrait. "They will take me down. You they'll hang.") With his power and prestige beginning to slip, Gorbachev needed all of the support he could muster in the United States. He had to offer something concrete in exchange for that support, and what he offered, to Chevron, was the Tengiz oil project.

Tengiz, a region in Kazakhstan, was estimated to be sitting on approximately thirty billion barrels of oil, more than two trillion cubic meters of gas, and more than six hundred million tons of sulphur. The Soviet Union simply did not have the resources to develop such deposits, and over the years, a number of foreign corporations from the United States, Saudi Arabia, and Turkey vied for the opportunity. At last, Chevron stepped in and proposed investing $1 billion over a two- to three-year period in a joint venture, but the manner in which it structured the deal was ill considered; it created a political bombshell that shook the dark corridors of power: the offices of Gorbachev and Kazakh president Nazarbaev.

From the outset, the project, which had already started just before the Soviet-American summit meeting in the summer of 1990, was mired in politics—and linked to a law that, when passed, would finally give Soviet citizens the right to travel or emigrate. Passage of the law was pending in the Soviet Parliament, and a sore point in the negotiations with the Americans. For decades the Soviet Union had been a prison. No one could leave. The issue of emigration had long been at the center of the fight between the Communists and the forces of democracy, and the American government was pressing hard for the passage of the law by making it a condition for granting the Soviet Union Most Favored Nation status.

Hard-line communists were determined to prevent its passage no matter what the cost in terms of trade (and in terms of lost profits). It is in the nature of diehards to die hard. Retaining power meant maintaining absolute control over the movements of their people. Relinquish that control, they reasoned, and you're history. Under pressure from both the Americans and communist hard-liners, Gorbachev turned the emigration and travel law into a ruse, just like the one in the Russian folk tale in which a con man sells his dog, which later runs back to him; he resells it again and again. Gorbachev "sold" the emigration law many times.

Gorbachev had to find something else to offer the Americans; his Most Favored Nation status was pending. At the height of American Gorbymania, Bush rolled out the red carpet for him and signed a trade agreement. In return, the Soviet Ministry of Oil and Gas signed a letter of intent with Chevron, offering them half the oil they drilled from the region and granting them permission to export it for profit. Twenty percent of the oil was to belong to Kazakhstan.

Both trade documents were really nothing more than symbolic exchanges between two presidents, in that the American trade agreement had first to be ratified by the U.S. Congress and the Soviet Parliament. The Soviet "letter of intent" was a long way from being a binding contract. In any case, the documents were doomed: both Gorbachev and the Soviet Parliament are gone.

Gorbachev's rhetoric about creating a free-market system was really just a dog and pony show for the Americans. He cut the oil deal by using the old Soviet-style *blat*, instead of genuinely opening the country to the market system. Blat is Russian for "connections," and because of shortages in Russia it rules practically all aspects of life there. If you have blat with a butcher, he will hand you a piece of sirloin at the back door while giving everyone out front bones. At times, it almost seems blat is behind every transaction. Even a plot at a cemetery is difficult to get without it. A Georgian decided to secure a place for himself at a prestigious cemetery in Moscow and offered a bribe to the cemetery manager.

"It is almost impossible," the manager told the Georgian, taking his money, "but let me see what I can do."

A short while later, the manager returned. Beaming, he told the Georgian, "The impossible has happened. I have succeeded in finding a place for you." Then he paused and added, "But you have to move in today."

A popular saying has it that when blat dies no one will be able to bury it. No one will have either nails or a coffin.

Once designated, Chevron immediately pursued high-level contacts in the Gorbachev government, which, under normal circumstances, would have been the right thing to do. However, the company overestimated the influence of these contacts, and underestimated the new, more powerful role public and scientific opinion was beginning to play. Perhaps there was no way Chevron could have been sufficiently sensitive to this new role. In any event, it rode into the Soviet Union like an emperor on horseback. It wasn't exactly greeted by cheering subjects; in fact, no one knew anything about Chevron. What's in a name? If you're on your home ground—everything. I would have advised Chevron to establish an image in the marketplace by talking to the scientists and granting interviews. Had

Chevron's directors been more familiar with the country, they would have known that such a major project would not escape the public scrutiny it came under, and might have been more prepared for the heat. ELF Aquitaine, the French oil giant, was much more sensitive to local problems and concerns, and as a result landed an excellent contract for a second oil field in Kazakhstan.

Napoleon once said, "He who wants too much will lose everything." He tried to swallow Russia and choked on it. The ministry thought Chevron was being too greedy. It objected to the provision that Chevron would keep half the oil it extracted. A bigger problem was that the deal seemed unfair to the Soviet people, just as it would have to Americans had the reverse happened in the United States. Imagine if a British or a French corporation set up shop in Texas and then proposed a similar arrangement. Chevron negotiated a noncompetitive deal, and it did not appear as though it was putting in as much money as it planned to take out. The notion of a foreign company cutting itself half the pie does not offend Russians as long as the company is anteing up its fair share of costs—and this was not clear with Chevron. When the information about the arrangement with Chevron leaked, the deal began to fall apart.

The Case of the 140 Billion came to light on a chilly February afternoon in 1991 at the Moscow International Airport, Sheremetievo-2. Colin S. Gibbins, a British citizen, was hurrying to cross the customs barrier. Gibbins had good reason to hurry; his modest-looking briefcase was as stuffed as a pirog (Russian pastry) with documents detailing plans for a $7-billion deal. Just as he was about to step across the last barrier, the heavy hand of the KGB fell on his shoulder.

Soviet newspapers announced that the affair led all the way to the Deputy Prime Minister of Russia. Spearheaded by Yeltsin, the Russian government, said the papers, had tried to sell 140 billion rubles at the rate of 18 rubles to the dollar—a sweetheart of a deal, considering that the official rate valued the dollar at less than one ruble. "They're selling Russia down the river!" nationalist groups screamed.

The authorities willingly disclosed the documents bearing on criminal case 18/5922-91 to journalists, describing the crime as an act of glasnost "run amok." On February 5, 1991, the case hit the front pages of newspapers around the world.

The true reasons for the scandal were once again rooted in the power struggle between Yeltsin and Gorbachev, or, to put it another way, between the Russian government and the Soviet government. In December of 1990, two months before the scandal broke, Yeltsin was winning the battle for supremacy with Gorbachev. He set a goal to establish a free market. He welcomed professional advice. His popularity was widespread and deep. Time was on Yeltsin's side, no matter what Gorbachev did to forestall Yeltsin's final victory and stir up trouble—such as cutting grain supplies to Russia or blocking the flow of hard currency.

Another Gorbachev maneuver was to have the Soviet Ministry of Finance and the Ministry of Justice cut practically all contacts with Silaev's Russian government. Ivan Silaev had become prime minister of Russia in June of 1990 and was fighting on Yeltsin's side. (Today, Silaev is Russia's trade representative in Belgium.) Try though he might, however, Gorbachev could not split the alliance between Silaev and Yeltsin, in part because Silaev had been personally offended by Soviet Prime Minister Pavlov when Pavlov was Soviet Minister of Finance. Pavlov had apparently collected evidence of Silaev's alleged "mistakes" in his capacity as a Soviet deputy prime minister in 1989 and then snitched on him like a schoolboy. Silaev never forgave him.

Concerned over popular unrest in the Russian republic, Silaev's government chose the only possible way of satisfying, at least temporarily, the widespread hunger for consumer goods: a deal with the West. But how? To export from Russia one needed a state license, and the Soviet government issued licenses unwillingly. (Now, of course, things are different. Pavlov is in jail.) Russia's hands were tied. The keys to the border gates were still in Gorbachev's hands. The easiest way—the only way—to import consumer goods was to make a so-called transfer deal.

Silaev assigned Deputy Premier Gennady Filshin to develop the economic basis for the transaction. Filshin's appointment was informal, a deal struck between a boss and his deputy. I have known Filshin for years, having first met him when I ran the Krasnoyarsk (Siberia) branch of the Economic Institute of the Academy of Sciences. Filshin held a similar position in Irkutsk. We saw each other at conferences and worked on reports together. I got to know him particularly well during an economic expedition to Mongolia in 1987. He is a flamboyant and controversial figure, and a strongly market-oriented economist. Filshin did a fine job with the economics of the transfer deal. But as a politician he lacked finesse, and this proved fatal.

Russia was prepared to sell 140 billion rubles and buy seven billion dollars. The idea was to find a foreign company to take the $7 billion and buy consumer goods and foodstuffs from the West, which it could turn around and sell in the Russian market for rubles. These rubles were then to be invested in chemical, oil, lumber, and metallurgical enterprises recommended by the Russian Council of Ministers. The Western partners in the deal would get paid in goods produced by these enterprises, and these they could export to the West to sell. Convoluted, yes, but potentially highly profitable.

A foreign company eager to do business soon materialized, and Comrade Deputy Minister of Trade went to Zurich to sign contracts for the first $2 billion. Hyposwiss Bank and Barclays Bank backed the seller. The mysterious Mr. Gibbins entered into an agreement with Eurofin, Ltd.

That the deal would have been beneficial to Russia was lost on Gorbachev, who was too busy trying to discredit Yeltsin. Although ultimately investigators could uncover no wrongdoing or violations, the "selling of Russia" played well to the press. Calling Yeltsin's Russian government on the "precipice of corruption," Oleg Moshaiskov, a member of the Soviet State bank board, held a news conference. Moshaiskov told journalists, "This crime proves just how damaging decentralization will be." Moshaiskov didn't know that Prime Minister Pavlov—known in Russia, with some affection, as the Shaved Porcupine because his hair stands up on end—had already prepared the way to lower the official exchange rate. In just two months, foreigners were able to exchange one dollar for 27.5 rubles. In March of 1993, the rate was 597 rubles to the dollar.

This fabricated Case of the 140 Billion, together with the tanks Gorbachev sent to enforce his "peaceful" solutions in Lithuania, emptied the final drops from his reservoir of support. The strategy didn't catch Yeltsin completely unawares. He understood that Gorbachev hoped to turn a reasonable way of getting hard currency into a criminal case. Russia's parliament under Yeltsin appointed a committee to investigate the situation, and the man chosen to head the committee was Deputy Alexander Pochinok. I found his appointment somewhat surprising.

Two years earlier, Pochinok had been a Ph.D. candidate in my institute in Moscow and often came to me for advice. Although proficient enough for a young economist, I thought Pochinok extremely naive when it came to the time-honored Soviet sport of political hide-and-seek. He entered the ring outweighed and outclassed, and the pressure was so intense it pushed him over the edge. When asked to comment on the case by *Commercant*, the most prestigious business newspaper in the former Soviet Union, all that the normally shy and retiring Pochinok could do was yell, "Do you want a punch in the nose?" Today, Pochinok is chairman of the Budget Committee of the Russian Parliament (which says a great deal about just how weak the parliament is).

My colleague Filshin was also hung out to dry. "I hold nothing against you personally," he was told by KGB chief Vladimir Kruchkov. For once this was true. Kruchkov was going after much bigger fish.

Gorbachev was trying to brand Yeltsin as a traitor to Russia, and Yeltsin, like any chess player finding himself in a trap, knew that he would have to sacrifice a piece. He chose Filshin, who resigned from his post. His resignation worried several of my American clients. Because Filshin had approved their projects, they were concerned that those projects would go down with him. I calmed their worries by explaining that Filshin had not violated the law and not only would not go to prison but was likely to get a new job and become a powerful figure once again.

I still wonder to this day how Gibbins found his way to this chessboard. He is a mysterious figure, and it almost appears as though he had dropped out of someone's sleeve in the middle of the game. Even his company, Dove Trading International, seemed suspicious. It is not registered in Britain but in South Africa, and was founded on February 23, 1990; the month and day mark the anniversary of the creation of the Soviet army. Perhaps this "dove" had flown onto the chessboard not from South Africa, but from Moscow. At any rate, he was only briefly detained by the KGB before being released.

The brouhaha didn't turn out so badly for Yeltsin, who learned an invaluable lesson. Had he publicized the deal from the beginning, Gorbachev wouldn't have dared break it. A master of bureaucratic infighting, Gorbachev threw a haymaker at Yeltsin. Yeltsin ducked and countered in the old Party style—by firing a deputy. He rewarded Filshin for taking the fall with a prestigious job, appointing him Deputy Minister of Foreign Economic Affairs of Russia. (Today he serves as Russia's trade representative in Austria.) Next time, Yeltsin knew better. He realized it would always be difficult for him to fight Party sabotage without starting a noisy squabble. Therefore, he followed Russian wisdom and "killed seven with one bullet" by issuing a decree prohibiting any Party activity in State enterprises—a move that greatly weakened its ability to meddle in policy.

Meantime, the Chevron-Tengiz deal had stalled. One year after the Washington summit, two Soviet committees issued a negative statement about the deal. The project, they said, would prove unprofitable for the Soviet Union, and although they were generally in favor of joint oil exploration, they suggested that the right to develop such a rich oil field be won through a competitive bidding process. There was no official word the deal was off, however.

Russians are fond of saying that the deeper you go into the forest, the more lost you become in the trees. Chevron made new mistakes. More articles criticizing the deal appeared in even the most progressive newspapers—the *Moscow News* and *Commercant*. *Moscow News* correspondent Mikhail Gurtovoy, a skilled and respected journalist from Siberia, with whom I had coauthored a book, wrote a series of investigative articles raising eyebrows around the country. Because of his investigative work, Gurtovoy was appointed, in 1992, chairman of a committee to investigate financial crime.

Chevron replied in a peculiar way: by writing an angry letter to the *Moscow News*. I don't know who Chevron's public relations advisors were, but they gave the company some regrettable advice. (In Russian, such advice is called "a bear's hug," meaning that you let yourself get trapped in a deadly embrace.) Sniping back through the *Moscow News* demonstrated total ignorance of the special role the mass media has started to play in recent years in all of the independent republics. Chevron had chosen the wrong target.

Debate about foreign investment is one of the hottest topics in the ongoing argument between the reactionary and progressive mass media. The market-oriented, progressive press practically always sides with those foreign companies beating the bureaucratic bushes to flush out opportunities for joint ventures. Newspapers such as the *Moscow News* and *Commercant* wholeheartedly support foreign investment, trumpeting its potential benefits whenever they can. Turning these papers against the Tengiz project was a notable achievement on Chevron's part!

Chevron's choleric and ill-advised letter to the *Moscow News* was accompanied by a note that read, imperiously, "Publish immediately." In Andropov's time, a newspaper might have responded immediately to a command "from above," but times had changed, and the order became the object of much joking among Soviet journalists.

In spite of all its mistakes and miscalculations (its underestimation of the power of popular opinion, most of all), Chevron eventually did sign an agreement with the Kazakhstan government in 1992. The conditions, however, were not nearly as favorable as they would have been had the deal been concluded earlier. Chevron's share of the profits was reduced, the cost of their investment increased, and Kazakhstan retained a much greater degree of control over oil exports. Yet Chevron was still right to sign the agreement, for through it they have gotten their foot in the door and will be able to compete with other companies (such as the French giant ELF Aquitaine) entering the Kazakhstan oil market. Kazakhstan oil fields are among the world's most abundant, and the quality of their crude is extremely high.

ACC's joint oil-production project was much smaller than the Tengiz project, and its approach was very different from Chevron's. It wanted to hold an auction to choose applicants that would offer the most to the region. Minister of Geology H., hoping to avoid the types of mistakes made in the Tengiz deal, wanted to wait and see.

I understood his thinking. No major oil fields had as yet been opened to foreign investors, and H. did not want to be a trailblazer. Trailblazing can sometimes be a rather unpopular pursuit in Russia. He had been instructed by Yeltsin to push ahead, but H. was well aware that people in higher positions than his had fallen from favor. He was in a tough spot.

Studying his face, I sensed that Minister H. might be willing to reconsider the matter. His concern was evaporating. He now saw that the company was run by dedicated people fully intending to participate in the ecological and social problems of the region, and he was impressed by their knowledge. I had been able to discuss the parameters of the deposit and the economics of the project with ACC before the meeting. For them, as for every American company looking to invest in Russia, the major question remains: When will the ruble become *completely* convertible? Since July of 1992, only small amounts of rubles have been convertible to foreign currencies; monetary reforms have not gone far enough. The frozen ruble has had a chilling effect on foreign business.

Not long ago, the manager of a British company, Semper Bio-Technology, flew in from London to consult with me about the opportunities in Russia. His company had developed a method for prolonging the life of fruit and vegetables by spraying them with a special coating. Such technology could be very useful in Russia, given the tremendous transportation and storage losses due partly to the country's immensity, partly to the legendary inefficiency of the Soviet system.

I introduced him to various ways of establishing sales and coproduction in Russia, and when he grasped the magnitude of the market, he couldn't wait to begin. In fact, he was all ready to book a seat on the first flight to Moscow.

"What are you willing to do with your ruble profits?" I asked him. "Would you want to look for barter deals or reinvest them inside the country?"

"Why bother?" he replied, his eyes shining. "I'll take them as cash and exchange them for pounds or dollars."

I started explaining the ruble convertibility problem to him: "You cannot simply exchange rubles for dollars. You can buy dollars at a currency auction with your rubles, or do a barter deal, or find some other way to turn your ruble profits into dollars or pounds."

I would have gone into greater depth but he had stopped listening to me. His eyes glazed over. Ten minutes later, he was gone.

His response was unfortunate, because he could have earned a handsome profit. From the moment he told me about his product, I had come up with a plan to put him in touch with the right people and the right companies, and to help him study the market so that he could establish a sales network and a joint venture.

Many Western companies are discouraged by the ruble's inconvertibility. The Soviet Union's erstwhile leadership not only imprisoned its citizens, it froze currency. Citizens today have more freedom of movement than they did, but not the ruble. It is still not freely convertible. The Communists used inconvertibility as a way of controlling travel abroad. Even when Soviet citizens were allowed to travel, they had no money. Unfortunately, Yeltsin's bizarre monetary reforms were no better than Gorbachev's, and consisted essentially of printing billions of new rubles a month. In 1991, there was a total of 176 billion rubles in circulation. By August of 1992, the Russian government was printing 275 billion rubles a month; in December of 1992, it hit 1 trillion. By the time this book is published, a fifty-thousand ruble note will be in circulation.

The situation of the ruble reminds me of a famous trick a Russian magician used to pull. He would take out a coin and, as if by magic, it would begin to run all over his body. No one could figure out how he did it. He had glued it to a cockroach. If the ruble ever becomes fully convertible, it too will start moving by itself, but not from trickery. Permitting it to remain internal funny money would be destructive. Total inconvertibility was a malignant tumor infecting every organ in the Russian economy. It killed the motivation of the labor force, made shortages worse, and, as I mentioned, discouraged Western investment.

There are ways around inconvertibility. Savvy foreign investors already know how to convert the ruble into hard currency, using not only the old methods of barter and countertrade, but some new tricks. They can invest rubles in dollar-producing businesses, or sell them at currency auctions, which are now common events and not, as previously, just fashion shows. In the free economic zones being created, every republic's currency can circulate freely and compete in terms of its "hardness."

A few Western economists, so-called experts on the former Soviet Union, claim the country lacks the reserves to back a truly international currency. I disagree. Russia, at least, is far from being a poor country. False statistics, concocted in the days of Stalin, have long concealed the true extent of Soviet gold and diamond reserves. For example, simple analysis of the correlation between Soviet data and the world diamond markets show that the country's diamond reserves are in fact quite significant. Between the Second World War and 1992, the Soviet Union sold no cut and polished diamonds larger than ten carats, and very few larger than five carats. Given that the Soviet Union, together with South Africa, was one of the largest diamond producers in the world, it is clear that almost all of these treasures had been stashed in a State diamond fund. As for raw diamonds, the Soviets came to an arrangement with De Beers Centenerary more than thirty years ago to sell them on the world market. In 1992, the Russian and Yakut republics confirmed that they had agreed to sell De Beers 95 percent of their entire raw diamond export. This will change, I believe, in that De Beers is starting to lose its grip on the market. Russia produces 30 percent of the world's diamonds and will soon begin to sell directly, rather than through an intermediary. World bankers know that Russia has always been one of the most reliable payers of interest. In 1991, an American official, speaking for the White House, confirmed that it had never defaulted on an official loan from the United States. (By 1992, however, the United States and the European community, together with the International Monetary Fund, deliberated long and hard before granting Russia new loans, because it had not paid the interest on its $65-billion debt. The debt of former Soviet republics has grown to more than $80 billion, and their hard currency debt today is four times their annual export revenues.) Russia is still quite capable of paying its way, but it is critically important for Western companies to distinguish between State debts and those incurred by private companies. Foreign lenders should be aware that the central government no longer backs the debts of private companies.

Russia has abundant natural resources other than huge reserves of precious metals and diamonds. It produces more oil, gas, steel, timber, and mineral fertilizer than any other country in the world, and is among the top two or three in nonferrous metals. This represents enormous wealth for the country, and backing for its currency. With time, the ruble will be able to hold its own in the world marketplace. There are better times ahead is what I tell skeptics who balk at doing business in Russia.

For the moment, though, the ruble cannot be easily converted, and its inflexibility compounds the economic crisis currently gripping the Russian economy. With inflation running at 15 percent in 1989, 25 percent in 1990, 150 percent in 1991, and a staggering 2,100 percent in the first quarter of 1993 (fifty percent per month), the ruble has lost purchasing power month by month, even day by day, and the hard-earned savings of those who saved them are dwindling to nothing.

Shelves in Russian stores are full, but cost puts what they hold well beyond the reach of the average consumer. The situation is similar to what was going on in Poland in 1987, and Russia is five years or so behind Polish reforms. Where they can, people resort to barter. Collective farms exchange five hundred tons of grain for a single ten-ton Kamaz truck, for example, or six tons of grain for one ton of cement. Feudal though it might be, bartering was the only means of survival for Soviet enterprises under communism. The best products were exported and sold for dollars, and the workers who produced these goods were robbed more blindly than any described by Marx. This, of course, is changing. One of the surest ways to motivate workers is to let them share in a company's hard-currency profits.

The American economist Thorsten Veblen viewed the formation of a monetary civilization as a negative development, but I think a monetary civilization reflects a healthy economy. Russia is not there yet, and it won't achieve that kind of fitness until the ruble runs free.

These were among the issues behind the discussion around the ACC conference table on that rainy afternoon. There was one more factor that day. Minister of Geology H. had not come alone. Soviet officials rarely traveled without another functionary peeking over their shoulders. Sending a Party drone along on trips was a practice widely used by the Communists to protect their comrades from the lurid temptations of "stinking capitalism." In the old days, the fear was defection; today, it is corruption. Accompanying Minister H. to ACC headquarters was the head of the International Department of the Ministry of Geology. I will call him Comrade Bribe Taker, for that's what he was—a retrograde, bought-and-paid-for hack, whose sole criterion for evaluating the value of a deal was the amount of personal profit he could syphon off it. The demise of the Communist Party does not mean that his type has disappeared.

Bribe Taker looked the part. Short, beefy, his neck as thick as a barrel, he sported smoked glasses so large that his jowly face seemed to do little more than provide a background for them. He fidgeted in his chair. The discussion so far didn't interest him in the slightest, since he had not yet located a bribe. He would have preferred to be out drinking or carousing. At last, perhaps weary of his disguise, he removed his smoked glasses. The sight of his hooded, bloodshot eyes confirmed my worst suspicions.

"Let me lay everything on the line," he said. "You try to show you are doing Russia a big favor and not talking profit."

"As you know from the agreement," ACC's president replied evenly, "we will not charge Russia for our services. We'll get paid by foreign developers."

Replied Bribe Taker: "We should study your proposal in greater detail. There must be some hidden agenda. You try to make us believe that the project is beneficial for all the parties concerned: investors, you, the enterprises, and even our State committee. This is impossible. You cannot satisfy the wolf and keep the sheep safe."

Discerning that the good comrade was attempting to lead the discussion into more personally profitable areas, I concluded that a change of scene would be beneficial. I made a crucial recommendation—lunch. Suddenly, the official's face brightened. Doing a first-rate impression of a human being, he grinned and said, "This we can understand." We adjourned to the Rainbow Room atop Rockefeller Center.

CHAPTER 2

Forging Ahead

Normally, moving a business meeting with Russians from an office to a restaurant pays off. Festive surroundings usually encourage the typical bureaucrat to loosen his government-issued tie. Unfortunately, the Rainbow Room—despite its well-deserved reputation for excellence—was not conducive to a productive discussion. Flamenco music rocketed off the walls. It reminded me of a Georgian restaurant called Aragvy, one of Moscow's best, where the music is so loud patrons pay the band *not* to play.

Listening to the president of the American consulting company, Minister of Geology H., and Comrade Bribe Taker debate the issues left me both satisfied and frustrated. I was pleased that ACC was not giving up. I also thought the American was missing the subtext of the conversation by not recognizing the differences between the two officials sitting in front of him. They were both simply "the Russians" to him. To me, they personified the ongoing battle between the Soviet Union's communistic past and its progressive present.

I had met them for the first time that day. Minister H. was one of the few new people in the government I did not know personally, and Comrade Bribe Taker occupied a relatively low-level post. There are almost eight hundred ministries and state committees scattered throughout the republics. Previously, a department head in a republic's ministry was little more than a feeble functionary. Now that the republics have gained real independence, the same official holds some sway over a project.

Minister H. and Comrade Bribe Taker were so typical and familiar to me that after one glance I was confident I would be able to help ACC structure a workable deal. Minister H. was arguing with ACC's president, but I could see that it would be possible to work with him. A geologist by training, he was less infected by bureaucratic prejudices than a non-scientist might be. Moreover, as Yeltsin's appointee, H. was committed in theory to cooperation with the West.

Comrade Bribe Taker, head of the Department for International Cooperation, was another story. He tried to come across as a simple Russian, his soul an open book, but he was in truth a cagey and artful thief who judged people from one angle only: whether or not they would offer him a bribe. Even if he got his payoff, it didn't mean he would keep his promise. His was a win-win situation. The bribe giver can hardly sue the bribe taker for not delivering the goods.

Trying to make himself heard over the flamenco music, the president of ACC shouted: "We would like to hold a bidding competition for international companies interested in developing the oil field. ACC's role will be to design a program for producing oil there using the most modern technologies, while protecting the environment and developing the social infrastructure in the region. The Russian government will get our services free. We'll be paid by future American investors."

Posing as the Great Patriot, whose one mission in life was to speak on behalf of Mother Russia, Comrade Bribe Taker smugly replied: "To be honest, we do not need your services. Russia has every one of the major oil companies begging for its attentions. They are ready to sleep on the carpet outside our door for the opportunity. Anyone who tries to bypass our ministry, like you tried to do, should know better."

Comrade Bribe Taker had raised his voice menacingly, trying to sound like a Cossack riding into battle, but I knew it was merely a ruse. He felt no genuine anger. In truth, he was incapable of being stirred by grand themes of national honor. Fattening his own wallet was what was on his mind.

Minister H. remained silent, but I could tell that his colleague's impudence unnerved him. Comrade Bribe Taker was behaving as though he were the minister, and H. was still too unsure of his new position to put him in his proper place.

ACC's president kept trying to advance his arguments, but when Comrade Bribe Taker donned his smoked glasses I knew that any further discussion was pointless. His emotional display was rare for a veteran bureaucrat. I concluded that he had been bought by some other foreign company interested in the same oil field. For ACC to win, we would have to go over his head.

ACC was understandably surprised and discouraged by this obstacle. Knowing that Yeltsin and the Russian Parliament were attempting to implement a free market, ACC expected that the Ministry of Geology would embrace them with open arms. The Americans did not fully appreciate how much time it takes to alter the collective bureaucratic mentality.

Whenever I advise my clients, whether a major oil, coal, or metallurgical company, I try to be realistic about the investment picture in the former Soviet Union. It had become clear to me in 1988 that the Soviet Union would fall apart within three to five years. However, I continually caution my clients against overdramatizing the degree of change in the country's business climate. Many elements of the old system—the republics' parliaments and governments, holdovers from the Communist Party, and the ever-present, ever-destructive bureaucratic mentality—will continue to function long after the breakup of the Soviet Union. This is a reality, and closing one's eyes to it is financially dangerous. I was gratified that the meeting I had organized had taken place at all.

I was raised in the heart of Siberia, on the banks of the Yenisey River, which divides the country into two equal parts. (The house I was born in served as a stopover in 1920 for the Nobel prize-winning Norwegian explorer and humanitarian Fridtjof Nansen.) In my youth, I traipsed over the very same oil fields north of Krasnoyarsk that ACC now hoped to tap. As a department chairman of the Siberian branch of the Academy of Sciences in the 1970s, a couple of decades later, I crossed the same sites yet again, helping to create a fifty-billion-ruble, ten-year development program for the region. (The program gave birth to an economy that flourished even under a repressive regime.) I knew that Western companies, working with already existing enterprises, could help the region develop into a highly profitable international project, especially since the land surrounding the oil field is a veritable treasure chest of gas, coal, aluminum, cobalt, platinum, gold, copper, and nickel. (This region produces 85 percent of Russian nickel; of all the former Soviet republics, only Russia and the Ukraine produce nickel: Russia, 91.8 percent and the Ukraine 1.9 percent.) Drilling for oil doesn't mean you want to throw away the diamonds you find along the way.

ACC was eager to gain a foothold in the region north of Krasnoyarsk because of what I had told them before they met with Minister H. I pointed out that if the treasures abutting the oil field were mined at the same time, the total cost would be cut in half due to what is called the local agglomeration effect. There is no doubt in my mind that the area will become Siberia's center of economic development in the coming decade. It offers many advantages to investors, including

- the Yenisey River, the major water artery between Asia and the Arctic Seaway, and a major river port fewer than 100 miles from the oil field;
- the world's largest nonferrous mining-metallurgical company, the Norilsk Concern;
- Norilsk, a city of 300,000, with a solid infrastructure, located a hundred miles from the oil fields;
- a half dozen gas pipelines, which could be used in developing new oil and gas fields, that connect Norilsk with the gas fields of Messoiaha and Solioninskoye;
- two substantial hydroelectric power plants (the Khantaiskaya HPP and the Kureiskaya HPP);
- Arctica, a sprawling agro-industrial complex, which breeds mink, sable, and deer, and harvests fish;
- construction companies that employ fifty thousand workers;
- one of the world's largest bituminous coal deposits; and
- practically unlimited reserves of construction materials.

Perhaps of greatest interest to foreign investors is that existing Soviet companies are themselves eager to participate in the development of Siberia. This will reduce the price of any new project, in that it will help spread costs around.

In the 1970s, there was scant trustworthy economic and geological data available on the Krasnoyarsk Region. I should mention that

American businesspeople find the scarcity of credible statistics about natural resources difficult to fathom. Reliable facts are precious; access to them was one of my biggest assets when I started consulting for Western companies.

Beginning in 1979, with the support of the Soviet Academy of Sciences, I organized several major economic expeditions to Siberia, the Far East, and the Arctic. The firsthand information I gathered on these journeys later enabled me to make accurate economic and political forecasts. Those of us who participated were members of the Academy and experts in our respective fields. Many of us had already traveled fairly extensively, but we all knew these expeditions were the experience of a lifetime. Our general goal was to evaluate the natural resources in these distant places, and the potential for using the Arctic Seaway as a route between North America, Europe, and Asia. My personal goal, and I kept this to myself, was to evaluate the potential for international cooperation in developing the riches of these uncharted regions.

The territory in question stretches from the sunburned Hakass steppes of southern Siberia to the frozen wastes of the Arctic, both regions in which you can travel for days and meet no one. These days it is not the Nansens or Robert Perrys who are exploring these regions, but economists and entrepreneurs. Firsthand information is far more valuable than government reports.

This is why I organized these economic expeditions. At the time, my countrymen were still living in a period of total prohibition, but some of us knew that the day would come when the irons and handcuffs would come off. We wanted to be ready.

My first problem was finding a ship powerful enough to take us through the Arctic Seaway. I approached the offices of the Merchant Marine. They wasted no time in turning me down. Other organizations were as eloquent as the ministry, and as prompt in their refusal. Then, one day, flipping through the directory of the Soviet Academy of Sciences, I came across the Department for Marine Expeditions, headed by the famous Arctic explorer Ivan Papanin.

Papanin achieved worldwide acclaim in the 1930s when he led Soviet expeditions from the North Pole to Greenland on a drifting ice floe. He was elderly now and came to his office only once a week to sign papers. Furthermore, I was told his department had never worked with economists. It administered huge ships used to control the movements of spacecraft. Papanin had a considerable reputation for speaking his mind and suffering no fools. "A mistake at sea will

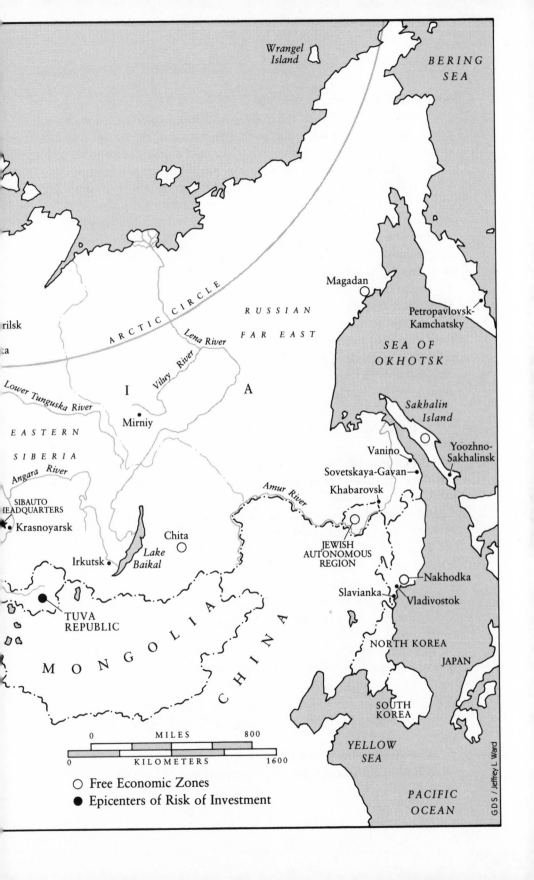

Wrangel
Island

BERING
SEA

ARCTIC CIRCLE

RUSSIAN

FAR EAST

rilsk

ka

Lower Tunguska River

Lena River

Viluy River

EASTERN

SIBERIA

Angara River

SIBAUTO
HEADQUARTERS
Krasnoyarsk

Mirniy

I

A

Magadan ○

Petropavlovsk-
Kamchatsky

SEA OF
OKHOTSK

Sakhalin
Island

Vanino
Sovetskaya-Gavan

Yoozhno-
Sakhalinsk

Amur River

Khabarovsk

Chita ○

Lake
Baikal

Irkutsk

JEWISH
AUTONOMOUS
REGION

Slavianka

Nakhodka

Vladivostok

● TUVA
REPUBLIC

MONGOLIA

CHINA

NORTH KOREA

JAPAN

SOUTH
KOREA

YELLOW
SEA

PACIFIC
OCEAN

GDS / Jeffrey, L. Ward

0   MILES   800

0   KILOMETERS   1600

○ Free Economic Zones
● Epicenters of Risk of Investment

sink you. Make one with me and I'll do the same." He was also a legendary drinker. Once, when he was drifting on his ice floe, Soviet authorities sent Papanin a special present: a crate containing two dozen bottles of expensive cognac. Papanin didn't like cognac, so he distilled the cognac back into pure alcohol and then drank it.

I made friends with his secretary by entertaining her with talk about growing up in Siberia, and telling her tales of polar wolf and brown bear hunts. These fascinated her; it was as though I was talking about life on the moon. After she had warmed to me a little she warned me against wasting my time trying to reach Papanin. He never received visitors, she said.

Interacting with secretaries in the former Soviet Union, and in the West, is a science all its own. Western executives are extremely secretive about their business dealings; Russians feel the same about their personal lives and contacts. In both cases, their secretaries can tell you a great deal. In the States, for example, a secretary's tone on the phone will let you know where you stand. Even before the executive picks up the phone, you can anticipate what he is about to say.

A major difference is that in the West, secretaries ordinarily have no say in actual business. Not so in Russia. There, secretaries might be intimidated by their bosses, but they are much more involved in business operations and much more at liberty to express their own opinions. The worst mistake foreign businesspeople trying to see Russian bureaucrats can make is snapping impatiently at the secretary. They will simply hang up.

To make an appointment in Russia, you either send an engaging letter (preferably one that will appeal to the bureaucrat's self-interest) or you become friendly with the secretary. That's how I got to meet Papanin. As luck would have it, while I was visiting the Department of Marine Expeditions one day, he happened to be in his office. His secretary let me through.

Papanin was a pudgy little man with a wispy crown of white hair. When I walked in I found him fast asleep at his desk. I felt guilty rousing him, but he seemed unruffled and greeted me with a choice selection of *mat*, or Russian obscenities. Mat is an integral part of Russian business life, and widely used by Russian workers and bosses alike.

When he had finished with the mat, I told him about the problems I had had in finding a ship for my expedition. "I had hoped that a letter from the vice-president of the academy would help me," I told Papanin, "but the Ministry of the Merchant Marine says it doesn't want anything to do with it. They told me I should stay home and read books instead of venturing out into the Arctic. I was hoping you'd come to my rescue."

My strategy worked. His eyes gleaming mischievously, Papanin exclaimed: "How dare they? What do they know about life? Penpushers! Have they ever drifted on a floe? They'd drown in a glass of water!"

He immediately phoned the minister of the Merchant Marine on his special government line, which connects the highest officials. He reached a man named Gushenko, let fly some of his choicest mat, and then demanded to know why respect was not being shown the academy. "Refuse them again," barked Papanin, "and I'll come and beat all of you over the head with a walrus dick."

Gushenko apologized—a very rare thing for a Russian minister to do—and assured Papanin that I would be given use of a seaworthy ship.

Papanin hung up, visibly stimulated by the conversation. He pointed to his chair and asked me, "Do you know what I'm sitting on?"

I hesitated, and looked at his odd-looking chair, which was made from some long, brownish bones. "No," I said.

"Walrus dick!" exclaimed Papanin, his eyes ablaze. "I collected them myself in the Arctic. One of the Arctic's wonders. Be sure to bring some back."

Having offered to me this pearl of wisdom, Papanin put his head back down on his desk and promptly fell asleep.

The Academy of Science's Arctic expedition lasted two months. We traveled 4,100 miles by boat; we flew another 6,835 miles in planes and helicopters. We visited sixty population centers, studied the workings of over two hundred enterprises and mines, and analyzed the largest natural resource deposits and ports along the Arctic Seaway. We saw oil derricks gushing sweet crude; the glow of torches on already discovered, but as yet untapped, gas fields; mountainous stacks of cut lumber rotting on the shores of Siberian rivers; and high-quality coal being unearthed by gigantic excavators. All I could think about were the opportunities that lay ahead. I was inspired by a desire to internationalize the Siberian economy. I knew that would be the only way to harness these boundless resources and to improve the lives of my countrymen.

Western companies have begun investing in the larger metropolitan centers—places such as Moscow and St. Petersburg. The Japanese are pouring money into the cities of the Russian Far East. But the real boom will begin when foreigners discover the wealth of the eastern and northern regions of Russia. What delays that boom is all the misinformation that, like a fog, blinds even the most sharp-eyed investors.

Based on what they learn from the press, most Westerners believe that the former Soviet Union's oil production is centered in the republics of Russia, Kazakhstan, and Azerbaijan (in the oil fields of Astrakhan, Shevchenko, and Baku), along the Caspian sea, and in the fields of western Siberia. Unaware of eastern Siberia's potential, many oil companies have already invested in these better-known deposits. The truth is that the Central Asian Republic's reserves have been diminishing for decades, and now account for just 6 percent of Soviet production, with Azerbaijan contributing only 3. The oil fields in Kazakhstan are more promising, but a set of factors, including ecological ones, will make the development of oil and gas production there increasingly expensive.

Siberia, on the other hand, produces nearly 80 percent of Russia's oil and 90 percent of its natural gas. Russia's gas exports accounted for 37 percent of the world's gas export. For the moment, most of this output comes from western Siberia, but, due to mismanagement and abysmally low worker incentives and productivity, yields there are declining steadily.

One reason foreign oil companies have looked only to the fields of western Siberia is that they are closer to population centers and are located in a milder climate. Another is that this is where Russian authorities have steered them. However, if a company drilling in these older fields hopes to get the same amount of oil they would in eastern Siberia, they will have to drill six times as many wells.

According to recent studies undertaken by geologists at the Russian Academy of Sciences, the oil reserves of eastern Siberia are larger than those controlled by all OPEC countries combined. Between 1979 and 1981, when we explored the Arctic regions, the Russian Far East, and various territories of Siberia, the geologists discovered that between the Yenisey and Lena rivers there was enormous untapped potential, particularly in the oil belt dividing the Taimir Peninsula from the mainland.

Gradual development is under way in eastern Siberia. These fields now produce only about twenty million barrels of oil a year—very little in global terms. It seems reasonable to assume, though, that eastern Siberia will exhibit the same rate of growth as western Siberia: from seven million barrels a year in 1965 to seven million barrels a day in 1980. Nearly forty billion barrels of oil have been produced there; exports earned more than $200 billion. It is estimated that by the year 2000, eastern Siberia, including the northern regions of Yamal, and the Gidan and Tazov peninsulas, will yield another 140 million barrels of oil each year, and billions of cubic feet of natural gas.

These conservative estimates, however, presuppose that Western technology and capital will be involved. In 1990, Russian oil wells yielded a dreary 20 percent of their potential. Were the expertise and capital of such corporations as Exxon, Mobil, Marathon Oil, Royal Dutch/Shell, and British Petroleum brought to bear on the region, there is no telling how high production might go.

To many foreigners, Siberia means blustery snowstorms and vast wastelands. Although these are undeniable features of the area, they don't by any means paint the entire picture. My native land is a country with a severe but stunning landscape, populated by strong and creative people and endowed with unparalleled natural resources.

I sometimes think that the Soviet Union's inability to develop the Arctic was a blessing in disguise, for it prevented its wonderful treasures from being pillaged by industrial development in an era of preecological awareness. Now that technologies, equipment, and human understanding are mature enough to prevent ecological damage, the time is ripe to forge ahead.

As for the Siberian weather? Everything is relative. At the end of the eighteenth century, the celebrated French diplomat Talleyrand undertook an expedition to the United States. Following his journey to New York, Pennsylvania, and Delaware, he wrote: "Significant difficulties will arise in coming to [these] new far-away regions. [They] have a very unhealthy climate, long and severe winters, and no roads necessary for good business connections."

History proves that if an entrepreneur has sufficient economic incentive, "far-away" regions can be brought within reach. The allegedly unpleasant and impassable regions of the northeastern United States have become the business center of the world—despite Talleyrand's misgivings.

Siberia might seem like it's in another galaxy to American investors, but it's actually much closer and safer than Saudi Arabia. Eastern Siberia is nearly America's next-door neighbor, located only four hours' flying time from Anchorage and seven hours from Seattle. Until 1867, Alaska was a Russian province. (Russia sold the territory for $7 million. Today, $7 million of oil is pumped out of Alaska in four hours.) Alaska is separated from several Siberian oil fields by a mere fifty sea-mile stretch of the Bering Strait. From some oil fields in the far eastern regions of Russia (principally those off Sakhalin Island and the Kamchatka Peninsula), an overnight oil delivery to Alaska could be organized without difficulty. In fact, in the spring of 1992, the MMM Consortium—consisting of McDermott, Marathon Oil (United States), and Mitsui (Japan)—won the right in international bidding to do a feasibility study of two offshore oil and natural gas fields near Sakhalin. Of course, the right to do a feasibility study is not the same as the right to begin drilling for oil. But it is a promising start.

American and Japanese consumers would benefit directly from the proximity of these reserves. Transportation costs to the West Coast of the United States would be a fraction of the cost of importing oil from the Middle East. Russian oil could even be pumped from tankers directly into the Alaskan pipeline.

The world's energy transportation routes and economics are going to change, and the Arctic Seaway, linking all of the northern regions to the warm-water Pacific, will become a very busy route—and an extremely efficient one. Foreign companies began experimenting with this route in 1980. The great eastern Siberian rivers, including the Yenisey, the Lena, and the Indigirka, create a natural transportation system for oil and other resources. The 2,000-mile-long Baikal-Amur Railway, begun in the 1970s, runs through the middle of northern Siberia and the Far East, connecting the oil fields with ports on the Pacific Ocean. From there, it is a two- or three-day tanker run to Japan, and another two days to Alaska.

Potential investors should be aware that development in eastern Siberia will be somewhat slowed by environmental concerns, which arose because of damage done by oil drilling in western Siberia. During the 1970s and 1980s, the Soviet regime ignored the ecological needs of the region. Less than 1 percent of the total oil investment went toward conservation. Now, to undo some of the damage, more than 10 percent of future investment will need to be allocated for environmental protection. Although Soviet environmentalists are not as anticapitalist as some of their American counterparts, and do not have the recourse of the U.S. legal system, they will put pressure on authorities to guarantee that the eastern Siberian wilderness is not ravaged. In former years, many of the big Siberian projects were facilitated by bribes to Soviet bureaucrats.

Development in Siberia under the Soviets was tremendously destructive to the environment. Exploitation brought devastation— human and ecological. Around a typical oil drilling settlement, all trees were cut down; near mines and oil fields, workers lived in appalling conditions (often, one room in a hostel served as housing for four people, furnished with a beat-up wardrobe, sagging table, and an ancient television set); entertainment for oil workers, who might number in the thousands, consisted of access to a single club (painted Communist Party red), where a dance recital by an amateurish group of Eskimos was considered a notable evening's entertainment. It is hardly surprising that workers drank too much; that despair and fatigue were rampant; that productivity fell.

Siberians will no longer tolerate this type of treatment, either to themselves or their home. Eastern Siberia is a beautiful wasteland, with endless tracts of virgin forests and mountains whose peaks jut into the clouds. Yes, the winters are cold, but the summers are warm and bright. The cities—Norilsk, Krasnoyarsk, Irkutsk—are attractive and cosmopolitan.

To conduct business here, foreign companies will have to invest in the social infrastructure and pay decent wages. Nearly half of any investment made in this area will need to go into transportation and basic services. However, at an estimated $8,000 per worker, it will still cost far less for these companies to upgrade Siberian facilities than it now costs to house and feed workers in Alaska or on North Sea oil rigs. In addition, the oil and gas deposits in eastern Siberia are buried deeper than those in western Siberia, which will mean further investment in geophysical and seismic equipment.

I have no doubt that an oil and gas development project along the Yenisey-Hatangsky trough will become one of the first major joint-venture projects in eastern Siberia. It will also offer lucrative investment opportunities to other businesses besides oil companies: the region needs everything from food processing plants to modern hotels to city services.

□   □   □

Full awareness of the awesome potential of eastern Siberia was what inspired the president of the American consulting company to continue struggling with Comrade Bribe Taker and Minister H. I had warned him, however, that when negotiating with Russian bureaucrats it is better not to show how aware you are of the rewards. I advised him instead to focus on the rigors of the project—the obstacles, delays, and costs. Doing that, I said, would keep the infamous Russian xenophobia from killing the venture in the cradle.

Even while Comrade Bribe Taker resisted ACC, his bushy eyebrows revealed how impressed he was at how well "these Americans" knew the situation in Siberia. If he had already sold out to some other investor, I knew that our only chance was to try to win time for ACC, so that we could go over his head. What we had going for us was that people like Comrade Bribe Taker are cowards at heart. He knew he would be watched carefully by his superiors, and that ACC was offering attractive terms to Russia. Should he strike a worse deal with another company and it become public, he would lose his job and what remained of his dignity.

ACC's difficulties underscore the concern a host of potential Western investors have expressed to me about making the appropriate contacts in the former Soviet Union and negotiating effectively with bureaucrats. I know the individual players—the heads of the republics, ministries, and the most powerful regions—so it is easier for me to predict how they will react to a particular project and how they will interact with one another. For example, the moment Yeltsin emerged victorious from the fray, I knew that the days of Soviet Prime Minister Rizshkov, a hard-liner, were numbered and advised my clients not to rely on either his promises or his connections. When journalists, politicians, and businesspeople ask me whether the time is right to invest in Russia, I say yes—but do so wisely and cautiously.

In many respects the timing couldn't be better. The new Russian government would prefer to sell its oil or any of its other products abroad for hard currency rather than to the Soviet republics. It will also be searching for foreign partners to conduct joint oil research, production, and sales. Of course, newcomers will have to compete with foreign companies already in the market. The age of monopolies is over. With its market-oriented economists, Russia will try to sell not just crude, but refined petroleum products. This is why eastern Siberia is becoming so attractive to petrochemical processors. They will be favored over those seeking purely extractive investments.

□   □   □

The Iraqi invasion of Kuwait demonstrated once again how closely economic and political interests intertwine, and how dangerous it is for industrialized nations to depend on a single source of oil. When Saddam Hussein invaded Kuwait, it was not so much his tanks or even his Soviet-made missiles that frightened the West; it was his potential use of oil as a weapon. Some people thought Saddam's vicious folly heralded another round of skyrocketing oil prices. But time is running out on the manipulation of oil for political gain. Saddam and his predecessors have banked too long on the assumption that the Middle East sits on the world's largest proven reserves of oil. They have not taken into account the prodigious oil resources hidden in Russia and Kazakhstan.

Even with its economy in a shambles, Russia and the independent republics remain the world's unchallenged leader in oil production. Official sources put production in 1989 at 11.6 million barrels a day; the true figure is closer to 13 million barrels. In 1990, daily output dropped to 11 million barrels. The Western press reported that the Soviet oil industry was in disarray. They pointed out that in 1991 Russia alone had produced 8.85 million barrels (Kazakhstan produced 0.5 million), and that by December of 1992 production had dropped to 7 million per day. Yet, that same year, Iraq, Kuwait, and Saudi Arabia combined produced just 9 million barrels a day, and all of OPEC a grand total of 24 million. That Russian oil producers have problems should be an incentive to foreigners considering investment. If things were running smoothly, they wouldn't need outside investment.

Although exports in 1990 declined by 140 million barrels compared to the previous year, Russia still exported 770 million barrels of crude oil. The country also exported 350 million barrels of oil products and 120 billion cubic meters of natural gas. Taken together, these statistics add up to one of the world's largest volumes of hydrocarbon export. Russia managed to do all of this exporting even though the nation is a grossly wasteful consumer of fuel (distribution is disorganized, the price of oil and gas is much too low, and heating and engine technology is very poor). Surprisingly, in 1992 Russia increased its export of oil by 17 percent to 463 million barrels.

Few in the West know about the potential in eastern Siberia; indeed, few Russians are aware of it. A cloak of Soviet secrecy has kept this oil out of sight and underground. The moment has arrived to bring it to market. In the years ahead, if more of this oil flows out to the world, crude prices will remain under pressure, making it virtually impossible for any Mideast leader to hold the world hostage. Interestingly enough, the Japanese understand this better than Americans. Their appreciation of Siberia's potential helped persuade their ever-prudent government that they could afford to antagonize Iraq by taking part in the economic blockade. As far back as 1975, Japanese corporations were exploring for oil and gas off Sakhalin, a Pacific island just north of Japan. Even given all of the uncertainties, they invested $25 million in oil and gas research in the Russian Far East, and invited American businesses to join them. Ignorant of the potential, Americans refused.

In 1991, the volume of oil production in the Soviet Union decreased by approximately 10 percent due to Gorbachev's diminishing power. In 1992, production of oil was dropping by 1.2 percent every month. This will change, however, and by 1994, we should see new growth in oil and gas production. It is true that Russians will need much of this fuel at home. Russians also desperately need foreign trade to buy consumer goods, however, and the fastest method of securing that trade is by boosting oil exports.

For American businesses in particular, it is time to think in terms of the Pacific Century. America and Russia live on opposite sides of a shrinking pond. A gradual relocation of oil production to the north and the east fits in with the overall forecasts for world economic development, which is shifting its center to the Pacific Rim. Americans should stop worrying about Mideast oil embargoes and start thinking about how to bring Russian oil to market. Some Mideast nations might be able to withhold their oil to punish the West, but Russia, hungry for development, will not.

During a lecture in Vienna, I asked the students in the audience which capitalist countries they thought were geographically closest to Russia. The majority of them answered either Austria or Germany. The answer, of course, is Norway, Finland, and the United States.

I had felt the proximity of the two countries strongly one midsummer night in 1980, when our expedition ship was slicing through the waters of the Bering Strait. I was standing on deck gazing out over the ocean. On one side was the easternmost edge of the Old World, and on the other, the westernmost edge of the New World, America, with all of its freedoms and luxuries—only five nautical miles away. An able-bodied sailor in a wet suit could jump ship and probably swim to its shore without any great effort.

I heard someone approaching, and suddenly the ship's captain was standing beside me at the rail. He seemed to guess what I was thinking. No doubt he had thought the same thought many times before.

"You are trying to see the States?" he asked. "Seems so close, right? And such a quiet night."

I looked at him. He was neither interrogating me nor trying to trap me into saying something he could later report to the KGB. He was speaking as a kindred spirit. I smiled. The night sky was bursting with stars, and the ocean sparkled, as if aurora borealis had been born in this nexus between two oceans, the northern Arctic and the Pacific—a slim silver line connecting two continents and two powers.

"The quiet is an illusion," the captain said. "In fact, this little strait is more stuffed than my grandma's chicken. You couldn't even begin to count the number of submarines and jets that patrol it."

"But the Bering Strait is shallow," I replied. "Only around a hundred feet deep. Too shallow for sharks."

He laughed at my reference to a class of Soviet submarine. We stood in silence as a small silhouette of a ship appeared in the distance.

"What kind of boat is that?" I asked after a moment.

"The American Coast Guard," replied the captain. "They're probably curious as hell why a Russian ship is hanging out here all night. Your trip is unusual for these waters."

I heard him sigh. Turning away, he wished me a good night. I listened to his footsteps receding into the darkness.

How close yet how unapproachable America is, I thought. I knew even then that the United States wasn't a paradise, but I would have given anything to enjoy its freedoms. A wave of anger washed over me. What is the point of all our expeditions? Our research? Soviet leaders may allot funds to mine natural resources, but hundreds of thousands of decent people will invest their lives and wind up with nothing. The communist bosses will pump out the oil and mine the diamonds, then sell them to foreigners for hard currency to buy the latest equipment for manufacturing missiles.

The Soviet Union is nothing more than a barrel without a bottom, I thought. Everything runs through it. Everything is wasted.

Staring out over the dark waters, I realized that for all my dreams I was just another slave. My ideas were locked behind bars, and my children's future was destined to the same fate—unless the Communists fell from power.

It was getting cold, even though it was high summer. Clouds, dimly lit by the moon, scurried overhead. It grew darker. The stars vanished. I headed for my bunk imagining the glorious things my countrymen could achieve if only they were given the chance. They needed help from the West, and from that country a mere five miles off the starboard bow.

CHAPTER 3

Dead Souls Awaken: The Russian Worker

Japan's greatest natural resource is its people. For the most part, I would say the Russian labor force is as qualified as Japan's—and as inexpensive as China's. Their professional competence and their reasonable salary requirements make Russian workers, from the point of view of foreign business, a real bargain.

I entered the Russian work force as a teenager in Krasnoyarsk, when I took a job as a construction worker at the Norilsk Combine in 1968. Norilsk is the northernmost city on the earth, and has a climate that makes Anchorage's seem almost tropical by comparison. Norilsk was for a long time one of the capitals of the Gulag system. A Russian acronym for Glaunaye Upravleniye Lagerey (Chief Administration of Corrective Labor Camps), the Gulag was a network of forced labor prisons established to enforce Leninist, and later Stalinist, ideology by silencing political and religious dissidents. Prisoners were frequently incarcerated without trial, and subjected to beatings and brutal conditions; untold thousands died before completing their sentences. For years after Stalin's death, the Gulag still enslaved the nation; today, it is but a bad memory. Today, Norilsk's claim to fame is as the site of the world's most extensive mining-metallurgical concern and the world's least expensive source of non-ferrous metals.

At the construction site where I began, the work team consisted of people known as *Banderovtsi*. Their name derives from the days of the Second World War, when these men had fought the Red Army under the banner of Ukrainian nationalist Stepan Bandera. For their efforts, they were branded criminals and given century-long sentences in various Norilsk labor camps. The crew of Banderovtsi I was assigned to was led by a man named Sergei. Every night, Sergei bought them vodka and listened to their horror stories about life in the Gulag. They seemed the best of friends.

Then something went wrong. Perhaps overestimating his authority over these men, Sergei started nagging them. He complained that they drank too much, and revoked their vodka ration.

One morning, while walking under an ore-smelting furnace containing nickel boiling at twelve hundred degrees centigrade, Sergei was doused in liquid metal and met an agonizing end. The rumor spread that his untimely demise was hardly an accident.

Even before Sergei's funeral, the foreman of our division offered me Sergei's old job. I was nineteen and broke, so I took it.

"How could you?" my mother cried when I told her. "They'll kill you, too!"

Her fears were not unfounded. If you took a handful of Banderovtsi to the meanest streets of New York City, the toughest local gangs would soon be begging for police protection. Yet, my short experience with them had already convinced me that even the Banderovtsi could be productive if handled properly.

There are a number of myths about Russian workers, from the toughest Banderovtsi to the most skilled engineer, that should be addressed. What Russian workers have in common is that they have been handicapped by seventy years of communism. They are still the most abundant natural resource my country has to offer foreign businesses.

Because any East-West joint venture will require a labor pool, it is of paramount importance foreign corporations understand the Russian worker. For instance, the Krasnoyarsk oil-field project the American consulting company was trying to put together was going to require thousands of workers. Should foreign companies such as ACC bring in foreign workers to ensure a high-quality product? The answer is a resounding no.

However, foreign companies should also assume that to get that high-quality product they will need to familiarize themselves with Russian working conditions and worker expectations. This can prove a challenge. Managing Russian labor, though it will yield the best possible results, is not easy. A good way to start is by appreciating the conditions under which the average Russian lives. Many of my students in Vienna were social democrats, much enamored of long-winded debate over good coffee. When they read my article "Russia: Capitalism Now!" in *Wohen-Presse*, a leading Austrian magazine, they accused me of abandoning socialist principles for degenerate capitalist ideologies.

"Go to the Soviet Union, that communist paradise, for a month," I would reply to them. "Get a Soviet passport. Live as the workers do. When you come back, we'll continue our discussion."

I wanted them to understand what it was like to live as a Soviet citizen, to have only vodka and potatoes in the larder and nothing in the refrigerator; to live in crowded apartments and share bedrooms and bathrooms with other families. Thirty percent of Russians still live in communal conditions, and they are generally squalid ones.

I would give the same advice to those in the foreign business community. Consider what the workers will think of your project and how they will look at it, I tell them. After all, they will be the ones producing the goods. Ignoring the worker was among the worst of the crimes committed by the communist regime, particularly in that it purported to represent and defend them.

What is the best way to get Russians reengaged in their work? Money is an excellent place to start. Some time ago I was asked by a Soviet military plant to help solve a mystery. An industrial robot sent to them by Westinghouse was constantly breaking down, and the plant manager was cursing the day he had ever ordered such an unreliable contraption. What was wrong with the damn thing?

When I visited the plant I asked the workers what they thought of the robot. At first they were surprised that anyone would care what they thought. Finally, one of them answered me in a characteristically Russian manner: "The more bear you serve," he said, "the more songs you get."

Translation: the efficient Westinghouse robot had dramatically increased the plant's output, but to keep up with the faster pace of production, the employees had to work twice as hard—yet their wages remained the same. So they avenged themselves by sabotaging the machine, and, predictably, production suffered.

The average earnings in Russia, as of 1992, is about $2.50 a week by my estimate of the Russian market rate of exchange. No one can live decently on such an income. President Yeltsin himself earns about $151. That's still a lot of money in Russia. A company manager earns about $80 a month.

It is worth noting that bureaucratic bigwigs still get nearly everything at a special rate. I often visited the residences of Soviet bosses; few American multimillionaires could match the magnificent level of luxury at which they lived. In Russia, people still call it "the communism behind the fence." A majority of Yeltsin's inner circle are old-style bureaucrats, and in 1992, Yeltsin officially permitted these officials to keep their villas, cars, and free memberships to health spas, hotels, restaurants, and childcare facilities. Russian officials have much greater access to State property than any American counterpart—even today.

The overwhelming majority of Russian people do not share in the benefits of "common" ownership, and the poorest 12 percent of the population has less than five square meters (about 54 square feet) of living space per person—a miniscule amount of space. Foreign investors would do well to remember this when organizing housing packages for their Russian employees.

The main difference between the ways the American and Russian governments spend money is that Americans live on credit and borrow from the future, the idea being that they will gradually repay the money over time. In the former Soviet Union, any government has traditionally offered false hopes of a more prosperous future, borrowed from the peoples' present, and then never paid them back. Even those miserable crumbs people labor so hard to gather over the course of a lifetime cannot be converted into real savings. Hyperinflation sees to that.

As a result, not only is the ruble inconvertible, but Russian citizens are also not "convertible." A friend of mine, a professor at the Academy of Sciences, couldn't afford the one-way plane fare to New York in 1993 (then 125,000 rubles) to attend a conference at which his work would have reached the right audience. When the most talented Soviet professionals—brilliant surgeons or groundbreaking writers—used to visit Western countries, they and their accomplishments often went unrecognized. When they emigrated, these luminaries became like Cinderella at midnight: everything they owned turned into nothing. All they had left was their talent. Nevertheless, many still choose to move to the West—a development being picked up by the Russian media. Recently, *ECO,* the most influential economics magazine in Russia (founded by Professor Abel Aganbegian), ran an issue with an alarming cover showing an hourglass with brains trickling through it.

Many know that they have a much better chance of building productive lives in the United States. The word is that Russian biologists, mathematicians, economists, computer programmers, and financial specialists are being warmly welcomed around the world. They have bought houses and cars and have developed an unwavering devotion to Western supermarkets, with their brightly stocked shelves and refrigerated cases teeming with roasts and steak and fish and fowl.

Still, these immigrants represent only a fraction of the storehouse of trained and educated people in the republics. "Labor resources" is just another economic term in the West, but in Soviet Russia the term took on real, and dehumanizing, significance. Many citizens who stayed behind were transformed into little more than a "resource." Humiliated and impoverished, they were ground down by the government until they became tiny cogs in the behemoth totalitarian machine. The pathetic irony of the boast "The Soviet microcomputer is the biggest in the world!" reflects the thoroughgoing idiocy of the old administrative system.

Market relations and political freedoms have eroded the old system, causing enormous relocation of labor resources both structurally and geographically. In January of 1991, Gorbachev legalized the status of foreigners working in Russia (again, not out of the goodness of his heart, nor some democratic vision, but because of the shortage of trained managers). Russian citizens can now work for foreign companies in Russia and abroad with the blessing of the State. For Western companies, this translates into a cost-effective, qualified labor force, and what they are finding is that all the Russian worker needs to match or exceed the productivity of his Western counterpart is capitalist incentives.

The morning of my first day as poor Sergei's replacement, I awoke with a start. It was pitch black outside, which was not surprising, since in Norilsk it is winter for nine months of the year. Winter temperatures can drop to minus 45 degrees centigrade, making dressing for work an ordeal: you must pile on layer upon layer of clothes until you look and feel like a stuffed cabbage—not that you care. You do anything you can to protect yourself from the ice-tipped lash of the wind. Waiting for the bus, your eyelashes freeze. Touch them and they'll snap off like matchsticks. Many people in Norilsk don't have eyelashes.

At least the buses run on time in Norilsk, because the city is the center of a huge industrial development. Ferrying people to work has been a top priority, an integral part of the technological process at the Norilsk Combine. As I was walking toward the plant, several of my friends tried to persuade me to reconsider my decision to lead the Banderovtsi. I'd end up like Sergei, they told me. I had to admit that icy winds or not, I had no wish for a molten nickel shower, but the job offered higher wages and I needed the money.

I had started working at the age of fourteen, when I was living in the Siberian city of Krasnoyarsk. My parents were divorced. My father was a well-known developer and manager in Siberia whom I rarely saw. My mother relocated to Norilsk; she was trying to bring up my brother and me, and wages were higher in the Far North. Life was hard and expensive, and I lived alone in the Krasnoyarsk apartment. I had no experience spending money, and the fifty rubles a month my mother sent me went fast.

I quit school to apprentice myself as an electrician. I had been boxing for several years, and my coach told me that my career would be finished if I didn't go back to school. I moved to Norilsk and started studying again, found another job, and continued boxing. At nineteen, I won the Russian youth middleweight boxing championship. How tough could it be to handle these Banderovtsi? I was young and foolish enough to think that if anyone could do it, I could.

By 8:00 A.M., the construction foreman led me into a cramped, windowless, locker room, where a group of burly men in hard hats sat playing dominoes (a common practice at Russian worksites) beneath a dim bulb.

"Men," said the foreman, even as he was backing out of the room. "This is Kvint, your new team leader. Now let's get to work."

The Banderovtsi glanced up, grunted, and then returned to their dominoes.

I put the daily assignment on a table in front of them and said: "This is what we should get done today. Any questions? I'm going to fight to get a truck with concrete. The steel girders have already arrived."

That the steel had already arrived stunned them more than did my young years. Normally, steel arrived after lunch, and often no one ever did any work until late morning.

One of the Banderovtsi walked off, saying he was going to look for a cigarette. I knew he was really going to check the construction site to see whether or not I was lying. This did not surprise me, because even at that relatively tender age I understood how the system worked. I also knew the man had good reason to doubt my word. The Soviets built things so slowly because it was almost impossible to pull together all of the required supplies for a project in time. Lost days and weeks were business as usual. In Russia, it is known as *prostoy*, idle waiting. The greatest of all Soviet myths was that the State would take care of anything. In truth, the State took care of nothing, and losses due to prostoy exceeded millions of mandays, and this does not include the time lost standing in railroad ticket lines. In 1991, thirty-five million man-days were wasted in ticket lines alone, and less than 75 percent of the would-be commuters actually got a ticket. In 1991, the amount of time wasted daily looking for services equaled the annual vacation time of 85,000 people. (Russians get an average of twenty-four vacation days a year.)

I did not inform my Banderovtsi that the day before I had managed with enormous effort to nail down an assignment and then secure the steel for the job. You can get steel in advance, but not concrete—it hardens too fast. For a crew to function efficiently, a team leader has to be ready to use his wits and his blat. I told the dispatcher that in the morning I'd need the first truck with concrete, and reinforced the urgency of my request by handing him a bottle of vodka, which substituted for hard currency—then as now. Unlike rubles, vodka can buy almost anything. The dispatcher nodded. We had a deal.

At 9:30 A.M., when I went back to the locker room, the Banderovtsi were still playing dominoes. I said nothing and went off to work with the steel: I was just a member of the team and it was part of my job. The workers joined me half an hour later.

"I'm not faking anyone's hours," I said.

Their hostile silence was deafening.

At noon, I was waiting at the plant's gates for my truck with concrete. I wanted to greet it as soon as it arrived, because, despite the dispatcher's having promised it to me, if someone else gave the driver another bottle of vodka, the concrete would disappear.

Soviet business life was and is a daily fight on every level—from the corridors of the Kremlin to a Siberian construction site. But when workers have proper equipment and materials, they function smoothly and effectively. This proved to be the case with my team. For the remainder of the day, the Banderovtsi were all business.

Before knocking off, I said, "Let's celebrate our first day together." This is a tradition that marks the start of a new job. In Russia, it will probably last forever.

I ceremoniously filled their filthy shot glasses with vodka.

The next day, about an hour before quitting time, one of the Banderovtsi looked up and said: "Hey guys, who's the youngest one here? Who will go get the vodka?" He was obviously referring to me. They were all over forty.

We were standing in the mud, and I noticed that the toes of his boots were missing.

"You go," I said decisively. "But not until the end of the day."

He glared at me.

"I don't drink," I went on. "And if you want to, then please do it after work. I'll join in with you on holidays."

The old Soviet production system was unproductive because it was a morass of disincentives. Moscow dictated what a Norilsk miner made and what a cotton grower in the south of Uzbekistan could earn (in either case, without any understanding of the specific working conditions or requirements), which led to apathy and irresponsibility. A worker fired for drunkenness at one place, for example, could simply cross the street and work someplace else for the same money, because, regardless of performance, all workers earned practically the same wage. If a team or a factory had a clever manager, wages could sometimes be above average, and this of course invariably increased the effectiveness of the work force. In the end, however, you got only what some bureaucrat in Moscow said you should get, rather than a market-driven wage.

To fatten their payrolls and to squeeze more money from the bureaucracy, companies inflated the number of employees and hired people they had no use for and who did nothing. Unnecessary workers were known as "dead souls"—from the novel of that name by

Nikolai Gogol. Even today, there are some twelve million of them. Westerners might be shocked by this, but in its way this situation might not be worse than a welfare system—at least people have to work. Still, the dead souls are a drag on production, and although on average Russians work no less hard than Westerners, they also have no incentives, and productivity keeps dropping. In 1990, these losses amounted to seventy billion rubles (given that the cost of raw materials is so much lower in the former Soviet Union, this means about $50 billion). In 1991, productivity fell by another 30 percent. At the same time, production levels rose in the companies that pay well, such as in the cooperatives or in businesses leased from the State.

In the bizarre economic world of the independent republics, two contradictory problems exist simultaneously: labor shortage and unemployment. Want ads seeking as many as twelve million workers are not unusual at any given time. Yet, in the Russian Republic alone, there were 1.5 million unemployed in January of 1993. I estimate that in the entire former Soviet Union, the number of unemployed fluctuated between 2.5 and 3 million. Among the republics with the highest unemployment are Azerbaijan, the Central Asian Republic, Kazakhstan, Dagestan, and Russia. Millions of make-work, dead-soul jobs are disappearing. As a result, in July of 1991, the authorities started to register the unemployed for the first time since 1930.

The labor shortage problem received wide publicity. The Communists tried to keep the unemployment figures a secret. The government cared nothing about production—only about the most efficient method of keeping its citizens in line. That was why, for instance, it was a crime *not* to work. A person without a job was referred to as *tuneyadets*—"one who eats in vain." This law was a convenient whip with which to lash dissidents into submission.

The celebrated poet Joseph Brodsky, who later won the Nobel prize, was sent to prison for "doing nothing."

"But I'm a poet," Brodsky is said to have told the judge.

"That's all well and good," replied the judge, "but I asked you what your job was."

In January of 1991, Gorbachev was finally forced to legalize the status of the unemployed (perhaps he was creating a legal basis for his own jobless future). This was no small achievement, in that extending social protection to those without work is a momentous step toward a free society. It came in the nick of time; millions of people will soon need it. (In East Germany, whose economy had been more efficient than that of the Soviet Union's, a third of the country's eight million workers lost their jobs after reunification.)

At present, however, new jobs in Russia are not being created at the same rate at which old ones are disappearing. Some industrious Russians have made a good start. As of January of 1993, more than 8,500 new cooperative technical consulting agencies and a total of 185,000 cooperatives have started up, employing more than 4,500,000 people. Today, in Russia, there are 408,000 joint-stock companies, 215,000 proprietorships and partnerships, 95,000 publically- and privately-held corporations, and 12,500 concerns and consortiums. This is a good beginning, and in the context of a full labor force, more than just symbolic. It shows that when the entrepreneurial spirit is given a chance, Russians are as quick as anyone to seize the opportunity.

The lack of proper incentives for workers, coupled with endless shortages, has long infected the Soviet system with the virus of theft, and it still hasn't recovered. Lacking any bargaining power to earn a decent living, workers are driven to stealing. *Nesuni* ("carriers") are everywhere: a worker at a meat plant will stow away as much as ten pounds of meat under his coat every day; at a rubber factory, a worker will take home as many Article #2s as he can carry (Article #2 is the official name for condoms, which are always in great demand and constitute a type of currency. I have never been able to find out what Article #1 is).

Theft persists not because Russian workers are any more dishonest than their Western counterparts, but because nothing belongs to anyone. Some claim that everything belongs to the bosses in the Kremlin, but most will say that the property belongs to the nation. "Since I am part of the nation," workers reason, "I'm not stealing—just taking what belongs to me."

This illness has a speedy cure. Those employed by cooperatives or who work in privatized industries, where a percentage of the property genuinely belongs to them, do not steal.

My crew of Banderovtsi worked admirably as long as the supplies lasted, but my luck didn't last. One day, during my first week on the job, the concrete ran out, and no amount of vodka could procure any. We were forced to sit and twiddle our thumbs. About an hour before the end of our shift, the foreman arrived and yelled: "Enough sitting around! Twelve trucks of concrete have just arrived!" Twelve trucks represented an enormous job for such a small team.

"It's not our problem if the trucks come at the end of the day," I replied. "Pay us for two shifts or throw the concrete away." By morning, of course, the concrete would set and be as hard as a rock. You'd need a crowbar to break it up.

"I didn't make you team leader to talk back to me like that!" he shouted.

"Then pick some other idiot," I replied hotly. "When it comes to work, I'm just another member of the crew."

He stormed off. If we worked a second shift for extra money or took an extra day off, he would have to justify it to his superior.

We sat in the darkness, the flashlights on our helmets projecting narrow, eerie cones of light. My workers were pleased that I had stood up for them, but they were jittery about the outcome.

"He'll be back," I assured them. "He doesn't want to pay for sixty tons of concrete out of his own pocket."

Sure enough, a minute later, the foreman was back. "I'll show you where lobsters spend their winters!" he shouted. "No extra money!" (In Russian, a place where lobsters "spend their winters" is supposed to be a very cold, faraway place. To use that threat in Norilsk, of all places, struck me as silly as it was).

A fierce-looking, broad-shouldered member of my crew carrying a crowbar approached the foreman. "You'd better shut your mouth, or else we'll do it for you."

The foreman blanched.

Hurrying over to offer my hand to the foreman, as if we had just patched up a mild disagreement, I said, "Let's shake on our deal. You pay us for the second shift and we'll unload the concrete."

He shook my hand limply and dashed off.

The concrete trucks pulled up. We heaved the steaming concrete ten feet. Each spadeful was huge and heavy, and my back hurt so much I thought my spine would snap. When I lay down during the brief breaks, I didn't know if I could ever get up.

"We won't get through sixty tons of this," one of my men said. I knew he was right.

Suddenly I thought of a simple solution. "The second shift is about to start," I said. "Let's give the workers a third of our extra money to help us finish the job."

That is precisely what happened, demonstrating once again that a little financial incentive goes a long way. Where free enterprise abounds, productivity flourishes. To cite but one example: in the former Soviet Union, private agricultural lots are as small as parking spaces in Manhattan, and constitute only 3 percent of arable land, yet they furnish 30 percent of the entire country's meat and milk products, and 60 percent of its potatoes.

How many really good unskilled workers are there in Russia? As many as 29 million. A popular Russian folk character (roughly the equivalent of Paul Bunyan) is a young man named Levsha (Left-handed), who was such a good blacksmith he could put a horseshoe on a bug. Russians are diligent, but the Soviet system tried to do away with creativity, just as it tried to do away with left-handedness. One typical example is the production of space reactors, which the United States decided to buy from Russia in 1992. The financial motivation for those who created these advanced reactors was small, yet they still took enormous pride in doing an outstanding job. Imagine what could be accomplished if there were appropriate financial remuneration in all industries!

During my Banderovtsi days, a Swedish corporation was invited to Norilsk to build a $30-million plant for the manufacture of insulating materials. I remember how excited the Swedish businessmen became when they saw how expeditiously the Russians worked—simply because they were well paid. In fact, productivity in eastern Siberia is 30 percent higher than in the European part of Russia, which is due in no small part to the fact that harsh conditions there mean workers earn more than twice what workers elsewhere are paid.

Labor was so cheap in the Soviet Union that Soviet managers frequently treated workers with less care than they did machinery, and gladly substituted human labor for machines to save wear and tear. Owing to a shortage of bulldozers, for example, my crew of Banderovtsi were ordered to dig out the iron-hard Siberian permafrost with shovels. In an effort to spare my workers from this hellish task, I illegally hired a bulldozer driver. In exchange for three bottles of vodka, he agreed to work during the night, for he had to be back at his state job with his bulldozer by morning.

I was inexperienced, however, and made a terrible mistake. I gave the driver his vodka before he started work rather than after. When I returned at 2:00 A.M. to check on his progress, he had already killed off the first bottle and was opening the second. I gave him a piece of my mind. He responded with some mat of his own. The next time, I knew better. Work first, vodka after.

As time passed, I came to enjoy working with my team more and more. Because of them, I formulated two critical lessons of management: neither frighten workers, nor, under any circumstances, give in to their demands. Treated fairly, they were first-rate workers, but because of their past "crimes," their official job rating was close to the bottom of the scale. Therefore, I couldn't pay them a wage based on the quality of their work. I decided to try to change their job rating. It was the only fair thing to do.

I approached the foreman about it. He immediately refused, explaining that they were former prisoners, zeks, and that he couldn't change their status. He was a liar, padding his own—and perhaps someone else's—pockets with my men's money. His rebuttal only whetted my appetite. After our unproductive conversation, I set off on an expedition around our construction site. By late afternoon, I had located a team that was overly friendly with our foreman. As I had expected, their job status and wages were far too high for the menial tasks to which they were assigned.

I reported what I had discovered to the foreman, who ignored me. I went to the head of the unit. "If you ignore me, too," I said, "I'll tell my workers you're cheating them. I'll go to the chief engineer."

The foreman and the head of the unit counterattacked with intimidation—by making what the Russians call a goat's muzzle. They sent two women with cameras over to monitor my team's performance. They wanted to prove we were slacking off. We responded, naturally, by stepping up our efforts. As I hammered nails into logs for sheathing, I felt like a monkey in a zoo. Who established the production quotas and the output rate for our team? What were they?

I put down my hammer and hurried over to the "estimate unit." When I got there, the head of the unit, an elderly woman, was busy eating her lunch: a hunk of black bread filled with good Norilsk sausage and a pickle.

"Please," I begged, "could you tell me what the output rate for my team is? I think someone is trying to trick us."

The silver-haired woman looked me up and down. What she saw was a pushy teenager in dirty rubber boots, overalls with deep pockets for tools, and a green fedora with a wide brim. She took pity and smiled. In motherly tones she told me that my team was indeed being underpaid.

I wrote a report to the administration and won my case. My Banderovtsi's wages increased substantially and I was happy for them. They were not murderers, after all. They were ordinary men capable of ordinary feeling and of showing respect—when it was earned.

Financial incentives are still the best motivators, but not the only ones. One day, I asked my crew when was the last time they had gone on vacation. Several replied that they had never been allowed to leave Norilsk. Western readers might be surprised to learn that Russian workers normally get eighteen days of paid leave; managers and engineers get twenty-four. In Norilsk, everyone gets forty-eight days. The Banderovtsi got the same amount of leave as the other workers; they just couldn't go anywhere.

"You know, there's a wonderful spa right here," I said. "Mud baths, winter gardens, all sorts of facilities." I knew of the place because my mother had gone there.

One man said, "Who would give us a pass?"

Rooms at the spa, like everything in the Soviet Union, were in short supply.

I went to the trade unions' committee in charge of distributing passes, and told them my team needed to use the spa.

"Those guys are *zeks*," an official answered. "Former prisoners. Zeks don't get passes."

"You'll give them a pass," I said, "and without a bribe."

They laughed.

I had managed to get a list of people who had been given passes the previous year by this committee. Predictably, the beneficiaries were mostly the managers and the trade unionists themselves.

"Trade unions are called schools of communism," I said to the trade union leaders. "Is that how you preach communism to the workers?"

In the end, I got the passes, my team got their vacation, and before long my team was the best at the construction site. I no longer needed to hover over them, and with my new time was able to pursue boxing and my studies.

A project of the scope the American consulting company was planning meant relocating a very large number of workers. Would they be willing to relocate? This is a question often asked by American companies. Russian history demonstrates that relocation should not be a stumbling block to new ventures. As far back as the seventeenth and eighteenth centuries, under Peter the Great, Russians volunteered to develop Siberia. In the nineteenth century, Russian Minister of Finance Yegor Koncrin implemented an incentive program that sent people to Siberia in droves. Citizens were given a substantial amount of money for settlement. So many Jews flocked to the new territory that Czar Nicolas I, a rabid anti-Semite, prohibited them from taking part in the program.

Even under the Communists, the Soviet empire continued to entice people into relocating to Siberia and the Far East—again, in exchange for significant sums of money. A program to build a major Baikal-Amur railroad through eastern Siberia and the Russian Far East attracted tens of thousands of people. They came voluntarily to work and live in the newly developed regions along the route. When a foreign corporation creates a project in an undeveloped region, it can count on the State to cover some of the expenses connected with relocating the labor force.

ACC's projects also raised the question of how Russian workers feel about foreigners. Xenophobic, anticapitalist propaganda has long been a destructive force in the former Soviet Union. Most Russians realize that cooperating with foreign businesses is the only road to a better life, but their minds have been poisoned for decades by an unremitting barrage of anti-Western propaganda.

Despite the propaganda, Russian workers have retained their own opinions about working with foreign powers. I remember a lunch break in a Norilsk copper-nickel mine, a mile underground. In the darkness, after hours of backbreaking work, their hands still shaking from pneumatic pick hammers, workers turn philosophical. Fidel Castro was visiting the area, and they were complaining that the government was lavishing money on foreign adventurers while its own people lacked essentials.

"Who needs that hairy guy, anyway?" said one of my team.

Yet, when former Prime Minister Pierre Trudeau of Canada was in town, he was warmly received by the workers. "Those Canadians are good people," was what they thought. "Just like their equipment. We could work with them."

Today, nearly everyone agrees that working with outsiders is beneficial, in that this invariably establishes new standards of productivity. Starting in 1989, for instance, the Chinese have been leasing land in Kirgizia. Local farmers grow twenty-three tons of tomatoes per hectare. The Chinese, on the same land, produce 100 tons. (In all fairness, the American seeds the Chinese used didn't hurt their cause any, but the difference was nonetheless striking.) So, too, the seeds of the American management system, transplanted to Russian soil, should yield a bumper crop. The former Soviet Union has everything it needs to improve its standard of living. Everything, that is, except the right system.

However, even when the old management system is replaced, not all traces will disappear. Mismanagement and waste under the old regime were enormous. Soviet secrecy and paranoia created an avalanche of lies that, as it picked up momentum over the years, overwhelmed everything in its path, including Soviet industry. If a foreign corporation launches a venture in Russia, its leadership should be acutely aware of this problem. Otherwise, it will suffer the economic consequences.

Here is one illustration. One morning, an engineer came to our construction site, pointed to the ground, and said, "Concrete for a foundation needs to be poured right here."

My team mixed and poured the concrete, and then laid the foundation.

The engineer returned three days later and told us we had put the foundation in the wrong place. "It needs to go ten feet over to the right," he said.

We were furious. You can't just move concrete. Besides, my workers hadn't put the foundation in the wrong place; they knew the plan of the building better than this ninety-day wonder of an engineer. We always carried tracing paper with us (there were no copy machines) and always double-checked the assignments. None of that mattered. We had to smash what we had built—an expensive and disheartening proposition.

Two or three years later, when I was head of a student construction team in Norilsk, the same thing happened. The proud but inexperienced students were outraged.

"That's ridiculous," one student exclaimed. "We won't do it over!"

"You'll do it as many times as you're paid for it," I said. "When they stop paying you, then you stop. Your business is to build. The engineer's business is to account for excessive use of concrete and cost overruns."

Such disorder provides fertile soil for fraud. If a foreign company decides to build a road in Russia, for example, it should watch out for the so-called Documents of Unseen Works.

What are the Documents of Unseen Works? To lay asphalt properly, you first need to spread sand, then pebbles, and finally the asphalt. The road requires a "pillow." In the Soviet Union, workers would often spread asphalt directly on the ground, bring in a roller, and call it a day. As the Russians put it, everything is *shito-krito*—buried and gone, hidden from sight. Because documentation might call for sand and pebbles, however, sand and pebbles have to be bought—whether or not they are actually used. If they aren't used, of course, the soil will move, the asphalt collapse, and the road disintegrate. Time and money are wasted. In 1991, losses connected with bad roads amounted to thirty billion rubles in Russia alone. Funds allocated for improving the infrastructure have about dried up.

Many foreigners believe that only Russians live in Russia, but, in fact, Russia is extremely diverse ethnically. Ethnic traditions are strong in every region, not just in every republic, and it is essential to take them into account before choosing a location for investment. Each region has its own ethnic conflicts, labor traditions, and economic history. A foreign company once brought in an interpreter who kept referring to Ukrainians as Russians. The Ukrainians were so displeased they almost cut off negotiations. There is also the story of the American accountant trying to land a contract in Tataria. He went to visit and brought along plenty of first-rate bacon, as he'd heard meat was in short supply. Only when he got there did he learn that Tatars, being Muslim, don't eat pork. Little things—but very important.

The Baltics, Moldova, western Ukraine, and western Byelarus still remember how capitalism works, since it flourished there until they were swallowed up by Stalin fifty years ago. The province of Chukotka, on the other hand, has been socialist since it ceased to be just a collection of nomadic tribes. Located in the northeast of Russia, Chukotka is roughly three times the size of Great Britain. In the 1950s, its Party boss and governor were each given an official car by Moscow. No one in that sprawling land had ever seen a car before.

The next day, the two cars collided.

Soviet bureaucrats always felt free to violate ethnic traditions. In the late 1960s, for example, they decided to introduce the Asian Tadzhiks, who for generations had been small tradesmen and cattle herders, to heavy industry. It took two decades and a small fortune to construct an aluminum plant in Tadzhikistan. Three hundred Tadzhiks were then sent to spend nine months at the Krasnoyarsk aluminum plant in Siberia, the second largest in the world, to learn about the industry. Only a dozen of them ended up going back to work at the new plant. The others went back to what they knew best—crafts and cattle.

The effects of modernization were more tragic for the nomadic northern Siberian nationalities, and in southern Siberia for the cattle-breeding ethnic groups in Hakassia and Tuva. Soviet authorities forced them to settle in towns. Their children were taken to city orphanages, where soon both urban and rural lifestyles became alien to them. Torn from their homeland and their families, they sought refuge in a vodka bottle.

I gradually came to understand the historical identity of the Banderovtsi on my crew. Their lives had been wrenched as violently as the Ukraine itself. During the seventh century, an ancient people who practiced Judaism, the Khazars, controlled the Ukraine. Two hundred years later, the Varangians from Scandinavia conquered the land and established their capital in Kiev. They joined with the inhabitants to form Kievan Russia, which remained a Russian principality until the thirteenth century, when, in 1240, the Mongols swooped down and conquered it. In 1392, the Grand Duke of Lithuania grabbed the Ukraine for himself, and in 1569 the area fell under Polish rule. The Cossacks rebelled against the Poles and managed to free the Ukraine; realizing that they could not survive on their own, however, they sought a treaty with the principality of Muscovy, which had been created in 1280. The treaty was signed in 1654, and according to its terms the Ukraine was supposed to retain autonomy. This is not how things worked out. Fighting led to the loss of independence, and the Ukraine was swallowed up by Russia in 1793. For over a century, the Ukrainians mourned the loss of their freedom, and in January of 1918, the Ukraine declared itself an independent nation. Four years of bloodshed followed. In 1922, the Soviet Union reconquered the Ukraine, designating it one of the original Soviet republics.

For seventeen years, the misery of the Ukrainians fermented. Then came the Second World War. Some of my Banderovtsi were little more than boys when the war began; the oldest among them then were just teenagers. Their fathers, proud and fearsome fighters, had recounted to them again and again the terrible, blood-soaked history of the Ukraine. Their homeland should be independent, they had told their sons, and they must fight for its freedom. The sons obeyed their fathers and fought to free their land. After the Soviet Union won the war and crushed the rebellion, the members of my crew were shipped off to the prisons of Norilsk. They didn't even speak Russian.

Today, their fathers and their fathers' fathers must be singing and dancing in their graves: forty-seven years after the end of the Second World War, the Ukraine is finally free. In 1991, George Bush, greatly underestimating the currents at work in the region, appealed to the Ukrainian Parliament to stay in the Soviet Union. But the Parliament was not about to bow to external pressure—not when the country was on the verge of realizing its centuries-old dream. It almost immediately voted for independence.

In 1968 I knew nothing about the politics or history of the Ukraine. I simply had a vague sense that my workers' lives had been shattered, and felt sorry for them. They were lonely, vulnerable prisoners of the past.

My mother once took me to Kolargon, which used to be a prison for the Quarterers—those who had been given twenty-five-year sentences. By the 1960s, its squalid prison cells were being used for storage. As I stood in the somber silence of the deserted prison, my mother whispered to me: "The prisoners here were innocent people. Most of them had done nothing to deserve their fate."

During the war, my mother had been a schoolteacher and later a consumer service manager. As part of her job, she was permitted to pick almost any of the workers from the labor camps. Rather than hire free people, she took the prisoners, and by so doing saved the lives of many.

I felt the same responsibility toward my men. I managed to secure them boots with solid soles, and warm coats. It was something of a miracle that I had been able to find them. Remembering that Ukrainians are a proud people, I put the coats and boots out on the benches and tables in the locker room before they arrived. Had I done otherwise, I would have insulted them, and they might not have taken them.

By the time I left my job as a team leader in Norilsk a few months later, they were coming to watch my boxing matches, and we often relaxed in the sauna together. Then the currents of our lives carried us off in different directions.

Although it is not necessary for foreign companies to import un-skilled foreign workers into Russia, given the quality and low cost of the labor force already in place, Russian companies desperately need to attract experienced Western managers. How will they get paid? In hard currency, if the company's hard currency profits depend on skilled management.

A tax for foreigners has been instituted by the authorities. (Taxation has turned out to be one of the few aspects of capitalism the Kremlin had little trouble grasping.) Today, any foreigner who lives in the country longer than 183 calendar days a year is considered a permanent resident and subject to income tax. In 1992, the Russian government helped matters a little by offering American businesses a special incentive: the abolishment of double taxation. However, these tax regulations, these—what shall we call them?—*refinements* are in general a nuisance and only halfway measures. You don't clean up a seventy-five-year-old mess without creating some new clutter.

Now for the good news. Over the last two years, in Russia alone, more than 8.5 million people have left State enterprises to work for non-State companies. By 1995, according to my estimate, 13 to 15 million more will have joined them as the semicapitalist economy blossoms, and by 1996, the private sector will employ 35 million people—out of a total pool of 62 million industrial and office workers. Dead souls are coming back to life. State companies, newly leased by workers, generally begin by eliminating unnecessary jobs and replacing them with necessary ones. These leased companies are among the best possible partners for foreign investors because the employees feel that they have a personal stake in the success of their venture and that brings out their best qualities. One of the smartest ways for a foreign company to invest in Russia is to buy an enterprise from the State, and to create a partnership with its workers.

CHAPTER 4

Inside
a Soviet Enterprise:
SibAuto

The best guarantee of success in the Russian marketplace lies in choosing a smart and reliable Russian partner. This way, whatever the Kremlin (formerly, home to the Politburo and Gorbachev; today, home of the Russian president and his staff) does or doesn't do, your factory will remain standing, you will still have access to raw materials, and, if the workers are well motivated, your business will continue to grow. Readers will have appreciated by now that I don't place much faith in the government, which still consists largely of former bureaucrats. Young or old, they are little different from their counterparts under the Communist Party.

When a foreign company considers investing in a joint venture, buying a company outright, or creating a shareholding company, it should learn as much as it can about the Soviet enterprise. Questions, hard questions, need to be asked and answered. How does its production system work (or not work)? How has the company survived a command economy? How much damage did the communist system do to the entrepreneurial spirit of management and workers? Is there any hope of fathoming the organizational structure?

Questions such as these are not so unlike those potential investors would ask were they considering investing in a company in Lima,

Ohio, or Flagstaff, Arizona, but because of cultural differences, and because for over seventy years Russia has been isolated, the answers are likely to be complex and incomplete. One needs more than a glance at an inventory or a balance sheet. This is why the advice I have given Western corporations extends well beyond purely technical considerations. Any Western managers worth their salt will want to know more than simply the latest laws or up-to-the-minute changes in Moscow's hierarchy—important as they might be. The keys to Russian business lie in the Russian business mentality.

Perhaps more than in any other country, business in Russia is predicated on personal relationships. If a Russian does not like you—if you do not hit it off—he will not do business with you, even if it might have been in his best interest.

Misunderstandings can sabotage the most promising deal, and—beginning the moment an outsider works through the door of a Russian business—they *will* arise.

The possibilities for miscommunication are endless. Imagine that the Russian businessperson brings a friend to a meeting with an American businessperson, and, with only the most amiable of intentions, the American asks the Russians, "So, how did you two meet?" Silence. The Russians will be very embarrassed. They are very secretive people generally, and with foreigners even more so. The nationality of a foreigner is unimportant; all that matters is that he is not Russian. (This doesn't mean a stranger on a Russian train won't tell you his entire life story, particularly if he senses you aren't interested.)

Cut off for so long from the rest of the world, Russians have an inferiority-superiority complex about foreigners and an idealized image of Westerners. If you are American, it is automatically assumed you are a millionaire. Yet, Russians will also sometimes refer to a Westerner as a burdock, a simpleton, someone innocent of life's cruelties. They, on the other hand, have lived with terror. Knowing how Russians have survived despotism over the centuries is critical to achieving success in Russian business.

Americans in particular would be amused at how the average Russian envisions them at the office: jeans, no necktie, feet propped up on the desk, Marlboro cigarette dangling out of the mouth; a nonchalant, almost cocky attitude toward the boss. Americans often find Russians terribly and unnecessarily formal. This is not without some basis, although Russian formality is only skin deep, like American informality. In the United States, just because you drift to a first-name basis with your boss after a drink doesn't mean you're best friends. In Russia, it might be years before two colleagues call each other by their first names. The new breed of Russian bosses might go on a first-name basis with an American after one drink, but this shouldn't be taken too far.

"Ivan thinks. . ." jauntily began an American at a meeting the day after he and Ivan had had a drink.

Ivan's face froze with embarrassment and rage.

Foreigners sometimes view potential Russian partners as somewhat primitive when it comes to commerce. This is a misconception. Because the Soviet economic system was so distorted, Russian businesspeople needed to become very sophisticated in their own way. Their skills are not rudimentary, just different, and their special Russian know-how will be invaluable to joint ventures. Where they might have been naive at one point about the international arena, even there they have become considerably more sophisticated. When perestroika began, and legitimate Western companies were still contemplating their investments, adventurers poured into the Soviet Union. They did enough damage to make Russians extra cautious. This is one reason why, when you visit a Russian official, it is always a good idea to bring as many documents as you can carry. Annual reports, brochures, stock reports, magazine articles—they all help legitimize the company in Russian eyes.

There are probably only five American companies with any name recognition in Russia: General Electric, DuPont, Ford, Pepsico, and Xerox. Even a high-level Russian manager might have no idea who Merrill or Lynch are, or what Citibank means, or even be able to identify a small number of companies on the *Fortune* 500 list. He will judge you based on what the name means to him. If you work for Salomon Brothers, he might assume you work for Israeli intelligence.

For their part, the first thing that comes to the mind of most foreign executives at the sound of the term Russian business is bureaucracy. After I told him I was writing a book on the Russian business mentality, a real estate broker in Connecticut looked stunned. "Is there such a thing?" he asked me. "I thought it was all just bureaucracy."

Many foreign investors still hold this view, which is why, when they come to Russia to do business, they often have done little thinking about what lies ahead for them after the bureaucratic stage. Connections with government functionaries, however important, will not bring long-term success. Concentrating solely on getting signatures on permission forms and not thinking about the next step can make you captive to a number of problems. Chief among them, as I will show, are shortages.

In Russia we often say that to really know someone you first need to sweat a *pood* of salt together. A pood is thirty-six pounds. Only after you have toiled side by side doing backbreaking, sweaty work with someone do you get to know what they're made of. Until very recently, foreigners couldn't get this first-hand experience because they weren't allowed to work at a Soviet enterprise. Now that has changed. Before signing any corporate marriage contract, outsiders should first go and sweat a pood—figuratively at least—with the Soviet enterprise: locate its aches and pains and its joys; find out what type of relationship it enjoys with the appropriate ministry.

Before anyone jumps into a joint venture, they need to fall in love—and the feeling needs to be requited. A study I conducted concluded that nearly a third of American-Russian joint ventures fail because the basis for the partnership was rocky to begin with. We will see in later chapters what the other major reasons for joint-venture failure are.

The problems I experienced while working at Siberian Nonferrous Metallurgy Automation Company (SibAuto, for short) some years ago are representative of what a Western company can expect to find at a Russian business today. It makes little difference whether the company bakes bread or casts steel. All Russian managers' headaches are similar—and they are very different from Western managerial problems. The differences are important to note because, as I have discovered from experience with Russians and Americans, although two parties might seem to be sitting across a table from each other, they are very likely facing in opposite directions. When I first started working in international business, my foreign partner and I spoke different languages (even though he spoke Russian). We were using the same words but giving them entirely different economic definitions. Things got so confused we tottered on the verge of breaking off our deal out of frustration. No one should want to walk a mile in a Russian manager's shoes, but this chapter will show where they pinch.

A Western corporation's primary concern is the marketplace: how can it get the fruits of its labor there quickly and efficiently? A Russian manager's fruit will get eaten, greedily, no matter how rotten it is, when it has made its way to the marketplace. The people are that desperate for goods and services. The Russian's nightmares revolve around supplies, and when a foreign company ties the knot with a Russian company, it shares his nightmares.

SibAuto's specialty was the automation of the diamond, gold, and nonferrous metal industry—an industry that contributed hundreds of millions of dollars to the Soviet Union. Desperate to increase their output, mine operators were in dire need of our equipment. We, in turn, were in desperate need of parts to manufacture that equipment. The mining companies would have been only too happy to purchase from abroad the parts we needed to manufacture the automation equipment for them, but, alas, they had no hard currency.

Shortages were generated by, and not merely endemic to, the Soviet economic structure—and arose from bureaucratic blindness. For instance, the State might place an order with an enterprise for aluminum window frames, promising its manager that the aluminum would soon be shipped from a plant across the country. Weeks would pass with no aluminum arriving. When the manager would try to contact the aluminum plant, he would learn that the plant was still under construction and might be operational sometime within the next two years.

This sort of frustration and absurdity still haunts every facet of life. In 1991, a friend of mine, a professor at the Russian Academy of Sciences, received a pass for a stay at a spa on the Black Sea. Looking forward to a little rest and relaxation, he arrived with several suitcases and a bicycle, only to find out that the spa had not yet been constructed. The blueprints were still on the State drawing board.

Stories such as these might be the stuff of high comedy, but the cycle of shortages is vicious and all-inclusive, and has gotten worse over the last few years. This is why I always advise potential joint-venture partners to think about how they are going to obtain the materials they will need *before* they sign a contract. Otherwise, the hydra of shortages will rear its ugly, multitudinous heads and devour the entire project.

McDonald's is a shining example of a company that prepared for the shortages it would face when it entered the Russian marketplace. Before it opened its first store in Pushkin Square, McDonald's established its own farm, where it grew potatoes and kept livestock. The company also trained local workers. When it went into operation, the Russian McDonald's franchise was nearly self-sufficient. Other companies were not as prepared. The lesson: the laws governing commerce might change, but shortages remain.

One of the first joint ventures between the West and Russia was a fashion magazine for women called *Burda Moden Russia*. The project became the darling of the joint-venture movement. When it was being created, I looked at the agreement and saw that there was no correlation between the joint venture's goals and the Soviet partner's capacities. I was far from surprised when the magazine folded in 1991.

In a discussion with *Vneshtorgizdat*, the official foreign trade publication of the Soviet Union, I said that the idea of publishing an affordable fashion magazine for Soviet women is an excellent one. Both German companies, Aenne Burda GmbH, which owns twenty-five percent, and Ferrostaal AG, which owns twenty-four percent, have excellent reputations. The Soviet partner also has experience in publishing. But I have two questions: where are they going to get the paper on which to print the magazine? And who will pay for the dollar expenses they incur bringing equipment into the USSR? I was told in response to these questions that Raisa Gorbachev herself supported the project and that she was going to arrange for everything.

The magazine was given a flashy launch. Moscow's first beauty queen was at the presentation, and—to give her blessing—Raisa Gorbachev. That was the good part. The bad part was that Raisa had arranged for hard currency financing only, and this, ironically, meant the project was undercapitalized.

Here is an example of a joint venture supported only by the Soviet bureaucracy, not also by the suppliers it needed. I warned the management about the problems they would face because it was clear to me that the administrative support wouldn't last, and that hard currency capitalization was insufficient. Further, the joint venture lacked the local support it needed. Having the blessing of the rich and powerful is fine, but someone had to provide the paper.

Indeed, the paper shortage turned out to be *Burda Moden Russia*'s major problem. This was 1987, and glasnost was gathering steam with every passing day. A growing number of newspapers were beginning to appear, and paper, always in short supply, became even more difficult to find. Central controls loosened their grip. Raisa's name started to lose its magic. Paper mills began selling paper to whoever paid the highest price. By the beginning of 1991, Raisa's husband was in trouble and so was *Burda*. But it was too late for the founders to change their partnership arrangements—they were in too much debt.

The founders of the *Burda Moden Russia* joint venture had made two basic mistakes. First, they relied too heavily on personal contacts. Although connections help, they aren't enough. Their second mistake was that the Western companies did not choose the right partner. One of the partners, at least, should have been a paper manufacturer.

Should connections fail, only a good partner and sound business sense will save a joint venture from bankruptcy. It is imperative to study and know what your possible shortages will be before you take the plunge.

When I was very young, my dream was to become a doorman at a garage. A little later I decided to become a cabinet minister. I would settle for nothing less. I studiously read all of the biographical entries of every Soviet minister in the *Soviet Encyclopedia*, noting that many of them held doctorates and that all of them had been directors of plants at one point in their careers. I forgot about becoming a doorman or a minister, but I did get a doctorate in managerial economics, worked as a department head at the Norilsk Concern, and then, at the age of twenty-seven, became Deputy Director General at SibAuto.

One bright winter's morning, soon after I started at SibAuto, my boss, Director General Tzaregorodtsev, affectionately known as Tzar, called me. At thirty-nine, Tzar was among the youngest men ever to serve in a director's position in heavy industry. Bright, quick, and ruthlessly demanding, Tzar was known for standing up for his principles even when it meant crossing swords with the authorities. He was very popular at SibAuto, and a respected figure in the region.

Tzar's voice on the phone sounded serious. "We're in trouble. The ministry inspector is on his way to Krasnoyarsk to take a look at our ghost building."

The "ghost building" he referred to housed a series of workshops. We had built it without the government's knowledge and hoped to keep its existence a secret.

"How did they find out about it?" I asked, swallowing.

"*Anonymka*," Tzar said simply.

I was immediately worried. Whenever anyone wanted to get someone in trouble, all he had to do was compose an anonymka—a slanderous, anonymous letter—and send it to the Communist Party, the KGB, or the militia. A neighbor who wanted your room in a communal apartment might write one; so might a wife or husband who wanted a divorce. Anyone could write an anonymka and accuse you of being an American spy digging a tunnel between Moscow and New York. These mud-slinging letters, often signed "A group of well-wishing comrades," could actually stand up in court, and were responsible for the deaths of tens of thousands of people under Stalin. Later, officials declared such unsubstantiated letters immaterial evidence. However, Soviet officials were masters of false promises. Anonymkas were nearly always damaging.

I knew we were in serious trouble. I hung up and called the head of our documents department, a retired colonel by the name of Holod—a pale, thin-lipped man everyone called Chancellor Frost ("holod" in English means "frost"). Word about our illegal project had leaked, I told him, and Tzar and I were in real danger. The lives of Soviet managers often were.

Who could forget what happened to Dr. Hint, a talented inventor and engineer, and a winner of the Lenin prize? An Estonian by birth, Hint had developed a machine called a disintegrator, which could pulverize virtually any substance. It proved very useful to a wide variety of industries and was soon in great demand. Hint founded a company to manufacture them, and it did extremely well. But the Soviet system could not abide his ingenuity, and in his fight for a fresh approach to manufacturing, he crossed the Soviet bureaucracy, which held that individual success was a sign of corruption. Hint was old and sick when they sentenced him to fifteen years in prison, where he died.

Ivan Hudenko suffered a similar fate. Hudenko had left a powerful position in the Agriculture Ministry to become the manager of a collective farm in Kazakhstan, where he wanted to implement progressive techniques. He achieved wonderful results and raised the standard of living of his farm workers to unheard-of heights. Soon he too ran afoul of the bureaucracy and died in prison. Even in those despotic times, hundreds of like-minded people around the country attempted to protect Hudenko and Hint, but to no avail. The sort of merciless persecution they suffered for their entrepreneurial independence lasted well into the days of Brezhnev and Andropov.

I was certain the inspector from the Ministry of Nonferrous Metallurgy would ask us where we had gotten the three million rubles to erect our ghost building. That the three million went into a building and not my pockets would argue against my going to jail, but it wouldn't stop the authorities from making life miserable for me. I might find a teaching job in a few years, but my corporate career would be finished.

"How could anyone have found out?" Chancellor Frost gasped, after I told him about the inspector. "We were silent as the dead about it."

I repeated Tzar's anonymka theory. Then I asked Chancellor Frost to contact Kozin, the head of our planning office, in the hope we could find out what had gone wrong. What went wrong speaks volumes about Soviet business.

Headquartered in Krasnoyarsk, with branches around the country and abroad, SibAuto supplied 85 percent of the automated machinery used in the nonferrous metallurgy industry in Russia, where, beginning in the mid-1970s, automation and geology were of foremost importance. Geologists became national heroes. Gold, diamonds, oil, gas, copper, and nickel fields sprouted up everywhere—though mainly in Siberia, especially in the Krasnoyarsk Region.

SibAuto was on the cutting edge of these trends, and mainly responsible for dragging the Soviet's nonferrous industry into the twentieth century. SibAuto was also remarkable because it was one of the first companies in the Soviet Union trying to become self-sufficient, meaning to base its production on actual customer orders, not the government. When I was there in the seventies, it had a long way to go.

My deputy director general position seemed tailor-made for me, for I could combine what I had learned as worker, middle manager, and economist. It was also a major challenge. The Russian nonferrous metals industry is huge, and was then generating enormous revenues. (Of course, the miners themselves generally wound up with nothing.) Yet, despite the scale of the industry, the government—Soviet and Russian—has never spent more than 3 percent of its capital investment on automation. By way of comparison, the United States spends 30 percent. As a result, 49 percent of the labor done in nonferrous metallurgy is manual. In jobs held predominantly by women, the level is 53 percent, a statistic that reflects the widespread exploitation of women in Russia.

There is a joke about a group of sociologists who decided to conduct an experiment about survival on a deserted island. They found three such islands and on one put two French men and a woman, on the second two American men and a woman, and on the third two Russian men and a woman. After a while the sociologists returned to each island to see what had happened. The French had formed a ménage à trois. The Americans created a company, in which the two men and the woman were competing for the top spot. When the sociologists came to the Russian island, they found the two men playing dominoes. The woman was missing. "Where is she?" asked the sociologists. "The people are in the fields," they replied. In Soviet industry, if things are bad for men, they are even worse for women.

A snapshot of me when I was at SibAuto shows me holding out a handful of sparkling, high-quality diamonds. It was taken when I visited one of SibAuto's customers, Yakutia Diamond, the largest diamond mining and refining company in Russia. Those gems represented just one day's work. With the automation systems I had planned for the company, I believed, SibAuto would turn one handful of diamonds into two. I also believed that if a small portion of the profits from this treasure trickled down onto the bare tables of Russian citizens, I could consider myself a success. I was confident SibAuto could make it all happen. But after my first week on the job, I realized SibAuto was an organizational and fiscal disaster.

First, the company's financial organization was tied up in knots. The manner in which orders were being placed made no sense; it reminded me of the way Trishka, a comic character in Russian folklore, patched his clothes. Trishka repaired the holes in his caftan by cutting out a piece of cloth from one spot and then sewing it onto another. The work was never-ending, and of course never-improving.

In the Soviet Union, an order would come in and the company would gear up for production. Then, out of nowhere would come a different order, this time from the ministry; it would assume top priority and scuttle the manufacturing schedule. The pattern repeated itself ad nauseam. On Monday, the ministry would want remote-control equipment and demand that every resource be allocated to its manufacture. On Thursday, it would change its mind and order a luminous separator. The Monday after that, it might decide what it most needed was a mobile nuclear power plant.

The result was that fewer and fewer orders got filled. SibAuto suffered from bureaucratic schizophrenia, and was in such a financial mess I soon began to wonder why I had left my post at the Norilsk Combine. We courted bankruptcy every day.

The state of affairs was brought home to me early on, as I was scheduling a meeting with our chief financial officer. I had asked my secretary, Nadia, to call him for me. Nadia was nineteen and beautiful. During those rare moments when she was not on the phone flirting with her army of admirers, she was a dynamic assistant. Actually, her steamy conversations provided something of an advantage. My telephone calls and visitors distracted her from her true occupation—winning and breaking hearts—so she dealt with them with blinding speed. Her method of answering the telephone was particularly effective. "Kvint's office. Name please?" Her style intimidated the majority of my callers. Decades of tyranny had made most Russians very wary about disclosing their name to a stranger, particularly over the telephone.

Nadia contacted the financial officer, and then came into my office. "He can't come," she told me. "He says he's busy."

"What do you mean, busy?" I asked.

"He's busy playing the accordion," she explained.

"During business hours?" I was first dumbfounded, then enraged. "Get me payroll. I don't want him to be paid for playing the accordion."

"Excuse me," said Nadia, "but you're new here and couldn't know this. He thinks his main job is playing the accordion with the Krasnoyarsk City Philharmonic."

If our chief financial officer was busier with his squeeze box than with the company's books, I was hardly surprised to learn that a bank had put SibAuto in File 2, which meant that it had judged the company bankrupt. We could borrow no more money, and whatever profits we generated would be seized to pay off our debts. Many of our employees had not been paid their salaries for months. SibAuto owed them a total of 340,000 rubles, a tremendous sum, considering that in 1976 the average salary was 158 rubles a month.

Yet, SibAuto was a technologically advanced company—a manufacturer of state-of-the-art automating systems for mines, refineries, and metallurgical plants. The systems it manufactured had multiple uses—from managing underground transportation, radio remote control, communications, and space geophysics to calculating material expenses and financial budgets. Why, for all its sophistication, was the company in such bad shape?

The answer was simple: the long arm of the State. Government meddling made our operations drift like a rudderless sailboat. The Soviet system was basically a confused system of prohibitions and exceptions, and it was nearly impossible to tell them apart. Its underlying logic was: "You can't do that; but if you want to do it, then go ahead. Just remember that you can't."

A second reason things were a mess was the lack of any real financial leadership. Tzar was a highly educated and very creative engineer, a first-rate specialist in mining techniques, and the co-creator of a number of inventions, but he was too enamored of engineering details to deal with organizational structures. In America, some managers start out as technical experts and use their expertise to climb the corporate ladder. By growing with the job and broadening their skills, they become effective managers and administrators. Others—and to some extent I place Tzar among them— have a more difficult time making the switch; they are wonderful technicians, but not qualified to lead a company.

In the Soviet Union, the overwhelming majority of managers began their careers as technicians and hence have no business training. This is why, as the country opens up, many are eager to learn more about management techniques and international business. Russian enterprises eagerly shell out scarce hard currency to send their managers abroad to study. These managers are a good revenue source for Western business schools. There are some Russian business schools, but not nearly enough that can teach international business as it needs to be taught. For example, in 1988, with the help of some colleagues from the Plekhanov Institute of National Economy, I helped establish the School for Young Managers in Moscow. Although the School was brand new and had no reputation to speak of, the competition to get in was tremendous. Bureaucrats used every ounce of their influence to get their children admitted. Every Sunday, these young people would come to the School, rather than go to the movies, to study the basics of the free-market system.

I felt that Tzar and I made a good team; our strengths and weaknesses complemented each other's. Besides, I was fired up for a challenge. Having first trained as a mining engineer, then as an economist, I was sure I could combine technical competence with managerial innovation and immediately came up with several ideas to get SibAuto back on track.

I learned fast that my freedom was limited. Initiative was still very much a punishable offense in the Soviet Union, and that made the life of a Soviet manager, as I have suggested, hell. Heart conditions and strokes were so common among managers that these ailments were referred to as "occupational" diseases. Managers in Russia continue to fight a war of attrition against the sort of insane system of restrictions and shortages I found waiting for me the moment I arrived at SibAuto. I routinely put in fourteen-hour days in an effort to correct it. Such hours might seem commonplace to the Western business community, which often works late into the evening, but the difference between Western and Russian managers is that Westerners have a financial incentive to work hard, whereas, no matter how hard they work, Russian managers wind up as poor as the rest of the population. Their incentive comes from a strong desire to beat the system and to accomplish something personally. If they succeed, that remains their only reward.

Every State company falls under the jurisdiction of a ministry or a governing administrative body that sets limits on a company's circulating assets: the working capital the company uses to pay its workers and buy spare parts or raw materials. Under communism, no company could allocate these funds for any purpose—such as to build a new facility or raise workers' salaries—but those stipulated by the State. Until July of 1992, only joint ventures, cooperatives, and wholly foreign-owned companies were free to determine the salary levels of their employees. (Today, managers are free to determine salaries; the problem is that they don't have enough experience to do it properly.) Even if an enterprise, such as SibAuto, operated on its own profits, or was leased from the State by the employees, it was still subject to a long list of governmental restrictions and, perhaps worst of all, passed along the lion's share of its profits to a ministry.

Every morning, as I was being driven to work, I brooded over our inability to control our own operating budget. I was eager to expand production. To do that we would need to attract skilled workers. The word around town was that our employees sometimes didn't get paid for months on end.

One Monday morning, as I was arriving at the office, I saw our head bookkeeper Gorelov standing near the entrance. He glared at me but said nothing. I nodded and hurried past. I knew that my age was a problem for some executives at SibAuto, many of whose middle managers were much older than I. Kozin, the head of planning, was fifty-five; our head of payroll, Puzirev, was fifty; Gorelov was forty-five (which is the average for middle managers in Russia). True to the meaning of his name (The Burned), Gorelov seethed every time my driver dropped me off. His resentment grew with each passing day. Whereas he, Gorelov, was forced to use public transportation, this kid Kvint was being driven to and from work. He didn't seem to care that my job forced me to rush around the city, while he could spend all day in his office. His anger tended to burn hottest on those mornings he arrived hung over. Gorelov was well known for dancing tight and hard with a bottle of vodka in the evenings.

Gorelov was so upset about my chauffeur he started sending Tzar memos on the subject. On one such memo Tzar jotted "I'll give you fifty percent of what you deserve" and sent it back to Gorelov. Gorelov exulted. He went around excitedly asking everyone what they thought Tzar's note meant. "Do you think he means I'll get driven to the office or home?" He wouldn't rest until everyone knew of his heroic stance.

That morning, as I passed by his glare, I had no notion what Gorelov had up his sleeve. I went to my office and started looking through the mountain of telexes, telephone messages, and papers. Most of the latter were bills and invoices, sometimes amounting to several million rubles a day. They were my nightmare. When I first started at SibAuto, we had no money with which to pay them. I thought the day would be spent like all others: doing battle against the army of restrictions governing wages, production quotas, and planning schedules. Restrictions were the soul of the Soviet economic system.

By 8:30 A.M., the telephone was ringing off the hook: the financial head of every SibAuto division across the country was trying to get through. After listening to their reports, I went to a planning meeting in Tzar's office.

I never liked these meetings. All we did was sweat—without really having accomplished anything. Tzar went into the details of every project and people bickered constantly over petty matters. Most of the issues raised in these meetings should have been resolved beforehand, so that we might confront the really pressing problems.

The meeting had barely begun when Gorelov jumped up and in a loud voice read Tzar's note at the top of his memo: "I'll give you fifty percent of what you deserve." "Right has triumphed," he concluded solemnly. "I just have one question. Does the fifty percent mean that the car will take me *to* the office or *from* the office?"

All eyes turned to Tzar who, grinning, replied, "Gorelov, say my whole arm represents hundred percent." He paused and extended his muscular left arm. "So, up to the elbow is . . ." Here, Tzar flexed his right arm and made a fist, then expressively patted his left arm near the elbow. "*Now* do you get it?"

Gorelov never mentioned the matter of the official car in public again.

After the meeting, I went back to my office and bumped into an engineer named Raccoon. His young wife had just graduated from college, and he wanted to know if there was any chance of my finding her a job at SibAuto. I happened to have heard of a position for which she seemed suited. Engineer Raccoon thanked me and walked off beaming.

Meanwhile, I had already decided on a course of action to dig SibAuto out of debt. I called Zelman, the plant director, to my office for a discussion. Zelman heard me out, but was emphatic in his belief that my plan wouldn't work. "Regulation number two thirty-five says you can't do that—and article number ten seventy-eight proves my point."

I had no idea what he was talking about, although I was getting used to being confused. I had written a dissertation, and worked as a laborer, a foreman, and finally as the head of a department at the Norilsk Combine, where I had devised plans for revamping the company's entire organizational system. None of that seemed to help at SibAuto. What I was facing here were nuts-and-bolts business problems about day-to-day operations. I had no clue how to deal with them. That is doubtless one reason I remain so sympathetic to the types of problems confronted by foreign investors.

I listened to Zelman, carefully recording his cabalistic figures 235 and 10-78 on a pad.

After Zelman left, I called in planning chief Kozin, who was a kind of corporate Sherlock Holmes, who always helped me decipher what others told me. Kozin came up with an interpretation of Regulation 235. I carefully wrote it down.

"By the way, get me a copy of the wording of article ten slash seventy-eight," I told him, feeling slightly more confident. "Maybe I'll find something in it we can use."

It became clear to me on mornings such as these that my task was to try to organize the company—to take formless protoplasm and give it an economic and managerial backbone. We were overwhelmed with orders because Soviet industry badly needed automation, but we had no working capital, and undercapitalization exacerbated our material shortages and the lack of spare parts. It was like starving to death in the doorway of a restaurant.

Checking our warehouses, I discovered an inventory consisting of over 100,000 various parts and other items—a veritable mountain of machinery. Yet SibAuto was still not able to fill its orders. Because there was no tracking system and no inventory control, the parts in stock were useless to us and the parts we needed were scarce. Discouraging? Of course. Yet this was and is typical of the Soviet system: plenty of resources and nothing useful. The rest of the world was eager to sell us the parts we needed, but we had no hard currency with which to purchase them.

The lack of working capital was the offspring of one of the grandest lunacies of the Soviet bureaucracy. If company A was profitable and company B bankrupt, a ministry would impound company A's profits and present them like a Christmas gift to company B. This way, even when an enterprise was flat broke, the State could blithely refer to it as a "company with planned losses," and bolster it with Company A's profits. The officious bureaucratic elves could then toast their clever wordplay. Until June of 1992, when Yeltsin signed a law permitting bankruptcy, there were hundreds of dead companies around the former Soviet Union that continued to be underwritten by the healthy ones. Today, by my estimate, about one-quarter of all Russian enterprises are bankrupt (the official figure, as of May 1, 1992, is 14 percent). The State funds but a fraction of them, and only if they produce goods for the State. The others are on their own.

The old system was particularly harmful to companies such as SibAuto, which couldn't invest the hard currency it earned from its exports. The Soviet Santa and his helpers had robbed it blind. Today, even as Russia and the other republics open their doors to capitalism, the long-term effects of the Soviet system continue to be felt. Company directors don't like it when foreign corporations approach them through a ministry. This is why Western veterans of the old Soviet marketplace, who relied on their contacts and friendships with the ministries, often lose out under the current system. When a particular ministry sends an American company along to a State enterprise so that they can come to a business arrangement, the ministry will probably try to keep part of the hard currency profits the joint venture generates. Conversely, if a State enterprise deals with a Western company directly, it can retain a good portion (roughly half) of its hard currency earnings.

SibAuto was like a barefoot shoemaker. It could design and manufacture automation systems for other companies, but it couldn't automate itself. We tried to remedy things by obtaining a Russian-made computer, and asking our talented pool of engineers from the Automation Management Systems department to create a program allowing me to keep track of the date products or parts entered our inventory and who had ordered them. It helped. I soon learned that most of our inventory had been gathering dust on the shelves for years. The drain on resources this caused was partly responsible for SibAuto's inability to pay its workers.

As useful as this information was, it didn't entirely explain where our operating capital disappeared to. Then I discovered that within SibAuto lived a deadlier enemy—a division known as Geophysica, which was a cover name for the department handling special types of space and underground communications equipment for the military. The head of Geophysica was a colorful character with a long, tangled beard, a pot belly, and a booming voice. He rarely changed his shirt—a fact obvious to anyone within twenty-five feet of him—and instead of a belt, he wore a rope. Everyone called him The Beard.

The Beard was an important man in the Soviet bureaucracy. He was a Ph.D. who had gotten a State award for his top-secret work, which he shrouded in a cloak of such impenetrable secrecy it verged on the ludicrous. Whenever I received a memo from his office I half expected to see EAT BEFORE READING stamped all over it.

Foreign investors must understand that, formerly, anything even remotely connected with the Soviet military was hidden by a veil of absolute secrecy. The discipline among those in charge of keeping secrets was higher than the national average. However, there was still a good deal of confusion—most of it multiplied by mind-bending idiocy. Every Soviet enterprise contained a department known as Department 1, whose workers (we all assumed) served the KGB. Their principal task was to guard State secrets. In no place in the country was the concentration of moronic buffoons as high. They saw to it that the documents classified For Office Use Only (or Secret, Strictly Secret, and Special Importance) never left the walls of the company. As a result of their frenetic classification, reams of ordinary engineering data available to anyone in one company might in another be classified Top Secret. Often, if a ministry refuses to provide Western businesspeople with information, they could obtain the same information without too much difficulty by simply going to the regional government or city hall. Foreign investors need to be aggressive about getting information, because by inclination and long-standing habit, companies won't divulge it. Furthermore, for the time being, Department 1s are still in business.

At SibAuto I had tried not to involve myself in the financial details of The Beard's division. The less you know, the sounder you sleep.

Still, to assess the situation, I was forced to find out whether his operation was as profitable as he claimed. I soon discovered that what the Beard was doing was "eating bread" (an expression that means to take more than you give) by taking bonuses intended for SibAuto's other units. He had friends in high places—many of them ramrod-stiff generals with more clout than brains. (In the Soviet Union, clout almost always beat out intelligence and industriousness.) His friends were effective at convincing Lomako, Minister of Nonferrous Metallurgy, to give The Beard what he wanted in the way of supplemental funds.

I took my findings to Tzar. "There are two people feeding SibAuto to the sharks," I told him. "The Beard, who is like a tapeworm, and Paraffin, the head of supplies, who couldn't find his own nose, let alone the right spare part."

Tzar shrugged. He thought fighting with The Beard would be of no use. His friends were too highly placed. I, on the other hand, was confident that we could beat both The Beard and Paraffin. There was always a way of getting around a Soviet bureaucrat. He is actually more vulnerable than you. All you risk in confronting him is time, and maybe money. However, if you prove to a higher authority that his decisions are inconsistent with State policies, he could get sacked. I have never forgotten what the head of a collective farm in Siberia once told me: "The weather forecast depends on your persistence."

By the time of the next semiannual company meeting, I was ready to make my move. This was my first presentation at SibAuto in front of the entire staff and some of the workers. Owed months' worth of wages, the workers were quick to jump all over me. "Where's our back pay, Mr. Economist? What about our bonuses?" they shouted.

"There are two people to blame for the mess we're in," I said, pointing to The Beard and Paraffin. "The Geophysica division carves its bonuses out of your salaries. And as for the warehouse, all you have to do is look at the figures to know how much money is being wasted there."

Before I could read my findings about the useless inventory to the workers, The Beard exploded. "Kvint, that's slander!" he said, turning bright red. Paraffin, an emaciated weasel of a man, whined. "How dare you accuse me? I've been like a father to this company. I do everything I can to save us from shortages, and this is how you thank me?"

"No one has used eighty percent of our warehouse inventory over the last eight years!" I shot back. "Yet we're still facing shortages."

The atmosphere grew tense. Luckily, our Party secretary, Partcomich (that is how Soviets used to refer to the chiefs of their company's Party Committee), was in the room. A wizened, dwarfish man, Partcomich was nominally in charge of "ideology," but he was also a clever, practical fellow with years of experience surviving the bureaucracy. He sensed that the workers were ready to tear The Beard and Paraffin apart, so he directed the attention back to me. "What do *you* propose?" he asked.

"Let's sell off what we don't need for next year's program."

A murmur of approval rippled through the room. "Geophysica's employees are paid twice as much as everyone else," I added. "The Beard's division uses three times more material per each ruble of finished product than the other divisions. He gets the capital he needs for whatever he wants from out of the common pocket, while the rest of us have to go to the ministry with our tongues hanging out just to get bare essentials."

The Beard sprang into action. "I'm the one getting the largest payments from my customers! I'm feeding you all! I just brought in three million rubles!" he shouted.

"Your cost base is so high that you bring almost no profit," I shouted back.

The Beard was too stunned to speak. In his many years of experience, no one had ever bothered to add up the numbers and confront him. "That's a disgusting lie!" was all he could say.

"Well," said Tzar, "let's take a look at the official report we sent to the ministry."

Rattling the saber of his connections, The Beard said ominously, "I carry out special assignments for the government, and anyone who is against it . . . "

"A special assignment doesn't give you the right to blow smoke in everyone's eyes, including the government's." I was really fired up.

The Beard jabbed his finger at me and said, "We'll see what the minister says!" Then, hiking his trousers up over the hump of his pot belly, he shambled out of the meeting.

It was quite late when I left work that evening. I walked home through the park—a wild tangle of sweet-scented vegetation that had once been part of the Siberian forest, the taiga. By some miracle, this remnant hadn't been destroyed when the city was built, and I was grateful for that. The benches were occupied by sleeping men who had imbibed more vodka than they could, but less than they wanted. I was suddenly reminded it was summer. I must have been more distracted by my battle with The Beard than I had thought.

The next morning, I got a call from my father, from whom I heard from time to time. He had met The Beard at the local government building and the Beard had threatened him. "Tell your son he's playing with fire."

"If you see The Beard again, tell him to go hell," I said. The phrase I actually used was more crass, but I knew I could count on my father to top me. He was a master of colorful expressions and creative obscenities—a true mat artist. In his day, when every telephone call was placed through a female operator, my father swore so lustily the State telephone authorities once disconnected our line.

After demonstrating that he had not lost his flair for mat, my father asked me why I wanted to tangle with The Beard. He was concerned that the man's connections could cost me my job.

"I appreciate what you say, but I have to do my job," I replied.

My father made The Beard the object of some more mat, and then we said goodbye.

I was certain The Beard would retaliate, but I still thought we had a good shot at beating him. After all, he had his enemies, too. He had effectively burgled the Ministry of Nonferrous Metallurgy in the name of the military. For decades, the other ministries had been unable to question the prerogatives of the Ministry of Defense. Now the tide was turning, and ministers throughout the Soviet Union might be ready to win back their fair share of funds from the military. I would bank on that.

Although I enjoyed my moment of triumph at the company meeting, I was still facing a terrible cash crunch, and the day when we would have to make payroll was drawing near. I had no money, but I did have an idea. During an inspection of the warehouses, I came upon the parts for an automation system sitting as idly as an unwanted bride. A plant in the Ukraine had vaguely expressed interest in the equipment. It wouldn't hurt to offer it to them again. I knew that the documents for payment would take two weeks to travel back and forth; I could use the two weeks to apply for a bank loan.

I spent the entire day calculating whether or not we could cover our debt. By day's end, the numbers seemed to work. I prepared the bill and sent it to the Ukrainian plant. Then I asked my secretary to connect me with Ptisin—which means "bird"—the head of our communications department.

Nadia strode into my office and delared melodramatically, "The bird has flown off with the young wife of engineer Raccoon." She read the telegraph held in her hand: "Love at first sight. Please fire me."

I felt sorry for Raccoon. I also wondered who was the luckier of the two men.

That morning I sent a bookkeeper to the bank with a copy of the bill to coax the bank into giving us a loan against goods in route; that is, on the allegedly forthcoming payment from the Ukrainian plant. At first the bank refused to talk to my bookkeeper, but in the end she managed to get them to look at the invoice for this Ukrainian would-be buyer and ultimately to give us a sizeable loan on the basis of it.

Now we had a little slack to play with. I could only hope the Ukrainian company would actually come through and offer to buy the inventory. They eventually did. At the end of each financial year, it was far better for a State company to purchase equipment than to leave money in its corporate account, since that money would likely be taken by the government. The practice of taking a company's profits continues, although today it goes by the name of taxation.

In an effort to increase SibAuto's profits, we sold off the back inventory in the warehouses. It took three months, but earned us three million rubles in cash. I then turned my attention to the mystery of why our main plant was in such a cash crunch. My hunch was that its director, Zelman, was playing games with me, even though the plant's warehouses seemed in good shape and I couldn't find anything amiss in paperwork.

As I was sifting through the reams of papers showing back orders, the problem came into focus. For approximately a year, the main plant had been gearing up to produce a system called, somewhat ominously, "Bazooka." However, shortly before work began, the customer changed his mind and the Bazooka project was scrubbed. At that point, practically all of the plant's working capital was tied up in it. Instead of trying to sell off Bazooka's parts, Zelman left them scattered in every corner. He also hadn't drafted the proper legal paperwork for the system; therefore, when the customer refused to pay for what had been purchased on his behalf, Zelman could do nothing.

Zelman's ignorance was understandable. SibAuto was in transition from a command- to a market-driven company, but for a long time had conformed strictly to the State Plan. When the rare private customer did come forward, the managers were unprepared to do the paperwork. When Zelman learned that his Bazooka customer would not pay, he tried to hide the debt by scattering it around, and in so doing managed to violate several laws simultaneously: inflating production numbers, squandering State property, and awarding illegal bonuses.

I assigned Kozin from the planning office to look into it. I had begun to appreciate Kozin's investigative skills. Once again he proved intelligent and cooperative, and his report effectively catalogued Zelman's nonsense.

One afternoon, the three of us met in my office. "My friend," Kozin said to Zelman, "we should drink one to the stretch ahead of you."

Zelman's face drained of color. "Why?" he asked.

"Because," replied Kozin, his eyes gleaming wickedly, "you're about to spend about ten years in the slammer."

Kozin was thoroughly enjoying himself. He enjoyed browbeating people, particularly those lower on the ladder. Zelman panicked, but then seemed to accept the situation. Like other Russian managers, a part of him was prepared for life's unhappy surprises.

"If you didn't line your pockets with the money, then relax," I assured him. "We'll try to handle the rest."

Shortly thereafter, we gave Zelman an official reprimand and fired him. Then Tzar appointed him chief technician of SibAuto, a job for which he was well qualified. If I hadn't hired him, he might have gone to prison. He was guilty of mismanagement rather than larceny, but several hundred thousand rubles were no joke.

The inventory sale gave us some working capital, and I was able to start thinking about worker's salaries and plant expansion. As I mentioned earlier, a Soviet manager was like a Gulliver tied up by bureaucratic Lilliputians, and I soon discovered I could neither pay salary bonuses to my employees nor begin construction on new facilities.

SibAuto desperately needed to expand in order to meet the growing demand for its products. The division that did most of our major automation work lacked plant space, and this meant that too much of the production had to be done on the work site itself. An enormous amount of money could be saved were the preparatory work done on the equipment *before* it went to the site, so that all that was required was assembly. However, SibAuto did not have enough facilities for this more efficient, and more profitable, arrangement.

Under the Soviet system, even if you had the means to build a new facility, you were forbidden to do so until you received State approval—and approval could take as long as a year to secure. Each ministry placed limits on how many construction projects could be started. Even if by some miracle you did get the go-ahead to build and then discovered during construction that there would be a cost overrun (and they are inevitable), you had to walk away from the entire project. No additional money could be allocated. This is still essentially the case today.

For this and many other reasons of bureaucratic bumbling, there are approximately thirty thousand unfinished construction sites in the independent republics—the *Stroyka s borodoy,* constructions with a beard, or "bearded sites" for short, so called because they simply stand there overgrown with weeds. Their large number is due in part to the ludicrous salary system, which allotted the highest wages to persons doing manual labor. For example, electricians were paid less than foundation diggers, and therefore were scarce. Workers would routinely complete one foundation and then start digging a new one to earn the higher wage. These bearded sites (construction 70-percent completed or less) should be of considerable interest to foreign investors. They can be had cheaply. In 1992, the Russian government began selling off these sites, but during the first six months of the year had managed to earn only half a billion rubles out of a total estimated book value of 3 trillion rubles.

Just as I was searching for ways to build our plant, another player entered the game. Director Galkin was one of our most important customers, and the head of a company in Sora, in southern Siberia—a mining operation that produced more than 30 percent of the Soviet Union's molybdenum, a metallic element used to strengthen steel. To increase his company's output, Galkin needed to automate his facilities. He contacted SibAuto and spoke to Tzar, who called me. We assured Galkin that we had both the technology and the know-how to meet his needs. What we didn't have were the facilities, or permission to build them.

We decided to organize a fishing trip with Galkin to one of the most beautiful places on earth: Lake Svatikovo in Tuva, southern Siberia—now a rather unstable region for investment, given the trouble along its border with Mongolia. This is unfortunate, because Lake Svatikovo would be an ideal spot for a resort. Because there is so much salt in the water, you can float effortlessly for hours. Its waters and muds are known for their therapeutic properties and are believed to cure skin diseases and, according to local legend, to counteract infertility.

In Russia, fishing is not just a sport, but an almost sacred rite. It is to a Russian what meditation is to a Buddhist. It is also a matchless opportunity to speak openly with your companions. During the reign of the KGB, everyone knew that offices were bugged and telephones were tapped. Only when you were out rowing on a lake or hiking through a forest could you feel secure enough to share your thoughts and dreams openly.

Even today, my clients experience this phenomenon. In 1991, for example, one of my American clients went to Krasnoyarsk (the first foreigners to be allowed in) for business negotiations. When he returned to the States, he told me with some surprise that in the office of his future partners, talk had been limited to friendly chatter. The really serious business negotiations took place when they were out fishing in the middle of the Krasnoyarsk reservoir.

Russians are still wary of talking too much in their offices. Despite the changes, Russia is still not an entirely democratic society, and people continue to fear for their jobs and their freedom. That someone else knows the essence of a conversation they are having with a foreigner—or even the fact that it had taken place at all—is still frightening.

Our fishing expedition with Director Galkin was arranged by Schetkin (Brush), the head of SibAuto's Sora branch. Schetkin was a giant of a man, with flaming red hair and a cunning smile. I had no idea what winds had brought him to Siberia, but I was glad we had him. He had an entrepreneurial spirit and undertook complex organizational tasks with enthusiasm.

Schetkin had also stocked an ample supply of vodka, and at the end of a successful day of fishing, we sat around drinking while Schetkin stirred a pot of glorious fish soup. Galkin's eyes were downcast and his voice mournful. Even the magnificent aroma of the steaming broth didn't seem to cheer him. "Using your automation is like trying to get milk from a billy goat."

"What *we* need is a building so we can assemble the automation equipment *you* need," Tzar replied. Suddenly, Tzar turned to me. "What's the point of having an economist around if he can't come up with an idea?" he snapped.

Between spoonfuls of soup, I confessed that in fact I did have an idea, but it was risky. Galkin and Tzar were intrigued and pressed me for details.

"The molybdenum combine has an excellent construction division, " I began. "We have no construction workers. Schetkin here has eighty-five fitters. What we could do is split them into a team of sixty, which will remain with Schetkin, and a team of twenty-five, which will go to Galkin. The team of sixty would have to do the work of the eighty-five workers. Organizing that would be Schetkin's and my problem. For the use of those twenty-five, Schetkin will give Galkin a bill for a hundred thousand rubles."

Galkin and Tzar were following me attentively, so I went on. "Galkin will send the twenty-five construction workers to SibAuto to build our facility. His bill will also be for one hundred thousand rubles. Then Schetkin and Galkin meet and they tear both bills in half. No one pays anyone anything, but the work gets done: we get our building and you, Director Galkin, will get your automation."

Galkin and Tzar bought the idea. There was no money in it for us. We also realized we were sticking our necks out, and that the long arm of the Soviet system would not hesitate to lop off our heads—but from the start, Tzar and I were committed to the effort, and Galkin wanted his automation. We all shook hands and our ghost building began to materialize.

CHAPTER 5

The SibAuto Saga, Part II

Every State enterprise has an employee who doesn't really do anything, but who seems nonetheless to be one of the busiest people in the organization. At SibAuto, ours was a kind, elderly lady with the odd name of Mrs. Radish. An imposing, portly woman, she spent all of her time traveling back and forth across the country to attend meetings.

Westerners have no idea how many important but pointless meetings are still convened in Russia despite the collapse of the Soviet Union. There are the innumerable standardization conferences, and the regular gatherings of the Society to Help the Army and Fleet, Voluntary Fire Brigades, Old Monuments Preservation, Technical Safety briefings, the Group for the People's Control, the Society of Water Safety, and on and on.

One representative from every company has to attend each of these meetings, or the company runs the risk of being chastised by government for negligence. The only conferences the boss attends himself are those that take place abroad. Soviet citizens were prisoners of their borders, and any opportunity to go abroad was welcome. Until 1991, however, the boss could go abroad only if he was *viezdnoy*. Very roughly translated, viezdnoy means "permitted to travel abroad." *Nonviezdnoy*, on the other hand, meant more than not being allowed to travel abroad. It meant the system didn't trust you. Until 1988, I was nonviezdnoy as far as capitalist countries were concerned. The Party probably thought I knew too many economic secrets.

For domestic meetings, it was convenient to have the formidable Mrs. Radish represent us. Attending every conference, she freed others to work. She sometimes even asked a question. Mrs. Radish exemplifies how inefficiently labor is still used in the former Soviet Union. Quotas define how much one worker should do per hour, but because of shortages, work sites generally lack the equipment and materials for the workers to fulfill quotas and to do a proper job. As noted, they spend more than half their time sitting idle, waiting for shipments that seldom arrive. Yet, at the end of the month, a worker needs money. He has to feed his family. If you pay him only 50 rubles, and you had promised to pay him 160, he will quit and go elsewhere.

This is where *pripiska* comes in. Pripiska refers to the practice of overstating the amount of work that has actually been accomplished. All construction sites are subject to inflated figures. Even during one of the rare normal months, a foreman will jack up the figures just to have something to add to those slow months when there aren't enough bricks or concrete to finish a job. What this means is that having twenty-five out of eighty-five workers assigned to a job elsewhere is not really so outrageous. If anything, it means that something might actually get built.

Our ghost building was going up, despite the fact that I was worried my corporate career might soon come crashing down. In the West, corporate budgets are broken down by category: salaries, benefits, advertising, supplies, and so on. As long as sufficient profits are being generated, no one pays too much attention if you shift some money from one category to another. You couldn't do this under the Soviet system. If you did it anyway, you ran the risk of anything from a reprimand to a prison term.

There is another managerial nightmare that still haunts the Russian business world. Perhaps the worst part of a Soviet manager's life was his inability to exercise discretionary spending. His difficulties were exacerbated by the fact that not all money inside Russia was usable. All rubles are not created equal. Most foreigners now realize that the ruble is not internationally convertible, and are prepared to use alternative forms of exchange. Even within Russia, there are several types of rubles that do not convert into one another. For example, there is a special type of "clearing money" that is not cashable and functions more as a line of credit. Soviet enterprises pay each other with this "money" in exchange for services, supplies, or raw materials. These checks can on very rare occasions be cashed, but only after great difficulty. Even when they are cashed by a bank, they flutter around the entire financial system like homeless moths.

In 1984, progressive Soviet economists launched an attack against the State's monopoly over property. In response, the central authorities permitted the creation of cooperative businesses—a public-private mutant created as a compromise between the warring factions. I mentioned earlier that today they make ideal partners for joint ventures, since they were the first enterprises to follow market principles. They were a welcome change. Finally, people could invest their own money in ventures and operate them free of many of the oppressive State restrictions. They followed no preset plan, and there was no limit placed on wages. Not surprisingly, their productivity levels immediately doubled those of State-run companies. They operated without proper facilities, but personal investment and initiative more than made up for that.

Today, these cooperatives can, though not easily, mix clearing money with the cashable type, which is why they have become vehicles for all sorts of speculation. For instance, a State enterprise can create a cooperative, and then transfer uncashable clearing money to this cooperative's account—money that an individual from the cooperative then exchanges for cash. In the summer of 1992, Russian managers were exchanging this money at a secret rate of one cash ruble for every four clearing rubles.

In June of 1992, Yeltsin signed a decree strictly limiting a company's ability to spend cash. Companies are now required to keep nearly all of their money in banks (which have not yet been privatized), and to use only as much as the banks permit. The Russian government would like to limit the cash deficit through this type of control; however, as with the printing of 1 trillion rubles, it is a half-baked attempt on Yeltsin's part to solve a serious problem. It is also another reason Russian managers are so eager to exchange their clearing rubles for cash.

This has significant implications for the foreign investor. If a joint venture sells its product for ten rubles in cash, it could probably sell the same product for forty clearing rubles. A foreign company shouldn't be surprised if a Russian enterprise approaches it to convert its clearing rubles into cash rubles. There is in principle nothing illegal involved, and there can be significant profit.

Clearing money was yet another reason for the widening gap between spendable income and the shortage of consumer goods. For years, this ocean of uncashable money did nothing to increase the public's purchasing power.

All of this goes to show that to run a business in Russia, you need to look for loopholes. I learned this lesson at SibAuto. Looking for a way to break, or at least bend, the bonds of economic slavery, I decided to turn SibAuto into what was called a scientific-technical corporation (STC). SibAuto was originally structured as a trust, and according to Soviet law, that made doing research there illegal. However, a scientific-technical corporation was permitted to conduct research, and the rules governing this activity were generally less restrictive. In addition, I created a payroll department, and asked our wiry, walleyed bookkeeper Puzyr (Vial) to run it. Puzyr was a pedant, an absolute requirement for the job I had planned for him: to convince the ministry to let us increase our workers' wages. Only a pedant was sufficiently long-winded and dogged to change a minister's point of view.

Until November of 1991, employees at State-run businesses couldn't receive bonuses exceeding 30 percent of their annual salary. Puzir and I studied all of the existing Soviet legislation in the field, looking for exceptions to the rule. Holing ourselves up in the library for hours, we unearthed legislation dating back to 1921; there was our ticket, signed by Lenin himself. There were, we found, many cases in which a bonus had been allowed to exceed the limit: bonuses for excess days on business trips, for recycling scrap metal, for manufacturing consumer goods, and for introducing new equipment, etc.

I also found ways of raising our employees' standard of living without giving them more money directly. I sent a portion of our profits to our trade union. They in turn gave the money to SibAuto's canteen. The canteen used the money to prepare sumptuous lunches, and for a mere thirty kopeks (a few pennies) our workers could eat their fill. SibAuto's lunches soon became famous. Our trade union chairman also helped matters by securing free passes so that we could reward our best workers with vacations at various spas.

We next turned our attention to consumer goods legislation. The

State allowed us to use 30 percent of our profits from consumer goods as bonuses for workers. The trick was to come up with ways of producing consumer goods. Technicians sweated for two weeks and finally came up with an idea. They said that given the type of waste SibAuto produced, and given our existing technical capacities, we could easily manufacture polystyrene chandeliers that looked like crystal. That seemed like a great idea. Chandeliers, we knew, were exactly the sort of luxury the goods-starved Soviet consumer would jump at. I passed their suggestion on to Tzar. He approved the plan, and at the next company meeting we announced that in two months we would start manufacturing plastic chandeliers.

A man named Kokish, a technician on Zelman's staff, was in charge of estimating the amount of materials we would use in production, but too lazy to get acquainted with the agendas for our meetings. Neurotic, impulsive, and frightened of anything new, he flew into a rage, springing from his seat at my announcement. "That does it!" he shouted. "I won't work at this madhouse any longer!"

With one final, baleful look, he dramatically flung open a door and swept out. There were two doors in my office and they looked identical. Kokish had gone through the one leading into a closet, where I kept a refrigerator and my coat. A nervous silence descended on the room. Everyone held his breath. We all knew that Kokish was now standing in my closet.

I waited for a minute, then said calmly, "Kokish, why don't you come out?"

Embarrassed, though with a certain dignity, Kokish slowly opened the door, walked out, and slid back into his seat. The rest of us choked back our laughter and with a significant show of willpower, continued the meeting.

"Why chandeliers?" asked Kozin. "Why not elephants?"

We explained the reasons, and at last managed to convince everyone. It wasn't long before our Waterfall chandeliers, with their sparkling ersatz crystal, were considered the height of fashion. We sold them for about $13 apiece, and couldn't get them from our plant to the company store fast enough. Lines formed outside our plant entrance. People bought them before they could be loaded onto trucks.

One might wonder why there is such a shortage of consumer goods when manufacturing them is so profitable to employees. Producers can keep a high percentage of the profit only if 80 percent of the materials used to make the consumer product comes from waste.

Why aren't Russian companies collecting or buying the billions of tons of waste produced in the former Soviet Union and recycling it? The question is a reasonable one. The answer is not. Recycling in the independent republics is handicapped because every industry answers to a different ministry and regional government. They don't share information about their waste products and therefore remain ignorant of the financial incentives of recycling it. The result is the real waste: a squandering of an enormous amount of time and money. For example, mountains of gravel—by-products of the mining of apatite, the ore used for aluminum production—cover half the Kola Peninsula in northwest Russia. Right next door to the mining complex is a construction company that spends thirty million rubles a year—guess what?—mining gravel.

But times are changing in the former Soviet Union. Cooperatives and private companies are demonstrating how easy it is to earn a profit by recycling, and some of the country's first millionaires made their fortunes exporting waste products.

Waste recycling is among the most profitable areas for foreign investment. If advanced Western technologies were employed, Russian industrial waste would be a richer source of profit than most mineral resources in Western countries. In 1992, for example, one American plant extracted sixty pounds of gold from every ten tons of Russian scrap. Foreign companies would do well to locate a region in which there is a substantial supply of usable waste, buy that waste, and then set up shop in an unfinished building and open a recycling factory and refinery there. I should add that the Russian government was quick to issue a host of restrictions as soon as they realized the magnitude of potential profits. This is why today it is more efficient for a foreign company to cooperate with State enterprises (especially those now privatized) than to try to go it alone.

SibAuto's 1976 fiscal year closed with a handsome profit, and we were rated the best company in the ministry. We paid off our debt, and it was with enormous satisfaction that I wrote in my diary: "For the first time, SibAuto has three million rubles to spend."

By law, we were supposed to return our surplus capital to the State, which allowed us to keep a mere three kopeks (3 percent) for every ruble of profit. Tzar and I found the rule unconscionable, and disobeyed it; instead, we used the money to start a camp for juvenile delinquents. We called the camp Boys of the North. Our idea was to encourage teenagers to straighten out their lives by making friends and learning a trade. Children are not officially permitted to work until fourteen years of age, but when the camp dormitory was under construction, the boys helped build it. They were thrilled to be involved, and in no time learned how to lay bricks, work with concrete and cement, and even drive a truck. They soon forgot about the streets and started down the road toward more productive lives.

The Communist State, in which, supposedly, "children are the only privileged class," would not have been at all pleased with the way we spent our profits; nor would the State have approved of my efforts to raise workers' salaries. The workers were on our side, of course, and as a result, production and profits were up, but none of that would have mattered to the bureaucrats. Tzar and I were past caring what the State thought. We knew we would be punished for taking such liberties with the system. I, for one, was sure The Beard was plotting against us.

At the request of the head of the gold and diamond division of the Ministry of Nonferrous Metallurgy, SibAuto introduced an automation system for a bucket dredge known as *draga*. A bucket dredge consists of a mining and gravity-preparation facility on a boat that can navigate small rivers. We went to the trouble of creating a research facility to develop the draga because Zshmurko, head of the ministry, was the first administrator willing to pay us for our work. That gave us real incentive, but in order for the research facility to be legal, we first had to apply for STC status—and in a hurry.

SibAuto's legal adviser was named Svetlana. Bright, but rather self-important, she claimed she was too busy with other responsibilities to fill out the STC application. I suspected that her connection to The Beard was behind her refusal. He had already tried to throw a spanner in the works on several occasions, and it now looked as though he had convinced Svetlana to join forces with him. I would have to go over their heads.

I scheduled a private meeting with our Party secretary, Partcomich. Partcomich and I had had our disagreements in the past. A young computer engineer by the name of Felner had once come to see me with a problem. His family had emigrated to Israel, but because he had worked with secret documents, he had been forbidden to join them. All Felner wanted was to be allowed to travel to Romania, the only place he could meet his mother, who would fly there from Israel. Felner had gone to Partcomich for a character reference. Partcomich turned Felner down—in a rather abusive fashion. He was drunk at the time and indulged in a few anti-Semitic slurs. (It would, however, be wrong to assume that only Jews help Jews in Russia. Those who helped me in Russia were mostly non-Jews. Russian Jews are very often hesitant to offer each other assistance because of the many years of antisemitic and anti-Zionist totalitarian propaganda.)

Immediately after Felner told me about the incident, I stormed over to Partcomich's office.

"What do you want?" he snarled.

I glared at him and said, "All Felner wants to do is go meet his mother."

Partcomich snorted. I felt my fists clench. I hadn't boxed in years, but I was experiencing a sudden urge to rekindle my career. "If you break Felner's back over this, I will never forget it," I said menancingly.

"I don't know why you're so upset, Kvint," Partcomich responded. "What does Felner matter to you? All right, all right, I'll give him his letter."

At heart Partcomich was a coward who detested any conflict with someone his own bureaucratic size; eventually we developed a distant but respectful relationship. I was confident he would help us circumvent our legal adviser. Were SibAuto registered as an STC, that would mean more revenue, and more revenue would mean a feather in Partcomich's little red cap. I told him about Svetlana's reluctance to prepare the papers.

Partcomich scowled. "Why can't we just make a joint decision between management and the Party?"

"We can," I replied. "I was about to suggest it myself."

"Done," he said, slapping his hand on his desk.

(Foreign investors take note: going by the rules will generally carry the day in any skirmish with the bureaucracy. There are no shortages of rules in Russia—you just have to find the right one to use.)

The next morning, Partcomich summoned SibAuto's legal counsel to his office and told her that if she did not do the paperwork she would be in direct conflict with the Party. Without a word of protest, she dove headlong into her assignment.

Although SibAuto was barreling down the right road, my headaches were never-ending. We dismissed Zelman as director of the plant for the Bazooka fiasco, and appointed him, as I mentioned, chief technician at SibAuto. (He later became the director of a margarine factory, where he invented several varieties of mayonnaise and revolutionized the eating habits of the entire Krasnoyarsk Region.)

One day, the perpetually dissatisfied Kokish stormed into my office. Even my secretaries could not repulse his advance: the older one didn't move fast enough, and the beautiful Nadia was engaged in a critical conversation about love.

"I won't tolerate that sniveler!" yelled Kokish. "Before Zelman gives me any order, I demand that he first ask my permission." Kokish had discovered a new postulate of management theory. What was most frightening was that he was serious.

Everything went wrong that day. Tzar was on vacation and I was overwhelmed with work. The telephone rang, and because Nadia seemed to have evaporated, I answered it.

"Hello," a voice said. "Glushkov here."

Glushkov was a lunatic inventor who had been haunting SibAuto's hallways for months, peddling his harebrained ideas and giving each of our department heads an earache.

Fed up with him, I screamed into the telephone, "What is this? National Village Idiot Day? Listen, Glushkov, I told you never to call me again. Can't you get the message?" I slammed the receiver down.

The telephone rang again.

"Glushkov here."

It was too much. Kokish was still buzzing around my office, infuriating me even more.

"Drop dead, you bastard!" I screamed—meaning both Kokish and Glushkov—and slammed the receiver down harder.

It rang again. By this point I was nearly out of my mind, but before I could formulate any more mat, I heard a voice say: "This is *Deputy Minister* Glushkov, from Moscow. I am in Krasnoyarsk, and not far from your headquarters."

"Oh," was all I could manage.

"This other Glushkov must have really been bothering you."

The Glushkov on the phone was then deputy minister in charge of finances for nonferrous metallurgy. He later became chairman of the Price Committee for the entire Soviet Union—a position he held until 1989, when, like so many other high-level Soviet bureaucrats, he became a consultant for private companies.

Kokish finally grew tired and left, and I got a chance to spend some time with Glushkov, whom I had known since I was a child. My mother had worked for the Krasnoyarsk regional government when he was a deputy chairman in the 1950s. I often accompanied my mother to work and had bumped into Glushkov a few times while racing around the hallways.

Before we parted, Glushkov promised to support my idea of creating an economic research laboratory to help develop automation for nonferrous metallurgy.

One problem was solved, but it created another. I knew that if SibAuto began to expand it would need a larger labor force. The ministry wouldn't allot us any money for construction of new residences, and one of our biggest concerns was not being able to provide new employees with what is perhaps the most critical and least available of all necessities, then as now: housing.

Housing problems are nothing new to Russians. Decades ago, my father, who was a noted developer and builder in Siberia, built two apartment buildings for his workers, thereby giving them a chance to escape the terrible slums in which they had been living. He wanted them to live in solid, modern apartments on the site of his construction enterprise in the Krasnoyarsk suburbs. City authorities created enormous troubles for him. My father had, it seemed, violated bureaucratic procedures by trying to speed up the process. Those cumbersome procedures are responsible for the housing shortage, which, if anything, has gotten worse. In 1993, the pace of housing construction was 58 percent of that in 1990—the lowest level it has been since 1975.

Our ghost building, and the boys' camp we had started, meant that Tzar and I had reached our limit on covert construction, but we continued to try to find a solution to the housing problem. While searching for a place to build SibAuto's new test facility, we heard about some vacant property in a place called Badalik, located some distance from the center of town and not far from the city's largest cemetery. No one wanted it—except us.

Badalik had three things going for it as a site for the test facility: location, location, and location. It was forty minutes from our headquarters, but only half a mile from the Trans-Siberian Railway, and very near the Krasnoyarsk airport. Best of all, it was next door to the Krasnoyarsk metallurgical plant, which received generous housing allocations from the military. Kuznetsov, the plant director, was in the process of building twenty high-rise apartment buildings. SibAuto acquired the Badalik property and work began on the test facility.

We sent a construction team to cut a road from Badalik to the new site, which meant that it went right past Kuznetsov's new high-rises. As people began settling into the new building's apartments, and as construction on our lot progressed, our new neighbors began asking us about openings at the facility. Our site was near their homes; if they worked there, they wouldn't have to worry about commuting. Many were tired of working in the dim, stuffy atmosphere of a metallurgical workshop. Our plant seemed to them a more attractive alternative.

Every morning, a ribbon of humanity happily wound its way from the new apartment buildings to our Badalik facility. To work a job a mere five-minute walk from home was utter luxury for these workers, a dream come true. As for the metallurgical plant, the loss of labor did not slow its production very long. The military immediately gave it more funding to replace the workers it had lost to us. The State's purse was open to Kuznetsov.

Foreign companies interested in doing business in Russia should remember that what prospective Russian employees value above all else is affordable and decent housing. Thirty percent of the population still live in communal apartments. The real estate market is beginning to heat up in Russia. Every year, more and more foreigners choose to settle there, and Russians with hard currency part with it willingly for houses or apartments. When the ruble becomes fully convertible, real estate developers with a presence in the market will doubtless earn significant profits.

One lovely spring evening, Chancellor Frost stopped by my office on his way home.

"I know you don't like to drink," he said. "How about some tea?"

He brewed some wonderful Siberian herbal tea in the kettle on my hotplate. While we sipped from our mugs, Frost came right to the point.

"There are three people out to get you—two carrying a stretcher, one with a knife. The Beard and Svetlana are carrying the stretcher. I caught our legal counsel thumbing through some documents, and it was obvious she was looking for something to nail you on."

I took in what he said, then asked, "Who has the knife?"

"Schetkin, the head of our Sora branch. Do you know him?"

"A redheaded giant with a cunning smile. He makes a delicious fish soup."

"I don't know about the soup," replied Frost, "but the smile I can believe. Schetkin was seen having lunch with The Beard. If I were you, I'd watch out for this Schetkin."

"How did you find all this out?" I asked.

"I served as a colonel and a chief-of-staff in the regional militia, so I have my ways."

Frost stood and bid me farewell in a formal military manner. "I also have my honor," he said.

I couldn't have agreed more. I wished I could have confided in him that I knew very well what Schetkin was up to.

CHAPTER 6

SibAuto, Part III:
Things Turn Around

One of the reasons we pushed SibAuto so hard into creating new technology was because of the scientific paradox created by the Soviet system. One-quarter of the world's scientists live in the former Soviet Union, but only a relatively small percentage of their discoveries directly benefit their countrymen. For instance, an advanced method for continuous steel casting was developed in Russia. Eighty-five percent of steel manufacturers in the United States and Japan adopted the technology; only 20 percent of our own steel manufacturers did. Paradoxes such as this stem from the fact that our economic system offered no incentives to put scientific discovery to industrial use, hence widening the gulf between technology and production and accelerating an economic decline.

When I was at SibAuto, all we could do was encourage our researchers and technical staff because we couldn't offer them monetary incentives. We told them their technology could save lives—and it could.

One morning, while I was in Tzar's office, a call came from the chief engineer of Yakutia Diamond. "Remember that bulldozer operator you talked to last time you were up here visiting?"

"Sure I do," replied Tzar. "Quite a character."

"Well, he's dead," the chief engineer said. "I need your help," he added.

Tzar and I went there as soon as we could. Yakutia Diamond mined the biggest diamond field in the world—with an enormous open ore pipe called Mirnay, located nearly a thousand feet beneath the surface. Gazing down from the top, I counted fifteen levels. The men worked the mine by drilling holes and filling them with explosives, which were then detonated. After an explosion, excavators loaded the shattered rocks onto dump trucks and hauled them to a refinery. Day and night, in three shifts, huge hundred-ton trucks crawled up and down the edge of the pit. Sometimes the explosions loosened mounds of rock that impeded the progress of the trucks. Bulldozers were brought in to push the rock back to the edge of the mine. However, the pit was rimmed with loose dirt and stone, and therefore unstable, and on several catastrophic occasions a bulldozer and its driver had plunged over the edge, tumbling a thousand feet to the floor below. That's how the poor man had met his death.

After we'd diagnosed the problem, our engineers modified a military invention and created a remote-control bulldozer. A driver could then stand in a safe spot and command the bulldozer's levers. If an accident did happen, the only casualty would be a piece of machinery.

Obtaining permission to manufacture our invention was far more difficult than actual production. Automating a safety device was an exceptional thing to do, and the bureaucracy didn't know what to make of it. The truth was, the Soviet regime held human life in no high esteem. On the contrary, Soviet propaganda regularly pontificated on the sacred preeminence of the State's property. The government once publicized with great fanfare a tragedy in which a young man heroically rushed to save a burning tractor and died in the fire! For the Communists, there was no question as to which one was more important. Difficult as it might be for Westerners to imagine, in April of 1986, when the Chernobyl nuclear power plant began to melt down, Tzar had to pull every string he had to persuade the authorities to allow him to bring in his automated equipment. Unprotected young soldiers and firemen were sent into the radiation; twenty-six people reportedly died and hundreds were injured. Experts believe that the effects of the accident will reach far into the future. Tzar finally did receive permission, and SibAuto's remote-control bulldozers and tractors saved countless lives.

When Tzar first approached the Ministry of Nonferrous Metallurgy about permission to build our machines, he was told by Bagrov, whose department oversaw SibAuto at the ministry, that without Fedirko's permission we wouldn't get anywhere. He was afraid it was too innovative an idea for the Party to allocate money.

Bagrov epitomized the bureaucracy: he never looked you in the eye, and he was known to stand up when speaking on the telephone to a superior. Fedirko, whom he mentioned, was the all-powerful Party boss of the entire Krasnoyarsk region, and his word was law. When I began at SibAuto, getting an appointment with Sizov, the region's second-in-command, was easy. It was far more difficult to get an appointment with Fedirko. Persuading him to visit our test facilities? Impossible.

This time we might just be in luck, Sizov told us. Fedirko was planning to attend the funeral of an old Krasnoyarsk bureaucrat (a happy coincidence, I thought). Because we had tested our bulldozer at Badalik, near the cemetery, Sizov said that he would do his best to convince Fedirko to take a few minutes out to visit our test site.

The plan worked. Fedirko was a towering, overpowering man with the face of a boar. When he arrived at Badalik, he stared suspiciously at our bulldozer. "So, this thing will go all by itself?" he growled.

"Anytime you want," said Tzar. "Just give the word."

"Then do it!" bellowed Fedirko.

Tzar pressed a button on the control he was holding and the bulldozer steamed ahead, dipping into a mound of gravel and performing perfectly.

"Can you make it come closer?" asked Fedirko, clearly eager to check whether there was anyone inside.

The machine approached the Party boss at full speed, lowering its massive scoop as though Fedirko were a pile of gravel. Tzar was grinning and chewing his cigarette in the corner of his mouth.

"Okay! Make it stop!" shouted Fedirko.

The bulldozer ground to a halt five feet from him. He looked inside the cabin and grunted.

"Want to try?" Tzar asked him.

"Why not?"

Fedirko took the control and like a child became engrossed, operating the bulldozer with ill-concealed glee. Recovering his boarish dignity and seriousness, he asked: "So, what is your regional plan for this thing? What do you need from me?"

I explained that in our villages there were three times as many tractors as drivers. With this remote-control system, one driver could operate three tractors simultaneously. I told him that we were already selling these machines to Yakutia Diamond, but that we had other systems, and that our laboratory was working on other models. I ended by saying that a program ought to be developed for the entire region.

"Do programs like this exist anywhere else?" asked Fedirko.

"No. We'd be the first," I replied.

"Then start one and I'll back you up."

Sizov helped me form a team, and we kicked off the first regional robotization program in the Soviet Union. Even the Kremlin took notice. The Communist Party's Central Committee, then the country's ultimate authority, issued a declaration praising our work. They were so pleased with Sizov they later elevated him to deputy minister of the interior. As for Fedirko, in 1986 Gorbachev appointed him minister for all State cooperatives.

Following on the heels of our success with Fedirko and the bulldozer, I naively thought the robot we developed for Yakutia Diamond would be met with the same enthusiasm. But in my excitement I forgot how pervasively destructive the Soviet system of financial disincentives could be.

I mentioned that SibAuto had developed a draga automation system for Yakutia Diamond's and Yakutia Gold's river operations. A bucket dredge consists of several huge shovels that scoop out sand and silt from riverbeds. What SibAuto did was automate the dredge with a 600-liter bucket—one of the biggest in the world. Every phase of the dredge's operation, from guiding it along its water route, to the remote control of the buckets, to the management of the preparation process, was automated.

After the first month of tests, a dredge using our draga brought up 7 to 10 percent more gold than did the old machinery. Our greatest achievement was our nugget-catch system. Before, when sand was sifted by the standard equipment, gold nuggets that weren't caught by the machinery were simply dumped. Miners would scavenge through the waste after their shift. With our draga, not one nugget escaped.

Our dragas were recognized as so efficient there was demand in South America to export them, but we weren't interested. SibAuto would have earned almost no profit from shipping its inventions abroad—a situation that to some extent persists today. The Rizshkov-Pavlov governments, and later the Gaidar government, still prohibited enterprises from being compensated for their hard currency export costs. It is no accident that in 1991 Russian exports fell by 29 percent. In 1992, the drop was 28 percent: in November of 1991, in an effort to move more quickly toward a free market, Yeltsin lifted most of the restrictions earlier governments had imposed.

A second reason SibAuto had no interest in exporting dragas was the terrible domestic shortage of them. We are not talking about the shoe industry here, but gold and diamonds. The country would earn far less hard currency from exporting our equipment than from stepping up gold and mining operations and increasing annual output from them.

Once our draga became fully operational, I felt as though we had traded in a seventeenth-century galleon for a nuclear submarine. However, when Draga-1 was assembled, the joyful gratitude we had been expecting from the gold and diamond miners at Yakutia wasn't forthcoming. Most of the miners showed no enthusiasm; some were even surly about it and grumbled under their breath. Why didn't they welcome an invention that would ease their labors, I wondered.

Within weeks, the situation went from bad to worse. The miners became openly and adamantly opposed to SibAuto's little technological miracle. They claimed our draga didn't work. When Nikolenko, one of our best engineers, heard this news, he was incredulous. "That's impossible," he said. "We tested the *draga* over and over, and under the toughest conditions. It works perfectly." Nikolenko was as solid a technician in the art of remote control as anyone in Europe. A small, intense man, proud and self-taught, he was one of the fathers of our invention. Perplexed, Nikolenko, some engineers, and I went to Yakutia to check on *Draga-1*.

I stood on the shore of a quiet, narrow river, the bank lined with stunted northern trees. How incredible, I thought, that this modest-looking waterway was loaded with diamonds. Suddenly, Nikolenko appeared with a look of horror on his face and a section of cable in his hand.

"You won't believe it," he said, his voice trembling with rage. "These barbarians cut the cable with an ax. We worked nights to create this miracle for them. Nobody in the whole world has a bucket dredge with an automation system like this one, and these savages go and destroy it."

We were standing in the middle of the Siberian taiga. The only possible cable cutters were the miners themselves. Why did they do it? I knew how they cherished any bit of equipment that could ease their backbreaking labor.

A cursory inspection of *Draga-1* gave us our answer. Installed on the unit was a meter that clocked the real time the machine was in operation. It indicated six hours—two hours less per day than the miners were supposed to work. If their actual hours were reported to the ministry, their salaries would drop. Because the miners did not share in profits, they were uninterested in increasing output, so they cut the cable to eliminate any tangible proof of their malingering.

Tzar and I argued to the ministry that the miners should be given financial incentives to use automated systems, but the monolithic Soviet system was unmoved by our appeals. It would take another decade and the full weight of seventy years of socioeconomic mismanagement before that happened.

When the paperwork for our proposal to become an STC had been placed in the bureaucratic hopper, I left for Moscow. Months earlier, I had sent representatives from SibAuto to the city to lay the groundwork for my visit. I knew very well that to succeed we would need not only to be persuasive, but come bearing goods.

Being a diversified company, SibAuto manufactured, among many other things, sophisticated telephone systems. Officials in the ministry needed telephones for their offices, but like so many other things in the Soviet Union, they were not readily available (nor are they still). We were doing them a favor by selling our systems to them.

Because supplies are always so scarce in Russia, you can never depend on receiving the official allocations necessary for production unless you have good contacts. If the State promises to supply you with raw materials of one type or another, that does not mean they will deliver them. When you find yourself waiting for a ton of cement, you can be certain there is another company waiting for that same shipment and that the bureaucrat will have to make a choice. He will always give the cement to the company whose contacts are strongest and who, at a later date, might prove most useful to him. This doesn't necessarily mean he is looking for a bribe, but he is building a friendship—one he might need in the future. This is how business gets done in the former Soviet Union to this day.

In pursuit of these types of "friendships," we dramatically stepped up the production of Waterfall chandeliers several months before our

STC paperwork reached Moscow. We ran into some trouble. The head of the regional trade department in Krasnoyarsk, feeling cheated of his slice of the pie, visited the local Party boss—whom he probably was bribing—and turned informer against us. He argued that what we were doing ran contrary to the best interests of the State, in that "the people" would not have access to our chandeliers. The truth of the matter was that our manufacturing chandeliers ran contrary to the trade chief's personal interests. Once he gained control of them, rather than sell them to "the people," he would sell them on the black market at astronomical prices and pocket part of the profits.

Kozin, our planning chief, and I, along with some of SibAuto's better minds, spent several late nights in my office drinking strong tea and trying to figure out a way of keeping the chandeliers out of the hands of the regional Communist Party.

One night, Lev Krasov joined us. Krasov was perhaps the most renowned figure at SibAuto and a member of Russia's parliament. "Another case of tea abuse?" he teased us. He was alluding to the fact that at work people hardly ever ask a companion to go drink vodka. They always ask, "Shall we go have a mug of tea?"

Kozin told Krasov our dilemma. He nodded sympathetically. "Let's not take the guy on by ourselves," he said. "This is what I would do. My friend Stukalov is a director of a television factory. . . ."

The television factory was among the biggest and most important companies in the city; not for its televisions, but because it also manufactured military equipment. This deadly secret was known by virtually everyone. Arms factories often used consumer goods as a cover for their operations. The same plant that manufactures the Snow Cap refrigerator also manufactures missiles. In 1991 and 1992, a lot of military plants were converted from military to consumer production. These plants are technologically advanced, and many of them already have a consumer goods division, which makes conversion easier. In addition, directors of these plants are well connected, military production having been the top priority of Soviet industry for so long. Former manufacturers of military hardware therefore offer a solid basis for joint ventures with foreign partners.

Krasov went on to say that Stukalov's father was director of Krasnoyarsk's largest State retail store, called Central. Through his connections he said he could arrange for us to come to an agreement with Central. This way, he argued, the trade chief's accusation that our chandeliers were unavailable to the general public would be groundless.

"I get it," said Tatiana, SibAuto's chief bookkeeper. "We give our chandeliers to Central, which will bring them profits, and in return, Central, which has all kinds of foreign consumer goods, will provide us with goods we can use to help us gain influence."

It was indeed an elegant solution, illustrating two important things potential investors in Russia need to know. First, you can waste your life fighting the paper pushers. They will always pull the blanket over to their side and take unfair advantage of their position. Second, potential joint-venture partners need to remember that in Russia goods are more important than money. Russians have money; the problem is they have nothing to buy with it.

Barter defines many business relationships between Russian enterprises. Even at the major military plants, barter accounts for half of the planned levels of production. Using the newly passed Law of Enterprise, a zinc mine, for example, is free to set up whatever barter arrangements it wants to trade zinc for materials it needs. Almost every successful joint venture uses this system to its advantage. It doesn't violate laws, nor does it ship products to the highest black market bidder. Instead, it sells its goods to whomever might provide it with items in short supply. Today, in addition to being important to domestic trade, barter accounts for nearly 10 percent of all international trade in Russia.

A century and a half ago, Russian writer Nikolai Gogol wrote his dramatic masterpiece *The Inspector General*. In the play, an entire town waits in terror for an inspector from the capital to come to scrutinize the activities of local officials. The day of judgment is at hand.

Today, in Russia, just as under the Soviets, the day of judgment comes every year in the form of a State financial inspection. An inspector comes to look at a company's books, searching for any irregularities. One morning, Tzar called. "Remember the anonymka?" he asked.

"Yes," I replied.

"Well," he said, "the inspector has arrived."

Inspector Mushroom had indeed arrived to look into the libelous claims made in that anonymous poison-pen letter mailed to Moscow.

When I met him, he was already frowning, his eyes narrowed to slits and his bald head glistening with perspiration. For an entire day, he filled out his reports and cataloged every inch of our facilities. He burrowed into our capital construction paperwork. When he came up for air, he asked the question I had been dreading most. "There is the cost of a whole building missing from the balance sheet. How did you build it without money? You must have dipped into the wage funds!"

"No," I replied, "we didn't touch the wage fund. That would've been a crime."

Inspector Mushroom scratched his bald pate. "So where did the money come from?" he asked.

"It was a gift," I answered, trying not to sound smug. "A gift from the Soviet people. They built it on a voluntary basis."

"I don't know how you did it," he said, "but it smells like jail to me."

"You're wrong," I said. "First you'd have to prove something was stolen, and no one stole anything."

Mushroom filled out a protocol form outlining our alleged indiscretions and went off to drink vodka with Schetkin, to whom he confided that he had never come across methods like ours before.

Then he left—and we waited.

During many long nights, long after the ghost building drama had unraveled to its end, I asked myself why Tzar and I had risked so much for SibAuto.

Our reasons weren't unique. Managers across the country risk their jobs because they want to do something significant with their lives, to accomplish something in spite of the pernicious economic constraints imposed by the State. This managerial drive to succeed often has more to it than simply the desire for profit. Although I have emphasized the daily deprivations those who live in the independent republics suffer, in the main, despite it all, they still manage to survive. This is due in no small part to those innumerable individuals who take the initiative and try to make life better for working Russians.

While the ministry considered Inspector Mushroom's findings, the anonymka fluttered about in the bureaucratic breeze, eventually landing on the desk of the chairman of our district's People's Control Board—the body that monitored citizens' adherence to rules. I was

soon summoned before the board to have my moral character eval-
uated. The chairwoman was a strict and elderly woman who wore
her hair in a tight bun.

After listening to my version of things, she said, "For the first time
I can see that there is actually a grain of truth in an anonymka." She
handed me the dreaded sheet of paper, and on it was a sentence about
my ability to "charm the leadership."

"You've won me over." She laughed. "I understand why you built
this factory."

My hearing went surprisingly quickly and we parted on the best
of terms.

My visit to the board solved the mystery of who had written the
anonymka. Although I couldn't discern who the handwriting belonged to, the legalistic tone of the sentences pointed to SibAuto's
legal counsel, Svetlana. I was also certain that The Beard was behind
it, pulling every string he had with military bureaucrats to oust me
from my deputy director's chair.

"What did I tell you," said Chancellor Frost when I returned to
headquarters. "Of course she and The Beard were in cahoots. But
how did they find out about the whole thing? That's the question."
The answer was simple: Schitkin. I had asked the redhaired giant to
spill the beans.

Question: Why doesn't the Russian economy work?

Answer: Because Russian managers talk about work in the sauna
and about the sauna at work.

The joke stretches the truth just a little, but it is an indisputable
fact that the sauna does hold a revered place in Russian business.
When the chief of the ministry's financial department landed at the
snow-covered Krasnoyarsk airport, Kozin took him straight to the
sauna. His name was Leshiy, which means "wood goblin," and I
knew that he would have a great deal to say about whether SibAuto
could keep its ghost building.

Our official black Volga was waiting for him on the tarmac when
he stepped off the plane and in fifteen minutes we were at the top of
Krasniy Mountain.

Centuries ago, Krasniy Mountain was a cossack settlement. Now
it is the main observation point for Krsanoyarsk. A million people
inhabit both sides of the wide and swift Yenisey River, one of the
mightiest in the world. The view is so magnificent it inspires people

to drink nothing less than champagne, rather than the more traditional vodka. While pouring champagne into Leshiy's glass, Kozin pointed out SibAuto headquarters and then showed him the plaque commemorating the spot where Popov, the Russian inventor of radio, had watched the solar eclipse at the start of the century.

We took Wood Goblin to the best sauna in the area, located in a secret military site outside the city. What the military did here, in the heart of Siberia, was anybody's guess. Perhaps it provided the safest hiding spot in the event of a nuclear war. Perhaps it was the observation point from which these modern cossacks could observe their comrades. One thing was certain: it had the best steam bath around.

Wood Goblin sprinted through the bitter January cold and freshly fallen snow, and ducked into the locker room. Once inside, he knocked back a tumbler of vodka and undressed. Two minutes later, a bare-assed government delegation proceeded in single file to the steam bath.

In Russian, drinking is called filling one's chest. Lazarev, our chief engineer, was a prodigious drinker and mistrusted anyone who refused a drink. His chest well stocked, Lazarev began telling a string of raunchy anecdotes, each one dirtier than the one before. In Russia, anecdotes are a way of life, a means of survival, and when people gather in the sauna it is a way of letting off—pardon the pun—steam. If you're offended by dirty jokes or drunkenness, you'll have to get over it if you really mean to do business in the former Soviet Union.

Lazarev proceeded to get roaring drunk and regale us with filthy stories. Things almost got out of hand when he offended a colonel who happened to join us in the middle of the revelry. The colonel greeted us stiffly, but politely. For some reason this set off Lazarev, who began yelling at the poor man. "Where are your papers?" he roared. "How dare you interrupt a top-level negotiation?" Lazarev's manner must have made the man think he was a high-ranking officer because he became very apologetic. This only infuriated Lazarev further. Finally, Wood Goblin interceded.

"Pay no attention to this slob, Comrade Colonel. Take off your coat and have a drink. And you, Lazarev, go take a cold shower or I'll throw you in myself."

Food provided us with relief. A stoic-looking sergeant brought in a plate of French fries, icy pickles from a wooden barrel, and Russian sauerkraut with cranberry. The atmosphere couldn't have been more conducive to good rapport, and Wooden Goblin, who had obviously had a lot of experience in such festivities, enjoyed himself immensely.

After the steam bath, he plunged headlong into a snowbank and then back into the sauna. Refreshed, he sat with us at a big, round table, everyone still in the buff. We ate and drank, and our late dinner turned into an early breakfast.

Our hospitality paid off. We got an appointment with the legendary Lomako himself, the Minister of Nonferrous Metallurgy. It was the only chance Tzar and I had to survive.

Lomako ("The Crusher") had an office on the twelfth floor of a skyscraper on Kalinin Avenue, in the center of Moscow. The offices on the twelfth and thirteenth floors of this building, where the ministers and their deputies sit, are more equal than those on the other floors—by one meter.

At 7:00 A.M., I was waiting outside the ministry. An hour later, Lomako arrived, his eyes bright and cheeks rosy. The Crusher stepped from his limousine, shook snow off his shoes, and strode energetically into the ministry. I watched him in admiration. Lomako was one of the last giants of the Soviet administrative system, a true survivor. His career had begun in the days of Stalin, before the Second World War, and he only retired quite recently (he died in 1988). He was, in my opinion, among the most intelligent and visionary government officials the Soviet Union had ever produced.

I was ushered into his office, and there he sat behind his huge desk in suspenders, a white shirt, and a short, wide tie. An assistant, young and pretty, was perched in a corner seat, holding a pad and pen, scrupulously writing down every utterance her boss made.

"What have you and Tzaregorodtsev done this time? I ought to drive you to visit the devil's mother. Another complaint about you: Inspector Mushroom thinks you should go to prison."

"To prison?," I replied. "For fulfilling your resolution and planning for the future of the molybdenum industry? The inspectors spent more money on airfare than we did on our building."

The Crusher studied me. "You always think you're right, don't you?"

"We follow the spirit of the law," I said, "and they make us obey the letter of it."

He glanced at the inspector's report. Then he noticed the anonymka in the file and his face filled with disgust. The former cossack leaned forward in his chair as though he were bestride a horse and galloping across the steppes.

"You're safe for now," he said, finally, "but this is the last time. One more violation and both your heads will roll."

That evening, I saw Lomako again as he was leaving. It was 9:00 P.M., and the man I saw shuffling down the corridor seemed old and tired. The years had taken their toll on him. The ministry collapsed not long after The Crusher's retirement. Prime Minister Rizshkov, needing to concede to the democratic forces, yet also afraid to jump into the free market, combined the ministry with others and formed one colossus. It won't stand for long.

As for Tzar, he was given a reprimand, one of many he has gotten over his career (and he is proud of most of them). I was not reprimanded and my record stayed clean. The ministry had to punish us somehow, so they ordered us to dismantle the radio-telephones we had in our cars. They said they cost too much—an especially counterproductive form of punishment I thought, given that SibAuto's branches were spread across the Soviet Union and had offices in eleven time zones.

At the next meeting of SibAuto's employees, I publically thanked The Beard for inviting Inspector Mushroom. His invitation had helped make the ghost building an official part of our operations and our balance sheet.

"Comrade Beard is so modest that he didn't even put his name on this very important document." I held up the anonymka.

Schetkin had played his part well. It was his idea to "leak" the story about the ghost building to The Beard over lunch. We had discussed the matter beforehand, and came to the conclusion that despite the risk it offered the best way of making an honest facility of it.

We had done it. We had turned SibAuto around and made it work. The company was on track and running smoothly. Tzar is still head of SibAuto, and his twenty-two years there has set the record for longevity as a Russian manager. Professionally, I was also on track. Several years of work at SibAuto would help me get a prestigious position in the Ministry of Nonferrous Metallurgy.

During my SibAuto days, I hadn't yet envisioned Russia's breaking away from the Soviet Union. My understanding of the political forces at work in the country came later. The world of free enterprise and the choices this would bring were closed to me. All I could do to reach my dream was deal with the same bureaucratic mess day in, day out. One day, gazing out of my office window, it struck me that I'd had enough of this career. Turning one Soviet company around was enough.

When I finally left SibAuto, I was proud of what I had helped accomplish. I believed the employees were better off, not just because they had more rubles and chandeliers, but because they were measuring their product by a different, and higher, standard of excellence. I'll also admit I rather enjoyed manipulating the system. In the end, however, all of the cloak-and-dagger machinations, although necessary, cost precious time. We could have done so much more had we not had to resort to them. Today, all across the former Soviet Union, millions of people are beginning to realize the price they paid to keep the Communist regime going. Just as I couldn't go back to SibAuto, so, too, are Russian workers ready to move ahead. They're ready to breathe the bracing air of capitalism.

CHAPTER 7

Finding the Right Key

Stand in Red Square in Moscow and face Lenin's Mausoleum and to your left you will see a small, unobtrusive-looking passage leading to the heart of the Kremlin—to the Soviet Council of Ministers and the President's Residence. The doors to these offices are closely guarded.

In my capacity as deputy director general of SibAuto, and later as a researcher at the Academy of Sciences, I went through these doors dozens of times. I was helping to compose regional programs and commerce laws. Behind Kremlin doors is where the top-level economic decisions are still made in Russia, and where the external forces that shape Russian business still operate.

Westerners who invest in a Russian business can expect its behavior and its fate to be shaped by the interplay among that company, regional authorities, and these Kremlin offices. Together, they compose the economic "program" for every region, listing economic objectives and development goals. I will have much to say about these programs and how they influence any decision to invest in a joint partnership.

In that SibAuto's customers were so happy with our work, why, I wondered, couldn't we facilitate the automation of companies in other industries. Tzar had always backed my ideas, and together we created one of the Soviet Union's first scientific-technical committees within the regional government. We held our first national seminar in 1977, at a time when only Japan and the United States were very active in industrial robotization. Later, I wrote the book *Industrial Robots: An Introduction*. The Kremlin took note of my activity and invited me to participate in drafting legislation for the Party Central Committee and the Soviet Council of Ministers.

The Kremlin corridors are tomblike—musty and dank—as though the windows hadn't been opened since 1917. When I wandered through them I half expected to run into Lenin or Stalin. The offices are ludicrously old-fashioned. Even as late as 1989, the office of First Executive Deputy Prime Minister Voronin lacked adequate office equipment; all it contained was fifteen outdated telephones and a crinkled and yellowing map of the Soviet Union. I have mentioned that SibAuto manufactured modern multiline telephones back in the 1970s, which, of course, were available to government bosses. But they stubbornly stuck to the outdated models—possibly out of the same impulse that led them to embalm Lenin's body.

After a number of years at SibAuto—years during which I was also helping to draft regional programs—I began increasingly to feel that I would be better off in an environment in which my ideas could reach a broader range of people and have greater impact. The day after I turned in my resignation at SibAuto, the deputy minister of the nonferrous metals industry and the chief of staff immediately invited me to Moscow.

The chief of staff had a flair for mat. Once, when I was on the fifteenth floor of the ministry, I telephoned him in his office, which was on the ninth floor.

"This is Kvint. Can I come to see you?"

In response came a flood of expletives, so I hung up and went down to his office. He was still swearing when I walked in.

"How did you get here so fast?" he asked, surprised. "I hadn't finished talking with you on the intercom. Anyway, we could offer you a position as a department head in the ministry."

I turned him down. By the time I had entered his office, I had already made up my mind. I didn't want to be a manager; I wanted to do research, to study nationwide issues involving management, and to work with people such as Professor Aganbegian, one of the shrewdest market economists in the Soviet Union. I got my chance when I was invited to join the Academy of Science. I had decided to join the academy because, I thought, that was where the "big science" was being done, rather than at the univerisities, which in Russia, unlike the U.S., are primarily teaching institutions.

Since its inception, the academy has played a unique role. In addition to being a major think tank, membership has always brought with it a special influence. Under the most tyrannical regimes in Soviet history, the academy has been the only relatively independent organization in the country. Because of the quality of its research, and its autonomy, it stands for prestige.

For me it was an opportunity to dive into serious economic research that I might later put into practice. I walked away from SibAuto one morning, leaving behind my wonderful office, chauffered car, and team of assistants. I had been asked to start the regional branch of the Academic Institute of Economics, to analyze scientific-technical progress and industrial organization in Siberia. I went to my mother's house to read, think, and compose my research program. After two weeks, my mother came into my room and demanded to know the truth.

"Tell me everything," she said, unable to contain herself. "Why did they fire you?"

I had difficulty explaining to her that the academy didn't care about office hours, but about ideas.

At the end of the 1980s, economic matters still revolved exclusively around the policies—and whims—of the Kremlin. Today in Russia the Council of Ministers continues to be heavily involved in practically every major economic program. Conflict between regional authorities and the central government is a constant problem. If anything, the conflict has gotten worse since the Soviet Union began disintegrating. Regions and individual enterprises have gained more independence than they previously held and are standing up for their interests. The Russian government generally sides with local government when it clashes with regional enterprises.

These conflicts make it difficult for foreigners setting up a joint venture to make all the right moves when dealing with the confusing array of ministries, political authorities, and regional bodies. For example, the best way to develop projects in western Siberia, Kazakhstan, the Central Asian Republic, or the oil fields north of Krasnoyarsk, would be to win a concession for all of the territory around the oil field and then form a consortium to develop it. Kazakhstan was the first republic to approve the concession law in 1992. Corporations—from petrochemical giants to toy manufacturers and restaurants—will find their niche in such multimillion-dollar projects. It is critical that a foreign investor understand how the economics of a project of such size tie into a regional program. I have spent a good portion of my life developing such programs. Many of them were adopted by the State and included in its regional development programs. I first started dealing with regional programs while at SibAuto. I continued studying the power structures within the Soviet Union because I wanted to know precisely how regional authorities functioned relative to the various ministries, the government, and the old-time Party bosses. How, I wondered, is such an immense region as Krasnoyarsk, whose size is one-fourth that of the United States, governed. Over the years, I learned the Byzantine logic of economic decision making at the top levels of the Soviet government, and how it gets translated at the regional level.

Equally critical to acquainting oneself with a regional program is getting the regional leaders on one's side. Very often, they, not the lumps in Moscow, have life-or-death power over a project. If they are progressive-minded, they will encourage cooperative developments with a foreign partner. Most are—the majority of regional authorities approve of foreign investment—but even those who are in theory in favor of such projects might need some persuading before they back a particular undertaking. My basic advice to foreign businesspeople is to pay a visit to the local boss. Interest him and involve him. Let him know that you have arrived.

Western investors naturally wonder what authority regional programs have, in the light of Soviet disintegration. They should rest assured that whatever government is in power, it will have to address the nation's dire economic woes. Regional programs have been developed to meet the country's economic and social needs, many of which were drafted despite opposition from the ministers. A more progressive government, recognizing the vital importance of these programs, will enact the necessary changes even faster. Encircled by economic chaos, no government, not even the most reactionary imaginable, is going to scrap them and start over from scratch.

□   □   □

I'll start with a success story. The German company Siemens, one of the world's largest energy equipment companies, has done extremely well in the Russian marketplace. Siemens beat out a giant American corporation in the same field because of its skill in navigating the corridors of power, and because it recognized from the beginning the importance of having a regional boss in your corner—in this case, the mayor of the second-largest city in Russia, St. Petersburg.

With a population in excess of four million, and many industries—shipbuilding, heavy industry, electronics, chemicals, brewing, publishing, food processing, and textiles—it was not surprising that Siemens and the U.S. corporation were competing for a project in St. Petersburg (at the time, of course, it was called Leningrad). Both companies wanted to strike a joint-production deal with a technologically sophisticated plant. I strongly advised the Americans to contact the newly elected mayor, a man named Sobchak, because he was a proponent of the progressive thinking then on the rise in the Soviet Union.

I informed my American clients that Siemens would probably invest somewhere between 380 and 500 million Deutsche marks in Russia, basing that figure on the guaranteed credit the West German government would give Siemens to invest there—given my perception of Bonn's interests in what was then East Germany, and on some information I had about Siemens' connections.

In August of 1990, I drafted a letter to Mayor Sobchak on behalf of the American company that, unfortunately, the Americans chose not to send. They opted instead to concentrate their efforts on the ministers in Moscow and the company in St. Petersburg. These were essential contacts, but insufficient by themselves. Siemens arrived at the same conclusion I did. In January of 1991, they established a cordial relationship with the mayor's office in St. Petersburg. Three months later, the St. Petersburg City Council approved the Siemens project and recommended that the plant sign an agreement with the Germans. The recommendation meant that they would help both companies cut through red tape. That was enough to persuade the Soviet managers to sign with Siemens rather than my clients.

The office Siemens opened was the first to be registered by a city council, rather than by the Kremlin. That has helped them enormously. There is a saying that "they who give once, will give twice." Once it established its presence in the marketplace, Siemens was able to expand its operations. The St. Petersburg City Council has provided Siemens with a large parcel of land, and there the German corporation, together with the city's construction organizations and various related companies, will join forces in building and equipping a power plant.

A stalwart advocate of cooperation with the West, Mayor Sobchak helped solve one of the basic problems facing Russian-foreign partnerships in general, and the Siemans project, in particular: convertible currency. Their efforts demonstrate how far a local politico will extend himself if he genuinely believes in the benefits of a business venture. For years, St. Petersburg has provided Finland with electrical power. Finland pays for this service in hard currency. At the urging of Sobchak, the city council permitted Siemens to participate in this contract with Finland, thus providing them with an opportunity to generate profits in a convertible currency.

Keeping in mind that even the most pro-business leaders in the former Soviet Union are sensitive about profits, as well as to the needs of the local population, Siemens drew up an agreement with the city council to construct a desperately needed medical center. For its part, the council committed itself to assisting in the joint production of medical systems and equipment, which will be sold domestically and abroad. Production was to start in 1992. In return, Siemens was granted a princely amount of space in which to establish an equipment service bureau and open a company store.

My estimate of Siemens' financial commitment proved accurate— approximately 500 million Deutsche marks. By contacting the right person at the right moment, the Germans received far more cooperation from the Russians than anticipated, and because of the extensive contacts they developed and the size of their investment, the Germans closed off a considerable portion of the Russian market to its American competitor.

However, the former Soviet Union is a land whose needs and markets are as vast as its borders. I advised my American client not to despair, and instead to establish relations with people outside the central government. I recommended in particular that they contact local authorities in the Far East, in that officials in this region are gaining more say in international projects. It was possible, I reassured him, to strike a deal in the Khabarovsk Region similar to the one Siemens struck in St. Petersburg. The region boasts a technologically advanced plant, is becoming a free economic zone, and its governor, like Mayor Sobchak, is a vocal proponent of cooperation with foreign partners.

Why are regional bosses becoming so influential? The answer, like so many answers in the former Soviet Union, is rooted in history. My American clients found it difficult to comprehend the importance of history to the Russians. To Americans, yesterday has the value of last year's snow. The future is everything, and the here and now is but a passageway to it. Russians, on the other hand, are deeply and painfully immersed in their past, and they look to it to help solve their current disputes and problems. In Russia, last year's snow still clogs the streets. Russians cling tenaciously to history, and to the strict order and tyranny of days gone by.

Thus, even though millions of Russian citizens have now resigned from the Communist Party and from its successors, it will continue to be a powerful force for a long time, especially in the provinces. It spent decades planting fear in people's minds, and it planted deeply.

A few months before the 1991 coup, a friend of mine, a minister in the new Russian government, paid a visit to a member of the Politburo.

"Listen," he said to the Party boss. "I had to pass through three cordons of your guards—KGB guys from the airborne division wearing shoulder straps. Nobody wants to visit you, anyway. Who are you hiding from?"

The answer is everyone. The Communist Party was not only a political organization, but the biggest corporate monopoly in the world, and it still wants to keep an eye on its money. The entrance of Party headquarters in the Krasnoyarsk Region used to be guarded by a wizened old soldier, his scrawny chest covered with medals. His job was to check Party cards or the passes of nonParty members. To get in to see the Central Committee, you needed a special pass. Party bosses have always maintained a distance from Party members, and still do. I once watched that soldier spend five minutes checking the credentials of a Party secretary from a big industrial plant.

"You know him personally," I said to him. "You checked his card when he came in. Why check it again when he leaves?"

"Many have entered the Party Committee carrying a Party card," he replied proudly, "and left without it!" The soldier's impassive face suddenly erupted into a toothless grin of pure triumph. "I'll remember the guy. He'll never get in again!"

The Party often expelled members on a moment's notice simply to instill a sacred awe of the Party's vengeful hammer. That hammer has much less muscle today, but it can still crush. The regional boss, as a representative of the longstanding Soviet power structure, oversees the entire legal system in his area. He can locate the skeletons in your closet, even if they belonged to the previous tenant; he can send an inspector to find something remiss about your operation and close down your factory; and he can deny you access to raw materials until you go bankrupt. He is his own private ways and means committee.

Before the central government began weakening, the local heavyweights were kept in their place by the national leaders in Moscow. But now that the Kremlin and Old Square (the former Communist Party headquarters) have lost their power, local authorities are filling the vacuum. Plenty of former Soviet officials have donned new clothing, but their way of holding and wielding power remains almost the same. Party bosses might have swapped their wolf's fur for sheepskin and hopped onto a governor's throne, but they are still wolves.

American businesspeople often come to the former Soviet Union with the illusion that a regional governor's position approximates that of, say, Governor Mario Cuomo of New York. Yet, when it comes to commerce, even the power of an American governor such as Cuomo pales next to the sovereignty of a regional boss. In the United States, an American company belongs to its owners. In Russia, the bigger part of major enterprises are still the property of the State. Any cooperative or private company is therefore even more vulnerable to the whims of a regional chieftain, since permission to continue operation—and the hard currency to do so—depends on his approval.

However, no governor, whatever his political allegiance, is either entirely inaccessible or wholly irrational. If you can convince him your project will be profitable and still improve the lives of the people in a particular area, he might become your ally.

When a foreign investor chooses a region in which to put capital, he should get a copy of the regional program and read it thoroughly before making any binding decisions. By the end of the 1980s, practically every region and city across the country were developing these programs. Becoming very familiar with its contents is worthwhile for four reasons.

First, each program lists which foreign technologies are considered vital to a particular region. In years past, regions and enterprises tried to squeeze enough hard currency out of the centralized powers to buy sorely needed equipment and technologies. Now that these enterprises are more or less independent, they are willing to barter for them—a fact not lost on a regional boss, who might well be desperate to get his hands on the very product you can provide. His desperation, of course, can be used to your advantage during negotiations.

Second, the programs indicate every region's export options, so you will see, *before* investing your money, what possibilities there really are for bringing the fruits of your joint venture to world markets.

Third, the foreign investment protection laws adopted in 1991, and the 1993 state and regional privatization programs, allow foreigners to buy State-owned property. Regional programs will indicate which companies are of greatest interest.

Fourth, reading a regional program will put you in the best position to evaluate your Russian partner and therefore minimize your risk. The joint venture struck between Mari El, an autonomous republic near the Volga River in Russia, and the Italian company Fata should illustrate the usefulness of reading and digesting what can be found on the pages of a regional program.

A center for the military's electronic and radio industry, Mari El was the site of a walloping number of unfinished, "bearded" construction sites. Authorities therefore decided to search for foreign investors interested in developing them. They began their search for partners by going to the international exhibitions in Moscow. There they met Fata. After learning about the frozen sites in Mari El from the regional program, Fata started investing gradually. They first lent money to complete the construction of an unfinished factory that belonged to the Ministry of the Radio Industry, one of fifty such sites the ministry has in Mari El (a fact also highlighted in the regional program).

By 1987, Fata had established a joint venture in Mari El to manufacture refrigerators. Within two years, this joint venture, called SovItalprodmash, had three operational factories—a total of 360,000 square feet of space and 2,730 employees. By 1991, the joint venture had manufactured 86,000 refrigerators. Projections call for 200,000 refrigerators by 1993. One-fifth of their output belongs to Fata and is sold worldwide for profit. Each year, SovItalprodmash also invests part of its dollar and ruble profits in the production of nine thousand thermic containers. Their cost benefit promises to be substantial. Inspired by Fata's success, other companies from Italy's Piedmont region became interested in the potential of the regional program, which led to the signing of an agreement between the Piedmont and the Mari El Republic. In November of 1991, Yeltsin abolished the ministry that supervised the Soviet partner; therefore, the company has become even more independent and flexible.

In light of the ever-changing situation in the former Soviet republics, regions, and economic structures, it is natural for foreign investors to wonder if the elements of the regional programs won't be as volatile, and thus useless. The short answer to that question is no, for reasons I have given previously. The importance of these regional programs will actually increase because of national instability. Regional plans are now designed to include and invite foreign investment.

I do not mean to paint too rosy a picture. One of the most treacherous obstacles to investment is that few people can provide foreigners with a reliable risk analysis of the proposed investment. Doctored information still infects the land. Only a handful of Russian economists have traveled very far outside their offices. As for foreigners, until recently, they have not been permitted to see the reality behind the facade of Potemkin villages, which have been a part of Russian propaganda since the days of Catherine the Great.

Even information from the U.S. Commercial Office in Moscow might not prove helpful; not because of propaganda, but because this office doesn't have access to the power structures and, like any bureaucracy, lacks business zeal. An American colleague of mine who went to Russia on business tried to gather profiles on four potential future partners from the Commercial Office. He could get information only about one of them, whose profile read: "No high [sic] education. Old timer [sic]. About 60 years old. Won't keep his position long." In fact, as my American friend eventually discovered, the man was considerably younger and had earned a Ph.D. in economics. He has had a very distinguished career, which culminated in 1992, when the government (Yeltsin is a friend of his) appointed him chairman of Russia's largest State-owned foreign trade company.

Let us assume a foreign businessperson knows about these pitfalls, but has located a project he hopes to pursue with a Russian or Ukranian company. He has acquainted himself with the regional program and has paid a visit to the local boss. What types of problems can he expect to confront when he tries to obtain permission from the authorities?

It would be ideal to have a precise, sure-fire, step-by-step guide to success, but it is impossible to explain every clause in every regulation, and to define every "if" in every Russian contract. Business in Russia can best be understood using a case-by-case approach.

The example of Gorevka, the world's biggest lead deposit, should serve as an excellent model of the decision-making process behind any large project. Discovered in 1956, the Gorevka lead deposit is one of the treasures of the Yenisey Mountains and among the richest mineral deposits on earth. Situated in one of the most beautiful places in Siberia—where the two great Siberian rivers, the Yenisey and Angara, meet—Gorevka (which means "grief") runs along the eastern shore of the Yenisey. Rimmed by forests of towering pines, the shoreline possesses a severe beauty. Not only is the amount of lead Gorevka contains astounding, but its geologic form: it is as though some giant took a massive slab of lead some four hundred feet wide and a mile long and drove it underground. The deposit also contains zinc, cadmium, and silver.

Gorevka was one of the targets of my team's 1979 economic expedition, when we were studying the natural and labor resources of the Krasnoyarsk Region. Our geologists estimated the amount of lead in one of Gorevka's open pits to be roughly 1.5 million tons. Experimental mining took place only three months a year because of the lack of construction materials and money. One hundred and forty-five million rubles (at the time, the dollar amount was about the same) would, we estimated, be needed to erect the first line of the preparation plant, and 32 million more to build housing for ten thousand miners. The enormity of the deposit inspired us. We were certain it would have an instantaneous impact on the international lead market. We also estimated that 60 percent of the lead deposits could be mined within twenty-five years at very low cost. No other deposit in the world could match Gorevka.

In addition to the world's richest lead ore, Gorevka also yielded ninety grams of silver per ton, which, even at our most conservative estimates, would deliver a profit of $35 million a year. At the time of our expedition, there was already a small pit and refinery on location, both run by Vassiliy Zentsov—a man whose energy could match the fierce Angara River. Any foreign company would be lucky to have him as a partner.

When we returned from the expedition, we put together a portfolio outlining what we thought were the most promising natural resource sites in Central Siberia. Gorevka was at the top of our list. We knew that for thirty years the Ministry of Energy had been toying with the idea of building a hydroelectric power plant there. We thought that idea was blatantly ridiculous. Who in their right mind would want to flood the land and drown the untold mineral wealth of Gorevka? You would be surprised.

Across the street from the Kremlin stood a gloomy, gray edifice called the Gosplan Building. Gosplan was the highest planning group in the Soviet Union, and a bloated parasite on the body politic. In early 1991, it changed its name to the Soviet Ministry of Economic Forecasting, and was later rebaptized as the Russian Ministry of Economics. Experience has taught me that no matter how many times you change the name of a bureaucracy, its essential nature remains the same. Bureaucrats are constitutionally unable to introduce or digest anything progressive, because by definition that would challenge the status quo from which they derive their power.

In the early 1980s, at a Gosplan meeting in which Gorevka was the topic of discussion, there were three major players: Baibakov (whom everyone called Lazybones), then Vice-Prime Minister and all-powerful chairman of Gosplan; Lomako (The Crusher), whom we've met, then Minister of Nonferrous Metallurgy, and former Vice-Prime Minister of the Soviet Union under Khrushchev; and Neporoshniy (Half-Full), then Minister of Energy. Joining this triumvirate were a selection of lesser lights, a collection of ministers and Gosplan functionaries.

The mighty trio exchanged ideas, whereas everyone else, awed by their power, sat in silence. The morning discussion dragged on. The audience was eager for lunch. Lomako concluded the morning discussion by saying, almost perfunctorily, "For so many years we have been unable to do anything about this lead deposit, a hoard of wealth sitting right under our noses, and now the energy minister here wants to drown it to build his hydropower plant. This is a crime."

Half-Full was a sly, gray-haired Ukrainian. He was upset and hungry. He had been poised for his next gargantuan project when The Crusher interfered. Half-Full had already had a disastrous experience with one big hydropower plant, and therefore had to temporarily stop construction on any new ones. His army of skilled and seasoned construction workers was dispersed and sitting idly. Sitting idle was not in Half-Full's nature. Under the Soviet system, gigantic projects were as critical to a minister as morphine to a drug addict. Without one, he might disappear from the agenda of the general secretary. (If they have an appointment with a minister, foreign investors should describe their project in the most grandiose terms possible. This can only help matters.)

Half-Full was also very aware this meeting could be decisive. His Sayano-Shushenskaya hydroelectric power plant was almost finished, as was as his Nadeshda copper metallurgical works in Norilsk. The Nadeshda works, which Prime Minister Kosygin had ordered him to build, had turned into a pain in the neck.

I can imagine Half-Full's thought process. *Suppose they start mining Gorevka,* it probably went. *In a couple of years, pulling every string I have, I might finally get permission to build the hydroelectric plant, but by then, my builders will have dispersed! If I do it now, I can keep my crew intact, relocate them, and start building. I'll reap a bumper crop of medals and awards. My research institute has calculated how efficient and profitable this plant will be. I think I'll order the director to rework his calculations, to make the proposed plant, say, ten percent more profitable.*

At this point, Half-Full might have grinned at the thought that this would give him the extra money he needed for out-of-pocket expenses; namely, the bribe he would need to pay The Crusher's ministry. He was certain this was the way to deal with Lomako: buy him. Everything and everybody had its price.

Here is a reasonable guess at how things went from there. During the lunch break, Half-Full approached The Crusher. "Listen, I've got an idea. I'll build you a dike that will keep some of the water out of Gorevka."

"Thanks a lot," The Crusher replied sarcastically. "Tell me why I should pay for your pleasures."

"But I'll pay for it, too," Half-Full replied.

The Crusher said nothing. He had already made it known he was in favor of mining Gorevka, but he also knew that would give rise to a host of problems. To begin with, he would have to push Gosplan and the Council of Ministers into including the site in the State plan. Not an easy assignment. Only then would the order go out to metallurgical plants to cast the metal needed to manufacture the equipment and underground transportation. Other industries would be needed to produce tools for miners, concrete, and housing materials.

If Gorevka were not listed in the State plan, The Crusher knew, none of this would be available. Construction in the Soviet Union depended on material, not on money. As I have suggested, this is still the case, although today, even if you are not in the State plan, your business can still work, in that enterprises are now permitted to increase the share of goods they sell on the world market in exchange for materials they need. At the time, however, this arrangement was not an option for The Crusher.

Standing there facing Half-Full, The Crusher's thinking probably ran like this: *The country is being starved to death, and the military is overfed. I phoned Ustinov, Minister of Defense. The military uses a lot of lead. Ustinov is a Politburo member and that might help. He buys lead for hard currency—at least $3 billion a year, even though a mountain of lead lies buried right in his backyard. He spends hard currency this economically besieged nation can ill afford."*

What The Crusher realized was that even if he killed the power plant, it was still unlikely he would be able to get Gorevka squeezed into the State plan within the next ten to fifteen years. He was seventy-five years old. In ten years, he'd be dead and buried in some cemetery—perhaps a good one (if a minister behaves himself, as a bonus, the government reserves for him a prestigious plot at a first-class cemetery). He was tired. Half-Full had too much going for him, despite his past mistakes.

They studied each other. Half-Full sensed that his adversary probably wouldn't be able to lay his hands on Gorevka. All he had to do was wait.

The Crusher looked out Gosplan's window down to Red Square, where hundreds of people, like insects, scurried through the fading afternoon light. He knew that if construction began on the power plant, the energy ministry would have to build a dike. He could say to Gosplan chairman Lazybones: "Look, you've spent a fortune on this dike. To make it worthwhile, put Gorevka in the State plan, too." Then The Crusher could use Half-Full's money and materials as a sort of down payment, an investment in his dream of mining the lead field.

He turned to Half-Full. "How high will the dike be?" he asked.

"A hundred feet."

The Crusher pursed his lips, so Half-Full added quickly, "You want 150 feet? Fine! I can allocate about a hundred million rubles for that!" The man had an expansive and generous nature when it served his interests.

The Crusher shrugged. He knew the dike would be about as useful to the country as a famine, but what could he do? The road to the mining of Gorevka ran past Half-Full's door.

Lazybones watched the discussion between the two ministers with mounting anxiety. Their disagreement worried him. Half-Full was pressing too hard. The Crusher could make trouble for everyone at the Central Committee. Who needed another fight?

The two approached him. They'd come to terms.

Relieved, Lazybones asked them to write a separate protocol documenting the agreement. "It's got to be put in writing."

It was a predictable response. Lazybones wanted no slip-ups, no loose ends, no convenient differences of opinion that would later get him into trouble. Russian bureaucrats protect themselves up to the neck in an armor of documents. The golden rule of bureaucracies is that signed documents act as shields. Had Lazybones not adhered to that rule, his head would have rolled long before. To persuade a bureaucrat to give you permission for something, or even simply to sign a paper, just show him another document signed by another bureaucrat.

Every foreign investor should know that a big construction project need be both approved by the local government and consistent with State programs. This is in their best interest, because, although they could bring in everything from abroad, foreign businessmen will find it much cheaper to use local currency and materials. Hence it is critical to have a robust and influential Russian partner.

Once it's in sync with a State program, a project will be flying around in the stratospheric rings of power. The air is thin up there. To survive in it, one must not underestimate the clout of ministers such as Half-Full. Multinational corporations such as Exxon are small peanuts compared to a minister of energy, who controls a kingdom of hydroelecrtic power plants that produce the energy for one-sixth of the planet's inhabitants. (His ministry provided energy for much of Eastern Europe as well.)

Foreign investors will find Russian energy very good barter, regardless of how it is arranged. Even with the former Soviet Union's 1992 energy output in a temporary decline (8 percent), energy is still plentiful and cheap. In the 1990s, economic transactions among independent republics will be carried out on a dollar basis. Oil formerly supplied by the Soviet Union to its satellite socialist countries and the Soviet republics for free is now for sale for hard currency, or as barter, as the Siemens case establishes.

The Siberian branch of the Academy of Sciences put me in charge of the Gorevka study because I had visited the deposit in 1979. I concluded that Gorevka should be mined and that the power plant could wait. However, the communist mob bosses had already cut their multi-billion dollar deal. Was it too late for me to interfere? I knew that the regional boss, Fedirko, might have some influence in the matter. To him, The Crusher and Half-Full were only ministers—two among the innumerable spokes in the perpetually spinning wheel of the Soviet bureaucracy. Fedirko, on the other hand, was a political leader. He could call Vladimir Dolgih, supervisor of Soviet heavy industry and the "official eye" of the Politburo, who would see that the matter reached Brezhnev's attention.

I have already argued that a no from a minister doesn't always mean no. In the United States, you have what is known as a rule of thumb. In the former Soviet Union, there is "misrule of hands," meaning that the right hand doesn't have the least idea what the left one is up to. If one ministry rejects your project, go to another. Cross the corridor and visit a different department in the same ministry. Whoever has turned you down will have at least one other bureaucrat above him; either go one step higher or rethink your strategy. Don't shrink from a fight. Don't be afraid to use tough words. That is the language every minister understands.

It was clear to me that getting the sluggish Fedirko to move would mean taking him head on. In my corner I had the Academy of Sciences, which operated at the highest political levels. Even the ministers were wary of its connections. A number of the president's advisors came from the academy. A minister knows that an academic's critique of his judgment, or his personal manner, can cost him his job.

Thirty years ago, The Crusher, clever as he is, nearly scuttled his own career by mishandling the academics. At the time, he was a deputy prime minister, and chairman of Gosplan. Professor Nemchinov, one of the founders of the Soviet Economic-Mathematical School, was the chairman of Gosplan's Scientific Council. One Monday, at 11:00 A.M., The Crusher phoned Nemchinov's office and asked to speak with him.

"He's at his dacha," a secretary said.

"What!" exclaimed The Crusher. "During office hours? Connect me with him immediately!"

When Nemchinov came on the line, The Crusher yelled at him. "You lazy bastard! What are you doing at your dacha!"

"Just what makes you think you have the right to talk to me like that?" Nemchinov hissed. "My job is to think, and I think everywhere, even in my dacha's bathroom." Indignant, Nemchinov slammed down the telephone. Then he called Nikita Khrushchev and gave him his opinion of The Crusher.

Khrushchev was no scholar himself, nor was he renowned for being especially polite, but he had some experience with scientists and he respected them. The next day, Khrushchev met with Deputy Lomako and said to him, in a phrase that was to become famous, "Your hat doesn't fit your head, Peter."

The Crusher was unceremoniously demoted to Minister of Non-ferrous Metallurgy.

This is a story any foreign investor would be well advised to keep in mind. The academy is not only an important source of information and professional opinion about a venture; on occasion, it can be used to trump the bureaucracy.

I finished my report to the academy, and then addressed it to Prime Minister Kosygin. Writing a report to a Soviet boss requires special skill, because it can make or break your project. A well-written report or letter can get you a meeting or a lucrative contract. My advice to anyone writing to a government official is that he begin the letter by listing his achievements *and* his deep admiration for the achievements of said official. If you start by complaining or demanding, he is very likely to put the letter down unread. After you've buttered him up and interested him in you, proceed to the magic word *"but."* That's when you bring up your problem.

Following these niceties, my report to Kosygin went straight to the heart of the matter. I outlined how much hard currency the Soviet Union lost buying lead, and how much it stood to gain if it increased its mining of it.

The lead market, I pointed out, is a shortage-driven market. In 1980, The Soviet Union produced only 285.5 thousand tons of lead (of which Russia produced 8 percent, Kazakhstan 72, and the Ukraine 20). That's roughly half as much as the United States. Lead is essential to a wide variety of industries: it is used to make storage batteries, nuclear power plants, cable sheaths, and medical equipment. If we attracted foreign companies, we could both upgrade the refined lead and substantially raise the country's profits.

According to initial projections, it would take thirty-five years to exhaust Gorevka. My report to the academy suggested cutting that time in half. This was technically quite possible, even without increasing our processing and refining capacities. Without question, all of the ore should be mined from the field before being flooded for the hydroelectric plant. To save time it made sense to process only the rich ore, storing the poor. The rich ore contained 5 to 7 percent pure lead, and Soviet enrichers and metallurgists had developed a technology that extracted 93 percent of the lead from the ore. This would bring faster profits and decrease the amount of capital investment. I speculated that in the years to come shortages in the world's lead market would increase. Gorevka could bring Russia billions of dollars in revenue and a leading position in the marketplace.

Foreign investors usually look at Gorevka as merely a deposit of lead, with some silver and zinc thrown in. I have always felt, however, that it would be wiser to approach Gorevka in a more complex manner. A multifaceted approach to developing other industries in the region could reduce costs by as much as a quarter. Working within the framework of a joint project, companies could slash their costs by sharing infrastructure needs and by making more efficient use of raw materials.

For example, the enormous oil and gas deposits throughout Siberia will influence the scale of business development there. One hundred miles of road connects the world's two largest gas fields: the Medveshie and the Urengoy. The Gubkin oil "treasury" is 150 miles from these polar deposits. Each deposit is so large that one would need to build dozens of roads to connect its several points. This is why capital investments in the infrastructure constitute 70 percent of total investment. Building anything in the north costs one and a half to three times more money than in Russia's more moderate climatic zones.

But, investment here pays off. In western Siberia, for example, petrochemical and chemical production have grown rapidly. Siberian economists calculated that were all of the region's industry developed together as a complex, the cost of the final products would drop 10 to 15 percent, and the required capital investment by 20 to 30 percent.

Right next to the Gorevka deposit is the Kansk-Achinsk Fuel and Energy Complex, which mines the world's largest brown coal deposit: 1 trillion tons. Soviet scientists have developed a unique technology of liquid fuel production based on this brown coal. The one critical element missing is financing. Oil deposits have also been discovered near Gorevka, on the Middle Siberian Plateau. Last, but not least, the entire area is encircled by the Siberian forest, with its abundant timber resources.

My report concluded by saying that everything about Gorevka argues for starting a consortium. Thousands of companies of every size and specialty will find it profitable to invest there. The director of the Gorevka combine, Vassiliy Zentsov, had been waiting for years to get the project off the ground. "I'll do anything I can to help, even write my own letter to the prime minister," he told me. "What do I have to lose? If they fire me, I'll go off into the *taiga* and become a fisherman."

Both Gorevka and the proposed hydroelectric plant were in Fedirko's bailiwick. Of the two, he would benefit more from the power plant than the lead field, in that the plant would create sixty thousand construction jobs. Like Half-Full, Fedirko did not want to lose the limelight after construction on the Sayano-Shushenskaya plant was finished, and the idea of starting another plant suited him just fine. The more jobs the project created, the greater his power would become, regionally and nationally.

Shortly after our report was forwarded to Prime Minister Kosygin, Fedirko called a Party meeting. This meant that Kosygin, or someone else in the Politburo, had read our report and agreed with our assessment.

"Why didn't you tell me earlier?" Fedirko thundered.

He already knew the answer. If we hadn't blindsided him and the other ministers with our report, they would have had it doctored in favor of the hydroelectric plant.

As this series of events so eloquently illustrates, the power structure in the former Soviet Union is complicated and labyrinthine. Leaders are more preoccupied with jockeying for control than with real business. Stalin designed the structure to divide and rule. Gorbachev kept it intact for the most part, although he did change a few names. It was because he looked back so much that Gorbachev stumbled and finally tumbled.

In a private conversation with Vladimir Dolgih, a secretary of the Communist Party Central Committee and a candidate to the Politburo complained: "I'm in charge of heavy industry, but I can't even fire a minister. A minister reports to the prime minister, and the prime minister reports directly to the general secretary." Dolgih was one of the most capable executives I'd ever met, but he too fell prey to high-level intrigue and was forced by Gorbachev to retire at an early age.

To break into the Russian market, one needs to understand how the power structure works. For starters, does the governor of the region have more power than the minister? This very basic question can present an enormous problem for a foreign investor, who has to negotiate carefully between them. The truth is, foreign investors need to have both the government minister and the regional boss on their side. In fact, strong relations have to be established with the people in power at virtually every level, even if the language—the dialect— used to win their support varies accordingly.

A good general rule is to avoid politics. The political views or preferences of the various bosses might not coincide with a Western- er's perspective on the future of Russia, or with the opinions of the more progressive Russian leaders. Even if a boss disagrees with some- one's views, he might very well help a joint venture and welcome outside investments—as long as one keeps one's political views to oneself. Political topics in the former Soviet Union can quickly be- come acute and personal. If someone dislikes—or even simply dis- agrees with—your political preferences, he might slam the door in your face. Limit discussions to business.

Even within the democratic camp, there are warring factions. In Russia alone, there are more than twenty-five registered parties and sixteen political movements. Pull the wrong string, and everything can come crashing down. I once listened as the chairman of a large American corporation discussed investment with a governor of a rich Russian region. During the discussion, the American chairman hap- pened to praise the mayor of Moscow. Although the governor liked Western investment, he happened not to like the mayor. Before the American could get down to business, his cause was lost.

As I write this, the local powers—the regional bosses, as I have been calling them—are gaining more and more power. Today, re- gional bosses have much to say about which ventures they will allow on their territories. Furthermore, public opinion will heavily influ- ence their decisions, since they answer to local interests, not those of some minister sitting in an office thousands of miles away.

Director Zentsov and I sat for hours in the reception area of the regional government offices, waiting to give our presentation, before, finally, we were summoned to Fedirko's office.

The regional boss greeted Zentsov by shouting at him.

"How dare you go over our heads and write to the central committee! What do you take us for? Potted plants?"

With a dramatic flourish, Fedirko passed Zentsov's letter around to the members of the regional committee. Then he sat back in his chair and glared at us.

Zentsov had known that his letter would make its way to Fedirko. The bureaucratic powers used to pass any letter along to the regional Party boss, no matter what it might say about him.

"How else was I going to get you to invite me to your office?" answered Zentsov, who proceeded to make his pitch. "Gorevka won't die by drowning in water, but by drowning in all these endless and useless meetings. You built the Krasnoyarsk hydroelectric plant, one of the biggest in the world, and it still doesn't generate enough electricity—and look how much grief it's brought us."

"What were the geologists conclusions?" Fedirko asked glumly. This was an uncharacteristic—and a less than halfhearted—stab at democracy.

Everyone in the room grew quiet. I knew from experience that Fedirko liked the truth only when it reinforced his agenda. Otherwise, a falsehood would suffice. Once, several years earlier, Fedirko announced grandly that the Krasnoyarsk Region would exceed its planned output by one billion rubles. He invited economists to a meeting and asked them, "How much over and above this one billion can we give back to the country?"

I was one of the economists, and replied, "None. Sixty percent of the factories won't fulfill their quota."

Fedirko despised forecasters who didn't agree with him. His bald spot, which was badly camouflaged by a long shank of hair, turned purple.

"Well then, how do we make it possible?" he roared.

"If the plant as a whole doesn't fulfill its quota, but some of its divisions do, or even have a surplus, you could add their surplus to the billion," I suggested. I was joking, of course, but that is exactly what he did. I never imagined he would take what I said seriously, let alone implement it as regional policy.

At this particular meeting about Gorevka, however, Fedirko had made a tactical mistake. We were disagreeing with him, and his usual amen corner of yes-men was absent. His ever-faithful chief geologist wasn't even there, and we had at our side a real geologist, an Order of Lenin winner by the name of Sherman. Sherman spoke eloquently and forcefully against building the power plant. Terskov, a well-known scientist with the academy, was also present, and he too voiced his objections to the power plant.

Outflanked by the scientists, Fedirko turned to me. "And what does the economist think?" he sneered.

I was ready for him. "Our country spends three billion a year buying lead, and that amount will grow as our needs grow. One of the biggest lead plants in West Germany has just had a fire, and that means world prices are going to rise. Moreover, we buy large amounts of lead from China, but our political relations with the country are very shaky. Yet here, right under our nose, is the world's biggest lead field. Instead of mining it, we want to flood it."

"We don't have the money for equipment!" shouted Fedirko.

"Any number of Western companies," I countered calmly, "would be happy to supply us with the equipment."

"We don't have the hard currency to pay for it!" insisted Fedirko.

"But we do seem to have the billions we already pay for lead each and every year," I replied. "Besides, there are at least five good reasons for opting to mine Gorevka. One, the foreign companies will take lead as payment. Working with them will also raise our technological level. Two, power plant construction will require thousands of people, and, as you know, there is a labor shortage in our region. We would be better off using what workers we have to build roads. Norilsk is cut off from the world. The only ways of getting to it are by air and water. Three, power plants always create environmental damage. You remember what happened with the artificial Krasnoyarsk sea? [In an effort to save time and money, the builders neither cut down the trees nor moved the cemeteries before the area was flooded. As a result, the water was polluted, the fish were poisoned, and coffins kept on bobbing up to the surface.] Four, following construction of the Krasnoyarsk power plant, the Yenisey will stop freezing in winter, and the water will evaporate. This icy steam is a major health hazard [it can cause considerable respiratory problems]. Five, the world's two largest aluminum plants are on the Yenisey River, and they need a constant supply of energy. This will be a problem when the Yenisey becomes shallow and there isn't enough water in the artificial sea."

The effect of our efforts was that although Fedirko didn't abandon the hydroelectric project, his bureau did write a letter to Moscow recommending the immediate construction of a mining apparatus that could mine some of the lead before the area was flooded, and that is what eventually happened. Between 1980 and 1989, an open pit was dug and 200,000 tons of pure lead (only a fraction of the ore's yield) were extracted. In addition, construction began on an enriching facility, and on the first part of the dike that was to protect the deposit from the Angara River. Unfortunately, all construction was temporarily halted in 1989, and the plans to build the second part of the dike, which would divert the Angara and permanently diminish the danger of flooding, never left the State drawing board. By the end of the 1980s, the Soviet government had lost its ability to invest in large projects, such as the mining of Gorevka. Plans to complete work on the infrastructure, and continue the mining, of Gorevka have all been drawn. They will wait until a foreign investor steps in.

Although the Gorevka story sounds complicated, the basis for our approach was fairly straightforward. Foreign companies trying to get permission to mine to a major deposit would do well to follow it.

1. We studied both the deposit and the State program dealing with Gorevka. Outsiders might not have access to all parts of State programs and will therefore have to use other sources, such as regional programs, ministry plans, and economic forecasts.
2. We formulated our point of view and outlined a project to develop the deposit.
3. We founded a solid enterprise by signing on with a capable director, Zentsov in this case. He was already very eager to organize production, which he did brilliantly.
4. We compiled closely reasoned and carefully worded arguments to persuade a regional boss.
5. We contacted the proper authorities. In our case, this meant a prime minister. Such a high-level official is not always necessary.
6. We waged an effective public relations campaign. Today, this is more necessary than ever.

When Robert Strauss was appointed U.S. ambassador to the Soviet Union, a friend of his said, "He'll teach them all about how to make money." The problem with that line of thinking is that the

Kremlin isn't interested in making money. It is interested in maintaining power.

In 1986, along with several other Soviet economists, I helped draft the Law of the State Enterprise and the new version of the Constitution. Generally, Soviet laws were drafted by the staff of the Council of Ministers, which invited professionals to help them compose it. These professionals would be assisted by members of the Central Committee of the Communist Party and other Kremlin and Old Square pen pushers. When it was finished, however, coauthorship was rarely acknowledged. By the time a resolution was adopted, most of your ideas were mutilated to such a degree that you were ashamed to admit parenthood. Only misplaced optimism makes you join in when the next document is under discussion.

We sent our reports to Gorbachev, and published our opinions in *Questions of Economy*, a leading economics journal. Our ideas never did make it into the final version of the law. Pen pushers might be the wrong term for these Soviet bureaucrats; they were more like erasers. At best, only 5 percent of the progressive legislation was put into practice.

But that was under Gorbachev. Today, things have changed. However artful, negotiations of any type would be of no use to any foreign investor were the legislative basis for business cooperation not in place. Over the last few years, the sum of the progressive laws passed has been impressive. Most of the barriers blocking the path between Russian enterprises and Western partners have been removed. Even more important, the State's monopoly on business activity has been broken. It is helpful to know about some of the basic laws that today facilitate cooperation with foreign investors.

The Law of the State Enterprise, adopted in 1988, contained some of the progressive seeds my colleagues and I tried to plant in it. Kremlin bureaucrats hoped the law would go unnoticed. However, workers and managers of the Uralmash plant in the Urals, for one, clutched at this law as if it were a life raft. Fed up with the destructive restrictions imposed by the Soviet government, they refused to fulfill the State plan Gosplan was imposing on them, and instead adopted their own production program using the Law of Enterprise. Gosplan fought back, but in the end, Uralmash got its way by gaining the overwhelming support of public opinion across the country.

In 1988, the government and Party also adopted a resolution liberalizing the rules of joint-venture creation and operations. On December 2, 1988, the resolution was made into law. A business revolution began on November 23, 1989, when the Legislative Basis for Leasing was adopted. This law defines the rights of individuals and enterprises to own property, which represented the first step toward a free market.

Between 1990 and 1992, under the guidance of Yeltsin, the Russian Parliament passed new laws breaking the Party's monopoly on power and the State's monopoly on property. Again, because the progressive legislation was widely supported by the general population—in particular, by the business community—the new laws were implemented almost immediately. In the area of business regulation, Yeltsin's government has done a good job; the business climate is vastly improved. First, it has eased the regulations governing foreign economic activity for private and State-owned companies in Russia. Second, it has allowed foreign insurance companies—such as the American International Group—which formerly were illegal, to enter the Russian market. Third, foreign and domestic investors used to hit a bureaucratic brick wall when it came to privatizing property. Today, the wall is coming down.

Reality has gradually forced the Soviet Parliament to adopt laws similar to the progressive legislation enacted by the Russian Parliament. On July 1, 1991, it passed the Law on Sale of State Property and Privatization. Together with a previously adopted legislative act dealing with foreign investment in Russia, this law establishes a legal basis for foreign companies to buy State enterprises. The republic of Byelarus led the way on this one by adopting a similar law even earlier. The law on investment in Byelarus set the minimum investment of start-up capital at $20,000. Most of the other republics have followed suit.

Also of interest to foreign investors is the Russian State Property, a newly created foundation that lists which enterprises are available for purchase. Their reports will teach the foreign business community things they need to know but might not think to ask, such as how eager the employees of a given Russian enterprise are to have their company sold to nonRussians.

New laws on land use make it possible for rental arrangements to be made for an indefinite period, or to buy land under the stipulation that improvements will be made to the property. Under certain conditions, Russia's Land Codex permits people to buy land for farming. The law on shareholding companies allows foreign companies to be partners in a business or even to run that business without a Russian partner. This same law permits Western bankers to be equal partners in, or outright owners of, Russian banks. The Law on Sale of State Property and Privatization allows foreigners to buy Russian companies and the land on which they sit.

Add to these laws the numerous progressive legislative acts and parliamentary decisions clarifying everything from private foreign ownership of land to taxation (eliminating double taxation, for example), and anyone will see there is already a solid legal basis for doing business in Russia. During 1991 and 1992, President Yeltsin and the Russian Parliament adopted nearly 580 legislative documents, nearly half of which touch on business, commerce, and foreign investment. They include contract laws and the regulation of financial markets; antitrust legislation and competition laws; security and bankruptcy priority rights; price and insurance regulation; tax laws; laws governing intellectual property, labor, and employment practices; and product liability and consumer protection laws. The list goes on. Knowing these laws and acts, and their wording, is one of the most effective arguments foreigners can marshall to their cause.

The climate in Russia is right for investment because the necessary legislation is in place. The first step investors should take is to look into those national, republican, and regional programs I have mentioned in this chapter. They contain detailed descriptions of a number of interesting projects and prospects. If a foreign venture fits in with the objectives of one of these programs, or would assist in implementing it, this by itself is a strong argument in its favor. The programs can be found at the ministries of economics and in the finance ministries of each of the fifteen independent republics. Industrial development programs are kept at each ministry; regional programs might be available through regional executive committees or at city halls. Foreign companies might also get help from consultants or local economists.

Becoming familiar with these programs is, of course, just the beginning. The next step is to prepare, with the Russian partner, a summary of the project in Russian. Such a summary should be part of a report containing charts and graphs depicting the stages, technologies, and efficiency levels of the project, and how they correspond to national, regional, and local goals.

It is also critical to get a professional or scientific recommendation from members of institutes such as the Academy of Sciences. Every Russian ministry has from five to fifty research institutes that can supply information and analysis. Choosing the strongest recommendations to present to the regional bosses and national ministers is key. They can create a snowball effect: one boss's recommendation can be critical in persuading another.

Other keys to success? Foreign businesspeople should make themselves available to the media—such as by granting interviews to both national and local newspapers. Take an official out for a business dinner (dinners are more acceptable in Russia than lunches). Make your pitch. Russians are more than ready to listen.

I was once wandering in the Siberian taiga when suddenly the breeze became as hot as the searing breath of a blast furnace. A forest fire. Panic-striken animals raced past me, their scurrying feet ripping at the leaves. Clouds of black smoke billowed above me and day turned into night. I sprinted through the woods, a fiery, choking wind at my back, until at last I reached the river.

A fire devouring a woodland is a truly horrifying sight. In the horror and confusion, the animals—prey and predator alike—dashed off together. Russians are also looking for a way out of the economic confusion and the welter of events, but they are no longer confused about one thing: they understand that economic integration with the outside world, in particular, with the West, is the only hope, the only path to the river.

CHAPTER 8

In the Land of the Free Economic Zones

When considering options for investment in the new republics, Westerners should focus particular attention on the newly established free economic zones. In December of 1988, I was finally declared "viezdnoy" and received permission to travel abroad. I seized the opportunity to visit and study free-trade zones in the United States and Belgium, as well as free economic zones and special zones of technological and economic development in China. I wrote up my conclusions for the Academy of Sciences. This time, rather than ignoring them, the government took my comments seriously— perhaps because one of our own, Professor Abalkin, director of the academy's Institute of Economics, had been appointed Deputy Prime Minister, and because a man I had worked with on the editorial board of *Eco* magazine, Ivan Ivanov, had also become a high-level official. Having helped draft the legislation that set up one of these zones, and having witnessed firsthand the battles that over the years have been fought over them, I know what types of opportunities they afford to foreign investors, especially if they are willing to look for the paths less traveled; that is, go east.

A free economic zone is a zone in which market-economy principles are given free rein. This means that business is unhampered by the old bureaucratic machine, or the bits and pieces of it that still remain. Here, investors have the chance to make the most of natural resources, labor, and transportation potential. Foreign businesspeople are granted up to a five-year tax holiday in these zones. They can own a company, rent or buy land, use foreign hard currencies, and, best of all, work actively with local entrepreneurs and private businesspeople instead of faceless bureaucrats. No two zones are exactly alike in the way they encourage business, each one being designed according to a local government's interests before being submitted for approval by the Russian and Byelarussian Parliaments—which have gone to great lengths to liberalize business practices. The Russian Parliament is even considering restoring business property taken from White Russians during the 1917 Revolution. The father of the late actor Yul Brynner owned a large nonferrous metallurgical plant and a port in the Far East in pre-Lenin days, for example, and there is a chance the family might be restored some of its property. Of course, the Russian government is not likely simply to give such properties back in the liberal way the Baltic states have, but it might at least lease the enterprises back to their original owners. This possibility is specifically provided for in the Russian republic's new Law on Property, enacted on December 24, 1990, and in regulations passed between 1991 and 1993, such as the Privatization Programs.

One of the most attractive features of free economic zones to foreign investors is that they provide a solution to the ruble problem. Investors can use rubles to buy construction materials, pay wages, rent land, and fund other operating costs, which saves an enormous amount of money. Even using a conservative ruble-dollar exchange rate, Russian labor costs are only 8 percent of those in America.

Foreign companies can also exchange rubles for dollars within these zones. Byelarus was the first republic to establish currency auctions. Russia, the Ukraine, and the Baltic states have followed its example. As of July of 1992, Russia and Armenia allow foreigners to purchase currency, as well as land and buildings, practically anywhere within their zones. This means that foreign companies can produce for rubles and export for dollars. Dollars can be deposited in an account outside the country. Businesses can also maintain accounts in dollars, from which they can withdraw freely at any time, within the zones themselves.

The oldest free economic zones in Russia are located in the Primorsky Region on the Pacific Coast, on Sakhalin Island in the Russian Far East, in St. Petersburg, and in Viborg near the Russian-

Finnish border. Others have joined their ranks: the Novgorod Region, the Kaliningrad Region, Dubna and Zelenograd (cities near Moscow), the Altay Region, the Kemerovo Region (a coal region in eastern Siberia), the Buriat Region (also in eastern Siberia), the Jewish Autonomous Region (located in the Russian Far East on the Amur River on the Chinese border), Magadan, and Chita, a region to the east of Lake Baikal, site of one of the world's largest copper mines, the Udakan, which is available for concessions. Byelarus, once again, is proving extremely progressive about developing free economic zones; it is establishing one in the Brest Region, the gateway between Poland and Russia. The infrastructure its government is building should make it one of the most active in all of the former Soviet Union.

The bad news is that between 1989 and 1993, first the Soviet, and then the Russian, government didn't draw up programs for these zones, and as a result, development is going slowly. It is one thing to set up a free economic zone, another to make it work. Before becoming independent, for example, Armenia and Estonia announced that their entire territories were free zones, but did so as a gesture of political autonomy rather than economic openness. From a financial standpoint, declaring an entire country a free economic zone makes no sense: eliminating all tax income would be lethal to any government. Since the disintegration of the Soviet Union, these two republics have no longer been advertising themselves as such.

In the following two chapters I will concentrate on the opportunities for investment in three areas: European Russia, the Far East, and the Far North. It is in these vast regions, I believe, that there is the least to be risked and the most to be gained.

With their offshore oil and natural gas potential, their stockpiles of minerals, acres and acres of timber, oceans of fish, and tourist potential, the westernmost points of European Russia are obvious, and lucrative, areas of investment. Any free economic zone allows foreign industry to operate virtually unfettered by Russian costs, but these areas have a particularly advantageous infrastructure of sea lanes, roads, and railways, and hence the easiest access to their free-market neighbors.

The Kaliningrad Region presents features of special political and economic interest, in part because Lithuania has for all practical purposes become completely independent, geographically separating

Kaliningrad Region from Russia and all other former Soviet republics. The region, which has a long history, occupies just over five thousand square miles, and has a population of 880,000 people. Prior to the Second World War, it was part of Germany, and was referred to as East Prussia; its capital bore the rather teutonic name of Koenigsberg. Stalin annexed it to Russia in 1946, renaming it Kaliningrad. Now only monuments such as the grave of the philosopher Immanuel Kant, located near the half-destroyed cathedral, are left to evoke the region's Germanic past.

By turning the Kaliningrad Region into a free economic zone (called Yantar, meaning "amber"), Yeltsin proved how forward-looking he was, for three reasons. It showed he was serious about moving toward a free-market economy, it demonstrated the level of autonomy he was willing to permit local governments, and it was testimony to his genuine interest in attracting European businesses. He might not yet have been conversant with the phrase "political risk of investment," but he appreciated from the beginning that any territory separated from the rest of the former Soviet Union by a democratic country would be of interest to the West. Poland, Czechiya, and Slovakia will doubtless invest in this zone—as will Germany, in that the region was once within its borders and Germans are sensitive to the pull of the past. The free Baltic republics will also be interested in economic involvement, since this region will afford close proximity to Russian resources, but not threaten their new-found and somewhat fragile independence.

The Kaliningrad Region has much to recommend it. To begin with, it contains a year-round port on the Baltic sea—the middle of Europe, essentially. The Neman River and a railroad connect it to Europe, Lithuania, and Russia. The region also offers an established industrial base—a car manufacturing plant, a ship repair factory, a wood pulp complex, and a fish processing factory—on which new enterprises might be built. Following the breakup of the Soviet Union, Kaliningrad took on a new role as an oil seaport; outside investors will be invited to join in the construction of the harbor and crude line. (What remains to be seen is how much costs will increase because the pipeline will need to cross Lithuania.) Last, the local government created one of the first commodity exchanges in Russia. So far, the joint-venture activity has been slow, mostly because of a lack of information. But the recent visit of Citibank First Vice-President Gary Skolnik, whose idea it is to create an international transportation company in Kaliningrad, is a positive sign of things to come.

Novgorod is one of the oldest centers of Russian culture, with historical monuments dating back to the tenth and eleventh centuries. By becoming a free economic zone, the region demonstrates the circularity of history. In the Middle Ages, Novgorod was the only independent republic located in what is today Russia.

During the early years of perestroika, there was great excitement as people debated about the types of reforms the country needed. One of the leaders in that debate was Professor Abalkin, then director of the Institute of Economy at the Academy of Sciences in Moscow (where I worked, at that time), and who later became Soviet Deputy Prime Minister. He organized a conference in 1987 to discuss the issue. We analyzed the failed reforms of 1965, the year the first serious debate about a market economy took place—and the year Khrushchev (for other reasons) was forced out of office. I argued long and hard that a market economy was the only way to go—as long as it had a distinctly Russian flavor. I drew parallels to the reforms of Peter the Great by pointing out that he had decentralized the management structure of the government, putting the boyars in charge of large regions and making them responsible for the regions' self-government. What Peter had really done, I went on, was to introduce free-market principles in Russia. (Of course, Peter's methods were totalitarian. When he ordered the hard-line boyars to shave off their long beards, in an effort to make them look more European, and they refused, he had their beards hacked off with an axe.)

Long before Peter, from the twelfth to the fifteenth century, the Novgorod Region had already been a semi-independent republic governed by the boyars' council and the popular assembly, the veche. The republic survived by exporting its crafts, and shrewdly protecting itself from the claims of Kiev (then the Russian capital), Moscow, and Sweden by maintaining excellent relations with its generals and retaining control of the military.

In 1988, when asked to list my choices for the first free economic zones, I chose Novgorod in the west and Nakhodka in the Far East. Not only was Novgorod an obvious choice because of its favorable location and economic potential (it is a center of the electronic and technical industry), but it had never really been Sovietized; throughout the Soviet occupation, its people had retained their entrepreneurial flair. That history, I knew, would attract tourists from all over the world. No one had the money needed to restore the monuments—the churches and palaces—but as soon as it became operational as a free economic zone, the flow of foreign tourists would bring in hard currency from neighboring European countries such as Finland.

Novgorod did become a free economic zone, but it wasn't easy. The local Party leadership had done a poor job of explaining to the population what would happen when the changes went into effect; therefore, people were unprepared for those changes. (The situation is not unlike what is going on with European unification.) In addition, chauvinists argued vehemently that Russian history was being auctioned off to capitalists. It took more than a year to deal with all these misconceptions. Now, at last, the region is well on its way to becoming a vital center for foreign, and particularly Western, investment. Sixty-five percent of Novgorod's industry consists of military plants that are being converted and privatized for domestic production. Foreign investment is welcome.

I feel strongly that investment in the Russian Far East offers the surest path to profit. Politically stable, because they were so isolated from the rest of the country, the vast territories of the Far East have all of the means necessary to keep business risks to a minimum. The Sakhalin, Primorsky, and Khabarovsk regions are especially attractive locales for investment. They already possess the infrastructure necessary for industry.

The Pacific Rim as a whole is becoming the center of world business activity. Fifty-two percent of the world's nations border the Pacific Ocean. With their tremendous resources and unexploited business opportunities, the Russian Far East and the Russian Arctic are destined to become major players in this rim.

Apart from the oil and gas potential, there are other industries that should attract foreign businesses. Timber, for one.

Like all Russians, I believe that forests are almost holy places. Wandering through them—one of my pastimes—has a restorative effect on body and soul. They also offer profits and tremendous opportunities, and cry out for foreign capital and know-how. Lumber resources in Russia are the world's most plentiful: there are endless expanses of Siberian pine and cedar, and literally mountains of lumber waste. Add these to the inexpensive local labor force and you have a powerful combination. What is needed now is foreign technology for furniture, paper, and cardboard manufacturing—and needed badly. Nearly a quarter of the Pacific region's lumber resources are to be found in the Russian Far East, yet Russian logging

The Krasnoyarsk hydroelectric power plant—third largest in the world—located on the Yenisey River, Siberia.

The oil-driven mobile power station *Northern Light*. Ships such as these are useful for joint ventures in regions where building a permanent power station is not practical. *Anatoli Polykov*

Opposite: One of our expedition ships, the *Valery Albanov* (named for a famous Russian explorer), going through the Jugorsky Shar Strait between the Barents Sea and the Kara Sea. Ahead of us is the *Captain Sorokin,* an icebreaker. Hours later, both ships got stuck in the ice and had to wait for the nuclear-powered icebreaker *Lenin*—the world's first—to help them through. *Above right:* The *Valery Albanov* crossing the Barents Sea in the western Russian Arctic. *Below right:* The *Lenin,* captained by the legendary Jewish sea wolf Grigory Entin, arrives to break the ice. The photograph was taken at 2:00 A.M. *Anatoli Polykov*

The port of Dudinka at the mouth of the Yenisey River, used by the Norilsk Combine, the largest nonferrous metallurgical plant in the world. *Vladimir Novikov*

A patrol inspecting an ice floe in the Arctic Seaway. Inspections such as these help with navigation and weather forecasting. The rifle is for protection against polar bears. *Anatoli Polykov*

Construction on a new tunnel for the Baikal-Amur Railway. The BAR has been in operation since 1984 and has become one of the most important arteries between eastern and western Russia.

The Bilibino nuclear power station, built on permafrost, is the only nuclear plant located above the Arctic circle. *Anatoli Polykov*

Air pipes connected to the Nadezgda metallurgical plant, part of the Norilsk Combine. (As a young man, I was a member of the construction crew that built the plant.)

The largest aluminum plant in the world, located in the Urkutsk Region in eastern Siberia. The world's four largest aluminum plants are located in this region. *Vladimir Novikov*

The SibAuto executive team (*left to right*): Me; Chairman Michael Tzaregorodtsev (known as Tzar); Deputy Chairman of the First Department (the security branch); Chief Engineer Lazarev; Dr. Aksenov, a SibAuto scientist.

A 1987 economic expedition to Ulan Bator in Mongolia. *Left to right:* Alexander Granberg, currently one of Yeltsin's most influential economic advisors and member of the Russian Parliament; Gennady Filshin, former Deputy Prime Minister of Russia and currently its trade representative in Austria; Dr. Valery Kuleshov, director of the Economics Institute, Siberian branch of the Academy of Sciences; and me.

A privatization voucher. Issued by the Russian government and available to anyone born before September 7, 1992, these vouchers can be used during auctions of State-owned enterprises. Foreigners can purchase them from private citizens. The building pictured in the middle is the Russian Parliament.

A typical oil and gas workers village on the Yamal Peninsula in the Arctic region of western Siberia. *Anatoli Polykov*

One of the Waterfall "crystal" chandeliers SibAuto produced from plastic waste (polystyrene).

accounts for a mere 6 percent of Pacific logging. A quarter of the former Soviet Union's forests are found in the Krasnoyarsk Region.

Siberian woods, on the other hand, spread out across 1.7 billion acres (American forests amount to less than half that number, or 760 million acres), totalling an area twice the size of Great Britain. Siberian forests amount to about 1.3 billion cubic feet of timber and constitute 62 percent of the country's—and 20 percent of the world's—lumber supply. Siberia also produces 25 percent of the country's wood and sawtimber. The opportunities are practically unlimited, and to date unrealized. Finland produces a fraction of the sawtimber the former Soviet Union produces, yet earns twice as much through exporting lumber and furniture. The Russian furniture industry is still extremely underdeveloped. The country spends close to $100 million of its precious hard currency buying furniture from abroad. In Russian lumber mills, 55 percent of cut logs are turned into scrap that is simply burned, in that there is no technology to do anything with it. There are the resources to cut it, but not refine it. In Siberia alone, almost fifty-three million cubic feet of scrap wood is burned annually.

It is clear that the Russian timber giant is hurting. In 1991, production of sellable wood and sawtimber fell by 15 percent and their export dropped 25 percent. Wood pulp exports dropped 18 percent, paper and plywood 30 percent. Why? Although the raw materials were abundant, relations between the republics has deteriorated, and equipment was in short supply. In 1992, log export grew by 8 percent, but the world market price for logs is ten times lower than the price of wood pulp, and seven times lower than plywood. In addition, as usual, there is the waste. More than $10 billion worth, roughly a quarter of all equipment imported, sits unused in warehouses. Unless foreign managers are brought in to help install, and to teach Russians to operate, the machinery, it will continue to sit in warehouses.

The waste of Russian lumber resources is staggering. Forty percent of all cut timber lies on the forest floor, rotting. Most of the timber that gets carted off is floated down the rivers, but 10 percent of that timber will be lost during the trip, some of it by drifting out into the ocean. For years, one Norwegian company has been collecting this lost timber and selling it for hard currency.

Despite the waste, or perhaps because of it, the opportunities are still prodigious. Between 1986 and 1990, the Soviet government exported 282 million cubic feet of lumber-processing waste, and

750,000 tons of paper waste. Eighty percent of it was sold for hard currency.

A close look at the far northern city of Igarka shows how attractive the timber industry should be to foreign investors. The city boasts all of the latest mechanized methods for loading lumber, most of which comes from Lesosibirsk, a city located where the Yenisey and Angara rivers join. However, Igarka lacks the technology and machinery to process lumber, sawdust, and chips itself, and that is where cooperation with the outside could prove most beneficial.

Although it lacks the charm of Vladivostok and seems somewhat primitive (the sidewalks are made of wood), Igarka is a fascinating seaport city. Years ago, as a student at the Krasnoyarsk Nonferrous Metals Institute, I got a summer job there loading lumber. I lived in a dormitory with the other loaders, who consisted of workers and students, like myself, doing a summer job. Above our bunks we wrote our professions. Docker, stevedore, and woodcutter were the most common. I wrote "Locksmith," and below it added in small letters, "of his own happiness." The inspector from Komsomol (the organization for young communists-to-be) was angered by what he called my cynical attitude toward labor, but as far as I was concerned, the real cynics were these young Komsomol bureaucrats, who did nothing worthwhile. Those of us who got up at seven in the morning to put in an honest twelve-hour day's work laughed at these lumps-in-training.

I liked the work. The morning polar sun and the unforgettable scent of the forest lessened the weight of the logs we carried on our shoulders.

I once counted vessels from twelve countries in the port. Igarka was always teeming with foreign sailors, who would socialize at their own club, called the International Club. The Komsomol, of course, forbade any of us from frequenting the place, which made it seem even more exotic. We all thought it looked like a medieval tavern, always brimming with sailors from faraway countries and blasting boisterous music. The club is still popular, but back then it was especially popular, particularly among the town's young women, who went there in search of diversion and foreign goods, and locals, who went in search of Scotch. Anything foreign was in short supply and therefore in great demand.

African sailors gave the tavern an exotic air. Because Igarka is situated well above the Arctic Circle, blacks in that city were as rare as palm trees. Soviet propaganda had always tried to teach its citizens to regard blacks as the archetypal victims of capitalism. One sailor challenged this image among Igarka stevedores and dockers.

One night, the sailor in question, an Englishman, after drinking a prodigious quantity of vodka, went off to visit a Soviet lady who lived in a dormitory. Although she apparently felt compassion for his victimization at the hands of the capitalist system, she didn't feel compassionate enough to let him in the dorm. Unwilling to take no for an answer, he tried to break in, but was hindered by an elderly woman, the door-*babushka*, who stood her ground. They got into a tussle just as two dockers from my team—also students at the Institute—happened to be passing by. The two dockers came to the aid of the old woman, and in the process decked the unrequited lover. When the militia arrived, they arrested all three of them. The next day, the local Komsomol boss decided to expel the two students from the organization for violating the rules of international friendship. A code was more important to Komsomol than a babushka. Expulsion from Komsomol meant they could also be kicked out of the institute. (Twelve years later, in 1989, being expelled from Komsomol was no longer meaningful. Millions of young people were quitting voluntarily.)

In an effort to aid my poor colleagues, I asked a friend of mine named Hots, the local TV news anchor and something of a celebrity, to go down to the police station. He did, taking with him an affidavit swearing that the students had been sober, and that it had been the English sailor who started the ruckus. The affadavit helped matters. The next day, in an effort to show respect to the code of international friendship as well, Hots took the students and me to the International Club to patch things up with the sailor. We didn't know his name, so we called him Paul Robeson, because Robeson was the only black any Soviet knew.

At the entrance of the club, Hots told the Komsomol guard that we were there to conduct an official interview with Paul Robeson.

Impressed, the guard let us in.

This international incident ended in a friendly, drunken binge, during which a besotted doctor gave our new friend a tattoo, proclaiming *Ne zabudu mat rodnuyu* (I'll never forget my mother), on his hand. He was delighted. He drank until his legs became wobbly, and we had to help him back to his ship. As we carried him along the bright streets of Igarka's polar night, our Paul Robeson, true to his new name, started belting out Robeson's hit song about Russia, "Wide Is My Motherland." The words of the song run: "I know no other country where a man can breathe so freely." No self-respecting Soviet drunk, even one delirious with white fever, would have sung such nonsense. They would sing songs both less inane and more politically safe.

We were fortunate the Komsomol boss never found out about our drunken revelry with the English sailor. Drinking with a foreigner was a serious crime, right up there with betraying the motherland. I wonder where that sailor is today—my African-English friend from that wild and white polar night, the one with the Russian tattoo on his hand.

My friend the news anchorman, Hots, was the only real casualty of that evening. While we were drinking at the International Club, he met a woman and they fell in love. Their marriage was happy, but brief. His wife became something of a demimondaine in Krasnoyarsk and left him. The experience left him morose, and poor Hots went on to become a government television correspondent.

Igarka demonstrates the immense opportunities awaiting foreign investors today in the lumber industry. It has everything necessary to absorb foreign technology and investment, and to generate profit from it. To begin with, the by-products of the lumber industry are of very high quality. I once visited the Belomor ornament factory, near the city of Arkhangelsk, where I saw local craftsmen use waste-lumber scraps to create beautiful latticework, dishes, and dolls. Their products are exported widely.

The Arkhangelsk, Sakhalin, and Khabarovsk lumber complexes are smaller than those in Siberia, but the problems and the potential to the foreign investor are similar. Thirty percent of the former Soviet Union's forests are located in the Russian Far East. Most Westerners think Siberia stretches all the way to the Pacific Ocean. In fact, the Russian Far East is a huge territory situated between Lake Baikal and the Pacific. It constituted 28 percent of the old Soviet empire. There are twenty times more acres of forest per inhabitant of the Far East than the world's average. The territory accounts for 40 percent of all lumber exported to markets in Japan, Australia, and South Korea.

Fortunately, people in the Far East do not view trees purely for their lumber potential. A huge national preserve called Terney, which is slightly larger in size than Luxembourg, has been set aside. Hunting, fishing, and even drinking from the river are prohibited. When I was reluctantly given permission to enter this vast territory, I had to bring my own drinking water. Precautions are so exacting that before entering I had to put on special plastic shoes and have my coat disinfected. Because environmentalism is a growing force inside the former Soviet Union (Russian Vice-President Rutskoy has even called for the establishment of a ministry for ecology and natural resources), any foreign company that can reduce waste and still make money will find a hearty welcome.

To many Westerners, the mere sounds of the names of former Soviet republics and regions are so strange and unpronouncable they conjure up a different solar system. This by itself can discourage investment. I once tried explaining the advantages of doing business in the Khabarovsk Region, situated in the Russian Far East, to an American businessman. The governor of the Khabarovsk Region, a friend of mine, had recently signed an agreement establishing direct flights between Khabarovsk, the region's capital, and the United States. This created even better business opportunities, I told him. However, the name Khabarovsk was off-putting and rang no bells for the foreign businessperson. That the region is larger than England and France together, possesses large ports along the Pacific, and is near both South Korea and Japan made no impression. I couldn't succeed in getting him interested in a place he couldn't find on a map. When I mentioned that the region included the Jewish Autonomous Region, with its capital in Birobidshan, his interest revived and he started to listen attentively to the opportunities.

The Russian Far East is the new Klondike. It has everything in abundance: diamonds, gold, non-ferrous metals, rare metals, coal, forests, and fish. During our arctic expedition, my colleagues from the Academy of Sciences and I went from Vladivostok, in the southwestern corner of this region, to the port of Slavianka, then on to the northern ports of Vanino, Sovetskaya-Gavan, and finally east to Sakhalin Island. We crossed Sakhalin on a railroad built by the Japanese and Russians before and during the Second World War, and from there traveled by ship to the Kuril Islands. Continuing northeast, we reached the beautiful port city of Petropavlovsk-Kamchatsky on the Kamchatka Peninsula, the volcano capital of Russia. Everywhere we went, we studied mineral and forest resources, energy problems, the use and replenishment of the ocean's biological resources, the fishing industry, the agro-industrial complex, local technological policy, manpower, and environmental issues. These places were thousands of miles of expanse; millions of tons of ore, oil, lead, and coal; millions of cubic feet of lumber and hundreds of factories: the possibilities seemed as endless as the horizon. When I saw the squalid conditions under which people worked and lived, I felt more determined than ever to see these possibilities realized.

Now, whenever anyone asks me anything about a specific location within these vast and unpronounceable regions, I almost involuntarily recreate a picture of the place in question in my mind, with its factories and managers, deposits and miners, ports and vessels, railroads and fields. Figures relating to the region's outputs and reserves, population, and exports start jumping around in my head. I know almost immediately whether a new project would work there or not, and what types of details would have to be worked out first.

When we returned from that expedition, we prepared a report for the government outlining the tremendous business opportunities of the Russian Far East. It read like a hymn to long-term, integrated planning. The authorities remained tone deaf.

Gorbachev tried to revive our findings following a trip he himself made to the region in 1986, but, as always, he only went half way. By 1989, it was clear that neither Gorbachev, nor his limited economic vision, would survive. A development project will work only if driven by an incentive system that includes everyone. Motivating workers and managers in Russia is a simple matter. It means helping with housing and providing consumer goods. Yeltsin grasped this idea. When, on July 14, 1990, it voted to establish free economic zones, so did the Russian Parliament.

The Russian Far East is attracting foreign business because it combines vast and untapped natural resources with a strategic geographical position. While the American government, together with the International Monetary Fund, continues to send food and grant loans to the bureaucratic staff of the Russian government, the Japanese have been quietly pumping money into specific industries in the Russian Far East. A Soviet-Japanese conference organized by Alexander Yakovlev, a former Soviet ambassador to Canada who became Gorbachev's right hand and a leader of *perestroika*, together with the Japanese Union of Entrepreneurs, taught me a great deal about what Japan was doing. The Japanese, I learned, were very shrewdly analyzing the current situation, and coming to practical, rather than theoretical, conclusions. They have proven rather less strong at long-term forecasting. Lately, the more into the future I have projected economic ties in the world economy, the more the Japanese role diminishes. I can't explain the mystery.

I also learned a lot about Yakovlev, who today is a chief analyst at the Gorbachev Foundation. When we were introduced, he suggested we go have a cup of coffee. Our conversation was casual, but this heavyweight politician gave me the impression of being a deeply thoughtful man—much more substantive, in fact, than the party ideologue I had taken him to be. He had in his time written scathing criticism of the American system, but from this conversation alone it was clear there was a big difference between Yakovlev's official writing and his private thinking. Slinging mud at capitalism was as obligatory for a Party official as wearing a business suit is to a New York investment banker.

Japanese academics attending the conference presented me with their papers on management. After reading them, I concluded that in Japan human relations are based upon corporate structure. That, I remember thinking, offered a new twist on traditional Marxist thinking, which posits that all human relations stem from production relations.

To Russians, and to Westerners, this theory is unacceptable. In Russia, even basic production relations are much more heavily influenced by personal contact than they are, for example, in the United States. The efficacy of any regulation depends to a large degree on which bureaucrat is applying it and to whom it is being applied. Paradoxically, Russian bureaucrats are on average far more flexible than their counterparts in most Western countries. An American officer will usually adhere strictly to the letter of the law, whatever the circumstances. If the law or regulations allow something, the officer will allow it. If not, forget it. A Russian bureaucrat, by contrast, is prone to his emotions. You can get his sympathy by crying, or his support by threatening him.

Mrs. Hazel Rose, a British representative of the pharmaceutical company Servier, is a hard-driving and successful businesswoman who travels to Russia often. Her work has helped save the lives of many diabetic patients. Combining business interests with humanitarian, she has substantial experience dealing with Soviet bureaucrats. Her daughter is as kind and clever as her mother, but also extremely shy. Once, when trying to get a tourist visa to visit the Soviet Union, the daughter encountered delays at the Soviet consulate. She came home without a visa.

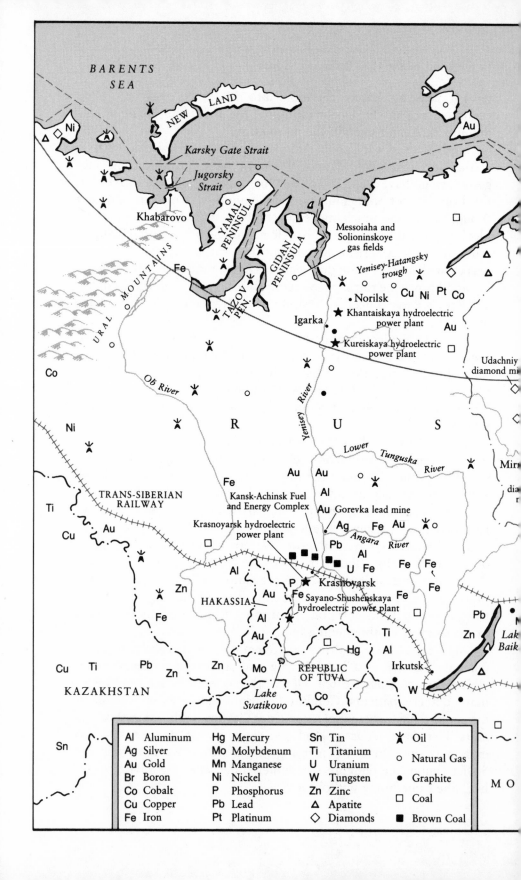

BARENTS
SEA

NEW LAND

Karsky Gate Strait

Jugorsky
Strait

Khabarovo

YAMAL
PENINSULA

GIDAN PENINSULA

TAZOV PEN.

URAL MOUNTAINS

Ni

Fe

Co

Ni

TRANS-SIBERIAN
RAILWAY

Ti

Cu

Au

Zn

Fe

Al

Au

HAKASSIA

Au

Al

Au

Mo

KAZAKHSTAN

Cu   Ti   Pb   Zn

Zn

Sn

Lake
Svatikovo

Au

Messoiaha and
Solioninskoye
gas fields

Yenisey-Hatangsky
trough

• Norilsk   Cu Ni Pt Co

Igarka

Ob River

Yenisey River

★ Khantaiskaya hydroelectric
power plant

★ Kureiskaya hydroelectric
power plant

Au

Udachniy
diamond m

R   U   S

Lower   Tunguska   River

Mir

dia
r

Au   Au

Au   Al

Fe
Kansk-Achinsk Fuel
and Energy Complex

Au Gorevka lead mine

Ag   Fe   Au

Pb   Angara   River

Al

Krasnoyarsk hydroelectric
power plant

P ★ Krasnoyarsk

Fe   Sayano-Shushenskaya
hydroelectric power plant

★

U   Fe

Fe   Fe

Fe

Fe

Fe

Pb

Zn   Lak
Baik

REPUBLIC
OF TUVA

Ti   Al

Hg

Irkutsk

Co

W

Fe

Messoiaha Fe

M O

Al	Aluminum	Hg	Mercury
Ag	Silver	Mo	Molybdenum
Au	Gold	Mn	Manganese
Br	Boron	Ni	Nickel
Co	Cobalt	P	Phosphorus
Cu	Copper	Pb	Lead
Fe	Iron	Pt	Platinum

Sn	Tin
Ti	Titanium
U	Uranium
W	Tungsten
Zn	Zinc

- ⚒ Oil
- ○ Natural Gas
- ● Graphite
- □ Coal
- △ Apatite
- ◇ Diamonds
- ■ Brown Coal

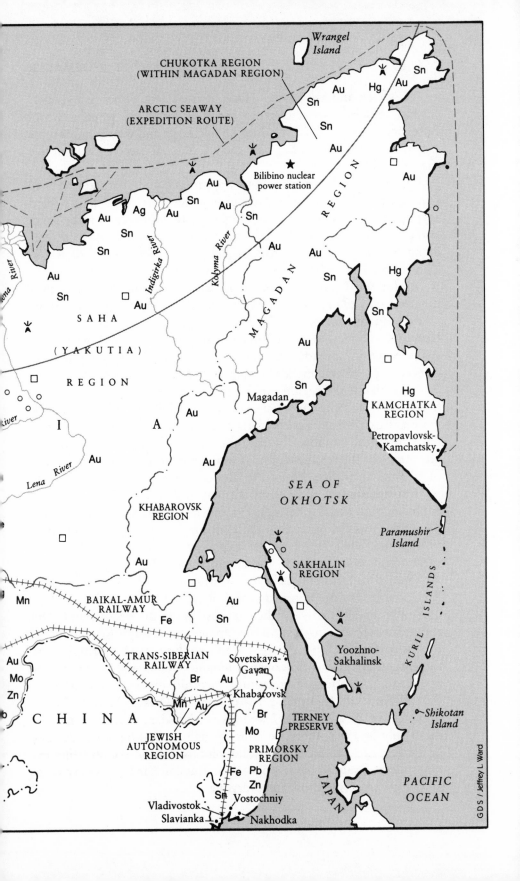

CHUKOTKA REGION
(WITHIN MAGADAN REGION)

ARCTIC SEAWAY
(EXPEDITION ROUTE)

*Wrangel
Island*

Sn

Au   Hg   Au

Sn   Sn

Au   □

Au

Au   Au

Au

M A G A D A N   ⌐
                        R E G I O N
Au

Sn   Ag   Au

Sn   Au   Au   Hg

Sn   Sn

Au   Au   ★ Bilibino nuclear
                            power station

Au   Au

S A H A   Au   Hg

Sn   □   Au   Sn

(Y A K U T I A)

Au

R E G I O N   □

□   Magadan   Sn   Hg
                                        KAMCHATKA
                                        REGION

I   A   Au   Petropavlovsk-
                                                Kamchatsky

Lena River   Au   Au

                        SEA OF
                        OKHOTSK

KHABAROVSK   *Paramushir
REGION   Island*

□

Au   SAKHALIN
            REGION

Mn   BAIKAL-AMUR   Au
       RAILWAY   Fe   Sn

Au   TRANS-SIBERIAN   Au
Mo   RAILWAY   Br   Au   Yoozhno-
Zn   Mn   Au   Sakhalinsk

C H I N A   *Khabarovsk   Br   *Shikotan
                                                    Island*
            JEWISH   Mo   TERNEY
            AUTONOMOUS   PRESERVE
            REGION   PRIMORSKY
                                 REGION

                        Fe   Pb
                        Zn   PACIFIC
                                    OCEAN
            Sn   Vostochniy
Vladivostok   J A P A N
Slavianka   Nakhodka

Sovetskaya-
Gavan

KURIL ISLANDS

GDS / Jeffrey L. Ward

"Go back and ask again," Hazel advised her. "If necessary, cry!"

Her daughter went back to the consulate, and when a Soviet bureaucrat tried to close the door on her, large and very genuine tears began streaming down her pale cheeks. She had her visa within five minutes.

"Everything depends on your appearance and character," Hazel explained to me later while recounting the story. "If *I* had started crying, everybody would have laughed. My approach is to be strict and demanding, and frighten the bureaucrat out of his wits by threatening to send a telegram to Gorbachev, or, even worse, to Raisa. That's how I get what I want." I admire her tactics.

As for the Japanese, their tactics are also quite clever, but in a different way. They regard investment as the best public relations strategy in the former Soviet Union. They are fully aware of the treasures to be found in the Russian Far East. Russia and the Middle Asian republics already account for 40 percent of Japanese imports of precious and rare metals; 70 percent of the region's exports go to Japan, which is the region's main trading partner. One hundred and fifty Japanese companies have already established direct ties with various Russian Far East enterprises, dealing in exchange rather than hard currency. In short, the Japanese are far from shy about taking advantage of the free economic zones. Japan accounts for 50 percent of all Russian trade with Pacific Rim countries.

The authorities are putting gas and oil fields off the coast of Sakhalin Island and other deposits out for bidding. American companies such as the Marathon Oil Corporation, McDermott International, and Shell Development expressed keen interest, but they earned only minor roles in the development. (The one exception is the Sakhalin Island Feasibility Study, in which Marathon Oil, McDermott, and Shell joined with Mitsui and Mitsubishi.) The Japanese will undoubtedly do their utmost to get the upper hand. The Americans are lagging behind the Japanese and South Korean investors, who are much better situated to grab business opportunities as they occur. So far, the American companies are having to play catch-up. Russian-American joint ventures have already been established in the cities of Mirniy, Yoozhno-Sakhalinsk, Petropavlovsk-Kamchatsky, Vladivostok, Nakhodka, Magadan, and Khabarovsk. As of July of 1992, there were ninety-eight operating joint ventures in the Russian Far East, with joint ventures in the region being established at a rate of ten a month. The Russian Far East is very large and very rich, with room for everyone.

Products manufactured in the Russian Far East are exported to fifty countries, including fifteen states within the Pacific Rim. The theory of "the closest neighbor"—that trade relations with the nearest neighbor are the most critical—explains the special role Japan, China, Taiwan, and South Korea play in Russian business. That is why, in 1988 and 1989, I argued tirelessly for the necessity of developing good trade relations with these countries and with Australia.

When I was serving as a board member of the Soviet Exporters Association, we invited and welcomed the first Taiwanese and South Korean business delegations ever to visit the Soviet Union. This was in 1989, and at the time there were still no diplomatic relations between the Soviet Union and South Korea. These visits therefore represented an important step in the warming of Soviet-South Korean relations, which have since grown to be much stronger than those between Russia and Communist Korea.

As for the Taiwanese, the Soviet ministries were still very nervous about China's reaction to our invitation, and told us we first had to make the same overture to China. I went to Beijing in 1989 to sign an agreement between the Soviet Exporters Association and the Chinese Association of Enterprises. Only then did we invite the largest organization of Taiwanese manufacturing and trade companies, the Importers and Exporters Association of Taiwan, to Moscow. Unfortunately, the Taiwanese themselves couldn't believe that Soviet businesses would be interested in them, so they didn't come prepared. The Taiwanese have not been the only ones to make this mistake. When foreign businesses come to visit, they should bring reams of printed material.

Khrushchev once called Vladivostok, one of the industrial and cultural centers of the Russian Far East, the "Soviet San Francisco." The city is indeed beautiful, its colonial-style architecture planned by the Russian merchants and American businessmen who frequented the city at the turn of the century. American businesspeople are slowly coming back.

America and Russia are too close together, literally and figuratively, to ignore each other. Alaska is in almost direct physical contact with the northern region of the Russian Far East, Chukotka. Among the few tangible results of the otherwise colorless 1990 summit between Bush and Gorbachev was the opening of several new airports for flights between the United States and the Russian Far East. Some Russian airplanes can now bring thirty tons of cargo per flight to Alaska. There are now regular flights from the West into Russian airports.

One of the region's newest airports is called Sun-Drenched Magadan by the Russians. The name drips with sarcasm. Located on the shore of the Sea of Okhotsk, Magadan was one of the capitals of Stalin's Gulag. Today, however, with a population of 190,000, Magadan is becoming the capital of a new type of system—the free-market system generated by a free economic zone.

Never in my trips abroad have I been as overwhelmed—not by the skyscrapers of New York, the sands of the Gobi desert, or the immaculate beauty of European cities—as I was when I visited the Guangz Hou free economic zone, located in the province of Guangdong in the south of China. I felt as if I had stepped into a time warp. Less than half a mile away from farmers tending the land with the same tools their ancestors had used a thousand years ago were people wearing power suits working in a skyscraper.

The contrast provides the best illustration of what entrepreneurial freedom can accomplish in only seven years. In China, however, economic freedom has not been matched by political freedom. Consequently, it is doomed to failure. The prospects in Russia are better. Not only is it more technically advanced than China, but the new political freedom will quicken and enhance economic development. Investors looking for opportunities in the Far East might be aware of the free economic zones in China, but by comparison, the Russian Far Eastern zones offer clear advantages: abundant natural riches, a much higher level of infrastructure and industry, a larger population of professional people, and a lifestyle more suited to Westerners.

The Russian Far East offers not only opportunities for long-term investment, but immediate opportunities for earning hard currency. One such opportunity involves the region's underdeveloped ship repair facilities. The ship construction market is not very active, but repairs still lag well behind demand. Repair facilities already exist in the modern port cities of Vladivostok, Vostochniy, Slavianka, Sovetskaya-Gavan, and Nakhodka. Pumping money into them will bring immediate dollar revenues. A joint Russian-American venture, Kamchatka Petfield, has already done exactly that, and is paying off.

With foreign participation, many State enterprises are fast becoming shareholding companies. This is why foreign companies can now own partially, or even entirely, ship repair factories and some port moorages. Japan's Mitsubishi Corporation has proposed to lease space and equipment, and to pay in hard currency.

The Far Eastern merchant fleet represents about 15 percent of the country's freight turnover. The ports previously listed, where the water never freezes, handle the bulk of foreign trade between Russia and its Pacific partners.

Not far from Vladivostok, merely a day away by boat, in fact, is Slavianka Bay, with its town of 25,000 people. Finnish companies equipped a local lighter plant with modern machinery to produce barges with deadweight of up to a thousand tons. The plant has huge floating docks, and, though there is a lack of technical specialists, repairs about 150 vessels a year. Vessel activity in the region is increasing. Should a foreign company create a joint venture with a plant there, it could instantly generate dollars by repairing the fleets of Western customers.

Foreign investors will find Russians eager to build new repair facilities. As the old Soviet repair factories have become more and more outdated, Russians have been forced to sell old vessels as scrap metal to Japan at bargain basement prices. Were the factories supplied with modern equipment, Russia would not be forced into making such unprofitable deals.

Here is yet another opportunity for foreign investment. The ships in the Russian merchant fleet are, on average, fifteen years old. Before long, there will be a shortage of vessels necessary to meet internal freight needs. This is a time of transition for the Russian shipping industry; privatization will help solve many of its problems.

During and after our Arctic and Far Eastern expeditions, we conducted a study of the various operational Russian ports: St. Petersburg, Petropavlovsk-Kamchatsky, Nakhodka, Vladivostok, and Vanino. We also studied ports that could be constructed efficiently and easily. St. Petersburg was the leading port at the time, but Vostochniy has been steadily gaining on it.

Today, the port at Vostochniy is the most technically advanced of any in the former Soviet Union. Vessels with deadweight of up to 150,000 tons can moor in the deep water. Loading them can take as little as twenty-four hours, because the port facilities are designed to handle rolling stock using the automatic delivery and wagon overturn systems. Six miles of container lines are available for use; meaning, for example, that it is possible to load six thousand tons of coal an hour. The specialized timber moorage provided by four mechanized lines is capable of processing a million tons of timber a year for export. The port of Vostochniy celebrated its twenty-third anniversary in 1993. It is now well on its way to becoming Russia's largest port, forming a unique transportation complex with the city and ports of Nakhodka.

Nakhodka is one of the world's transportation hubs, located at that strategic point where all sea lanes of the Pacific Rim and Southeast Asia meet. The shortest land route to Western Europe begins here, and almost eighty thousand foreigners pass through every year—mostly Japanese, Americans, and Koreans. The city has trade, tanker, and fishing ports.

The port of Vanino on the Pacific Ocean holds special significance for international trade development because it is a terminus of the Baikal-Amur Railway, (although, technically, the BAM—as it is called—finishes at another port near Vanino, the Sovetskaya-Gavan). From Vanino, ships can go directly to California or to any Asian country. This combination of railroad and port is ideal for dealing with international freight.

Vanino is also the gateway to Sakhalin Island; a train-ferry line connects Vanino with the Sakhalin port of Holmsk. The head of the Russian Merchant Marine, Yuri Volmer, has recommended that a feasibility study be conducted to find out if another train-ferry, Vanino-Sakhalin/Nakhodka-Japan route might be possible. The project is currently under study, as is another: a sea lane between Magadan and Rotterdam via the Arctic Seaway. In 1991, the Association of Small Businesses of Japan decided to invest $1 billion to develop the seaport at Vanino, and another half billion to renovate the rail system leading to the port.

I first went to Vanino by train from the industrial center of Komsomolsk-on-Amur with other members of our expedition. As we approached the port, the leviathan ocean freighters and towering loading cranes became visible through the morning fog. I remember it was a clean town, as bright as if it had been fashioned from the morning light. Usually, my appreciation of the beauty of any landscape is filtered (and sometimes hampered) by my perspective as an economist. Wherever I go, the first thing I look for is a power plant, so that I can estimate its capacity and fuel consumption. I can usually estimate how many people live there. The number of ceramic insulators on the pylons tells me about the electrical capacity. If I know how many tons of cargo are delivered to a settlement of geologists exploring for oil, I can estimate how many feet down they have drilled.

I sometimes wonder if this sort of skill is taught in secret service training schools. I do know that most economists are not trained to look for interrelationships, and that this leads to fundamental and very costly mistakes in planning. For instance, the city of Minusinsk is located in a sunny valley in southern Siberia. The climate is so warm that even watermelons grow there; Minusinsk tomatoes are famous among connoisseurs worldwide. But the real wealth of the region resides in its natural resources; in particular, molybdenum, gold, titanium, and aluminum. The gigantic Sayano-Shushenskaya hydroelectric plant, the world's second largest, supplies energy to the mining complex that digs for these ores. When the Soviet government authorized the construction of twelve electrotechnical factories in the city of Minusinsk, they didn't call for the building of a single cafeteria for the thousands and thousands of construction workers. Not one. In those days, the military still gobbled up all available funds; all the consumer goods industries got were the leftovers, barely enough to fill a doggy bag.

Once, after a busy day in Louisville, Kentucky, on assignment to General Electric, I was dining in a beautiful rotating tower-restaurant with GE senior vice-president Richard Kask. Kask should serve as a model for the perfect businessman. Humane and honorable under any circumstances, he is one of those relatively rare Americans who has a feel for Russia and knows its history, culture, and manner of doing business. This is not surprising; his ancestors were Russian nobility.

We were discussing the opportunities afforded by free economic zones in the Russian Far East, with all of their skilled labor, good ports, and ample natural resources. The tower rotated slowly over the Ohio River, which reminded me of the Siberian river Ob. Looking at the Ohio's silvery curve, however, I almost involuntarily calculated the local port's turnover. River transportation is not widely used in the United States at the moment, but that will change. Soon, river transport will be revived—in part because modern ships are nearly nonpolluting. Looking with the eyes of an economist often hampers me from appreciating a landscape for its natural beauty, but it has the compensation of helping me make the connections that might help revitalize cities or even entire regions.

It was with these eyes that I surveyed the town of Vanino. Judging by the size of the cranes I saw, I estimated each one could handle between five and forty tons. This meant the port was of medium size. Because of its location, it was clear to me that it could be larger.

Soon, I was standing at a train-ferry loading point. Twenty-six coal-laden railway cars were loaded onto a ferry in under two hours. In twenty-three hours the ferry would cover 144 sea miles and moor at Sakhalin Island. Timber to Japan and South Korea, machinery and food to Vietnam, and manufactured goods to Magadan and other Arctic ports of Russia are all shipped from Vanino. The paperwork takes longer than the trip.

At Vanino, our expedition boarded a ship and made for the port of Sovetskaya Gavan over seas with waves reaching ten feet. Sovetskaya Gavan usually serves as a harbor for military vessels, but it was clear to all of us that it could also become a major base for ocean fish harvesting. Seven percent of all fish harvested in the Far East, mostly salmon, is processed here, and all of it is exported overseas or to the tables of the ruling elite. The conversion of the military to peacetime industry presents countless opportunities for foreign investment; besides fishing, Sovetskaya Gavan would be a logical place for ship-repair ventures.

The port of Petropavlovsk-Kamchatsky, home to a shipping company of the same name, is located farther to the northeast. Kamchatka Shipping, the major company there, is still State-owned and suffers from significant problems: twenty-eight of the firm's fifty-one vessels will be decommissioned and scrapped over the next few years because of age and wear. The ministry plans to replace only one-quarter of the hulls. In 1991, the capacity of the company was 170,000 tons below what it should have been. Ninety percent of all goods delivered to the Kamchatka Peninsula arrive by sea, and Kamchatka Shipping handles most of it. The ministry has estimated that each year the gap between the peninsula's needs and the shipping company's capacity will increase by 1.5 million tons.

The most picturesque port in the region, Petropavlovsk-Kamchatsky operates principally as a fishing and trading center. Our ship spent four days there while we studied the port facilities; this was something of a treat. Even Russian citizens have to obtain special permission to visit the city. The first thing you see when you wake up in Petropavlovsk are steaming volcanoes. There are no fewer than twenty-nine active volcanoes on Kamchatka. Even the communist regime couldn't diminish their productivity. Three or four volcanoes erupt around the clock.

The Volcano Institute organized a terrifying lecture about the apocalyptic properties of the eruptions, which left me feeling so dizzy I had to go outside to get some air. As if fulfilling the grim prophesy of the lecture, a huge volcano covered the city with a blanket of smoke. Later, a helicopter took us directly over the dead volcanoes' craters, and we gazed down in fascination at the deep blue lakes inside. They seemed harmless enough, not at all like what we had learned from the fire and brimstone lecture.

When we arrived at the city of North Kurilsk on Paramushir Island early one windy morning, the entire city was enveloped in thick smoke—not from factories, but from ash spewing out of the volcano Alaid on the neighboring island. The streets were covered with heavy black ash—basaltic ash—weighing three pounds per square foot. Feeling bold, we decided to approach the giant Alaid by ship. As we got nearer and nearer, the sky seemed to disappear and the deck was covered in ash. The enormous volcano hung over us. Some members of the expedition began to panic. We were economists, they said, not volcano specialists. We had absolutely no business being there. Others less timid argued that the closer we got to the volcano the better we would understand what the local population has to live with all the time. One doctor even went so far as to demand we dock and explore the volcano. I, too, felt seduced by Alaid's power, but I was also responsible for the lives and safety of the expedition and asked the captain to steer away.

I can imagine a prospective investor's reaction to all of this. First he learns how horrendous the Russian bureaucracy is, and next he is told about the natural uncertainties in this part of the world. It is true that Paramushir is not a place designed for capital investment, but it is a good place for joint scientific research that could benefit everyone. The local seismic station can send information about an earthquake to any part of the world, and that type of information saves lives.

The fishing industry offers yet more opportunities for economic development in the Far East, which accounts for 40 percent of the former Soviet Union's fish harvest: 95 percent of its salmon, 75 percent of its herring, and 100 percent of its crabs. Every dollar invested in fishing—and there are more than twenty fish processing plants in the Far East—returns about $12 in net profit. This is true even though most of the plants were built in the last century. The Kuril Islands still have factories built by the Japanese, which they abandoned after the Second World War.

The Far Eastern Center for Underwater Breeding held a dinner in honor of our expedition. We were served caviar of sea urchin, which allegedly promotes male virility. I noticed that all of the men were consuming it with genuine enthusiasm. The feast took place at the Zarubino settlement, where a major fish factory exports $20 million worth of canned squid a year; again, in spite of outdated equipment and shortages of cans. The settlement is located in a highly strategic position for business ventures: it has its own fishing port with a one-million-ton annual capacity, and an eight-mile railroad connects it with the major railway leading to China and Korea. Like so many other fishing ports, it will need foreign investment to realize its full potential.

I have already extolled the natural resources of western Siberia. The Russian Far East, on the other hand, affords opportunities that should also be of great interest to the informed investor. Sizeable gas and oil fields have been discovered between the Lena and Viluy rivers. The Kamchatka Peninsula and Sakhalin Island in the Pacific, and offshore areas along the eastern coast of the Sea of Okhotsk, also boast rich deposits of oil. The coal mining industry in this region provides 13.5 percent of all Russian coal, and it, too, has a promising future. Verifiable coal deposits are estimated at nearly thirteen billion tons. Russian geologists believe that probable recoverable reserves are at least fifteen times this figure. Half of these immense deposits can be brought to light through the open pit method, the most efficient and least expensive method of mining (also the most ecologically damaging, however, meaning that compensation for post-mining clean-up will have to be taken into account).

A daunting task facing the Far East is the building of its own iron and steel industry. The Jewish Autonomous Region, located near the Chinese border, suffers from a terrible shortage of metal. There is only one metallurgical plant, even though the iron ore deposits in the region are so large they would be sufficient to keep an integrated steel works in operation, at an annual capacity of up to ten million tons, for almost ninety years.

Nor is there only iron. Some of the richest tungsten, tin, boron, and titanium deposits are located in the Far East. Western technology, combined with Western-style labor motivation, could increase mining and refining tenfold. These metals are themselves a convertible currency. In the Magadan Region, by my estimate, every dollar invested in gold and nonferrous metallurgy should yield a $15 return. It is no wonder that several Alaskan gold companies have come to the region to explore investment possibilities.

The uninitiated outsider might also not know that tourism in the Russian Far East presents unexpected promise for foreign investment. The climate is wonderful, particularly along the coastal territories of the Pacific and on Sakhalin Island; resorts are springing up. High-quality mineral water and thermal baths—along with the natural beauty of the landscape—point to a very profitable tourist trade.

The Kamchatka Peninsula contains an abundant supply of geo-thermal energy (and two of the first geothermal power plants in operation). Here, you will also find the Valley of Geysers, a natural fantasy world, in which geysers and steam jets produce an unearthly effect. The earth seems to float, and from beneath the grass rises steam. The water is legendary for its healing qualities.

Another place of wonder is Shikotan Island, one of the Kuril Islands, formerly part of Japan and now a part of Russia. Shikotan will eventually become a free economic zone, and a place for joint investment with Japanese companies. Economic agreement, it is hoped, will resolve the Japanese-Russian conflict over who has claim to the island. A military base is located on the shore facing Japan. The waters around these islands are clear and pure. The shore is called The Emperor's Beach because Japanese emperors used to bathe there. Hot mineral springs merge with the ocean water, and when you emerge you feel restored and renewed, ready to take the weight of the world on your shoulders. This area offers a golden opportunity for anyone wanting to develop a tourist industry; as the area's econ-omy develops, economic interests will eventually push the military out and open up the island to tourism.

Given that in the Russian Far East the population density is only one person per half square mile, potential investors might be under-standably concerned about labor resources. The concern is un-founded. They should keep in mind that the rest of Russia is on the verge of large-scale unemployment. Overmanned factories in western Russia will soon have to slash their payrolls if the economy is to become competitive, or even more productive. In exchange for jobs and freedom, Russians will willingly move to the Far East. Foreigners should not think that Russians are creatures of a breeder-feeder state that takes care of all of their needs.

As a Siberian, I know that Russians are not afraid of challenges, but I do know they loathe uncertainties. Once they see the goal, they are extremely diligent about working toward it. They are the most industrious and freedom-loving people I have ever met. Having been for so many decades places of exile, Siberia and the Far East are eager for a change. There are eleven time zones in the former Soviet Union. The Far East, seven to eleven hours ahead of Moscow, is the first to greet the rising sun. With all of its wealth, the Far East now contributes only 2.5 percent to the former Soviet Union's GNP. The bulk of its riches lie untapped and waiting for development.

CHAPTER 9

Free Economic Zones, Part II: Making Inroads Northeast

When I was an undergraduate, one of my professors, a Colonel Katashov, who taught in the military science department (all universities and institutes had them), posed this rhetorical question during a lecture: "What is the most essential element of victory?" He paused for a beat, and then answered triumphantly: "Access roads!"

The colonel's point is well-taken and can be applied to other kinds of victories. Transportation is also a key element in creating and sustaining economic development. As the Russian Far East's economy becomes energized by activities within the free economic zones, the Baikal-Amur Railway will play an important role. It is already a first-rate transportation system, connecting Europe with the countries of the Pacific Rim. Even before completion, it was carrying thirteen million tons of coal a year to Japan.

The BAM (Baikal-Amur) Region refers to the 965,000 square miles of territory adjacent to the new railroad, which is located north of the old Trans-Siberian Railway. The region is developing a dynamic construction industry, and towns—populated mostly by young people who have come there to increase their earning power and raise their standard of living—are waiting for investment.

☐ 167

Meanwhile, the grand old Trans-Siberian Railway continues to be active. It is the main artery for transcontinental container service; 82,000 twenty-foot containers a year are moved along the railroad. Japan, Hong Kong, Australia, the Philippines, South Korea, Taiwan, and a total of twenty-four European and Asian cargo companies use this land bridge between Asia and Europe, which takes twelve-and-a-half to fifteen days to cross from end to end.

Shipping via the Arctic Seaway would be even more efficient than the railroads, and offer distinct advantages over traditional water routes. It would cost companies half of what it does to use the Suez Canal, for example—whether their point of origin is Antwerp or Japan. To ship one ton of cargo from Munich to Japan using the European and Trans-Siberian Railway costs about $215; using the Arctic Seaway would lower the cost to $110. The seaway is 3,500 to 4,000 miles shorter than the Suez or Panama Canal routes for ships traveling from North America or Japan to Europe.

In 1984, the Canadians used the Arctic Seaway to ship cargo from Vancouver to Lithuania. The trip took seven fewer days than it would have had they gone via the Panama Canal and was 1,500 miles shorter. In 1985, the trip was repeated—this time in the winter—and it was still faster. The Yeltsin-Clinton summit conference of April 1993 took place in Vancouver not only for political but also for economic reasons.

Year-round navigation has become the key question regarding full exploitation of the Arctic Ocean as a transportation route. Russia has the world's largest fleet of marine icebreakers; about twenty-five, including three that are nuclear powered. However, there is still a need for more icebreakers of different classes, as well as for specialized transport ships. Generally, however, the way can be cleared for year-round commercial shipping.

The eastern sector of the Arctic Seaway is 3,500 nautical sea miles wide and there are a few political uncertainties involved in this part of the Arctic zone. Russia considers the Arctic Ocean a domestic waterway, a claim not recognized by international marine law. I would guess there is a secret agreement between Russia and the United States, since the latter all but acceded to the Soviet annexation of Wrangel Island in 1926. The territory of the island is roughly equivalent to the size of Delaware and Rhode Island together. Wrangel's location is key, and were the United States to become a presence in the area, that would doubtless help with internationalization of business in the eastern sector of the Arctic. As international cooperation increases, especially between Alaska and Chukotka, it would be more beneficial both to Russia and the rest of the world to recognize the Arctic Ocean as a free enterprise zone.

Five firms have formed a consortium called Global Air Transportation Systems and Services to study air traffic control and navigation issues in the former Soviet Union. The consortium consists of the three U.S. corporations Westinghouse Electric, IBM, and AT&T; the other two are C. Itoh of Japan and the Deutsche Aerospace, a subsidiary of Daimler Benz. The partners signed an agreement with the Aeronavigatsia State Research and Development Institute of the Soviet Ministry of Civil Aviation to conduct a study of the Soviet air traffic system. The consortium estimates that it will take roughly $10 billion over the next decade to bring the Soviet system up to international standards. When it is finished, however, the system will generate substantial profits. When investors begin to realize what kind of riches await them in the Russian Far East, the demand for trans-Siberian flight routes will be enormous.

I have already called the the Russian Far East the next Klondike. I don't make the comparison lightly. Most gold and diamonds are mined in the basins of the Kolyma, Indigirka, and Upper Amur rivers. More than 95 percent of Russian diamonds are mined in Yakutia at the Mir and Udachniy mines. A $2-billion investment in upgrading mining technologies would increase diamond production 20 to 25 percent.

The return on investment in Russian gold and diamonds would be high because both industries are currently in equally bad condition. Both suffer from the same shortage of advanced machinery and equipment, and they were both crippled by bureaucratic bungling. The automation system SibAuto designed for the diamond industry covered all aspects of the business, from mining to refining. All except one. Diamond cutting belonged to another ministry at that time, and therefore remained a manual operation. Not until 1992 did the Russian government create the Committee for Precious Metals and Stones, which is responsible for all foreign trade of diamonds and gold. (Any foreign exportation will require a license from this committee.)

When we at SibAuto tried modernizing diamond mining operations, we encountered one ridiculous restriction after another. For example, a truck driver was not permitted to leave the cabin of his truck until he arrived at the refinery and his truck unloaded. Authorities were afraid he might steal diamonds from the truck. If his truck broke down, he was supposed to radio a repair crew rather than leave the cabin. The automated diamond draglines SibAuto manufactured helped increase diamond production from ore by 10 percent, and production at the diamond factories by 15 percent, but it could not influence diamond prices on the world markets. In 1990, Western newspapers ran headlines about a "sensational" diamond deal being struck between the Soviet Union and De Beers. Actually, there was nothing sensational about it. The Soviet Union had been dealing with De Beers for thirty years. It was just that, until recently, very few knew about it.

There has been talk that rather than continue to use De Beers, Russia might put the diamonds on the market on its own. Attractive as it might be to do this in theory, the head of the Diamond and Gold State Committee confided to me in 1989 that, unlike the gold market, the diamond market lives by advertising. Advertising keeps demand from falling. De Beers spends millions of dollars each year on advertising alone. "We can't afford to do that," he concluded. "If we throw the diamonds on the market without De Beers, prices would drop. So, ultimately, it won't be profitable to us."

Gold is another story. Siberia's largest gold reserves are located along the Kolyma and Chukotka rivers, and in Yakutia. Gold mining in this region has a long history. When the Russian nobility revolted against Czar Nicholas I in 1825, he punished them by exiling many of them to Siberia. Some of them turned out to be shrewd businesspeople. They leased Siberian lands, hired managers, and started mining for gold.

Large-scale gold mining on the Yenisey River started in 1838. By 1847, there were 119 active gold mines, which produced 90 percent of Russia's gold—twenty-one tons. Later, gold miners moved farther east. Gold brings one of the highest return on investment of any of the region's natural resources, because production costs are so low. In Yakutia, in the town of Kular, producing one gram of gold costs no more than buying a pound of meat.

Soviet-made gold-mining equipment is efficient enough, but unfortunately is designed only for river mining. Methods for mining gold deposits in other locations are the most archaic imaginable. The gold industry in Siberia is still poised for a boom because the technical revolution has not yet helped it realize its full potential. With foreign technology and incentives, gold and diamond yield could increase threefold.

Can a Western company, for example, simply walk in and begin mining for gold? Yes, as long as they obtain the special license for the particular gold field a company would like to develop. Recent legislation permits foreign companies to invest in gold mining, and some of the richest gold deposits are found in regions being turned into free economic zones. This constitutes a major change in attitude on the part of the State, which in the recent past has not been as enlightened.

In 1977, SibAuto's deputy general director for scientific research, Lev Krasov, and I went to the city of Khabarovsk. We were to visit the Primorzoloto (Coastal Gold) Company, whose headquarters were tucked away on a quiet side street.

The head of the company was a nervous-looking man named Tarakanovsky. We could tell just by looking at him that he was haunted by something. When he learned that Krasov was a member of the Russian Parliament, he stiffened visibly. I could tell that if we intimidated the man, we wouldn't get anywhere, and I tried to signal this to Krasov.

Krasov took my cue. "Tarakanovsky," he said, "you wouldn't have anything for us to drink in that safe of yours, would you?"

The question visibly relaxed Tarakanovsky. He broke out a bottle of vodka and began to tell us what was worrying him. It seems an inspector was checking up on his company, looking for possible violations in his dealing with the gold mining cartels. At the time, these so-called gold mining cartels were the only legal outposts of capitalism inside the Soviet Union. They consisted of entrepreneurial gold mining teams allowed to mine deposits the State companies had already picked over. Ironically, the cartels were extracting more gold from these "depleted" mines than the State enterprises had when the mines were still pristine.

An entrepreneur named Vadim Tumanov had created one of the most successful cartels, and saw to it that cartel miners earned salaries of up to forty or fifty thousand rubles (at the time, the equivalent of about $25,000) over one nine-month season. That amount of money, even five years ago, could buy a first-class villa near Moscow. (The purchasing power of the ruble in the Soviet Union was then much higher than that of the dollar in the United States.) Because the cartels were so productive and profitable, the State was constantly breathing down their necks.

Just before we met with Tarakanovsky, someone had written an anonymka charging him with providing the cartels with virgin deposits and new equipment. The author of the anonymka said he himself, a state official, had only been shown well-worked deposits and supplied with worn-out equipment.

Tarakanovsky denied the charge, but he knew he was in trouble. He insisted to us that he had not given any new deposits to the cartels; and as for their machinery, they somehow obtained it in Moscow and paid for it with their own money.

Right then, an investigating officer opened the door to Tarakanovsky's office. He was working on a different case, he announced—one involving the Communar cartel at the mine in Hakassia, southern Siberia. He had come to see whether there was any connection between this case and one in Georgia.

In Georgia, the militia had arrested a black marketeer who was making a fortune reselling tomatoes (resale is now legal). During a search of his house, the militia found some gold dust. Possessing gold dust was then, and still is, a crime. The State has a monopoly on all gold mined and on licensing any foreign company to mine it; if a private citizen is found possessing gold, it means it is stolen.

The chemical composition of the gold revealed it had been mined at the Communar mine in Hakassia. Authorities arrested the head of the cartel and temporarily shut down the operation. They later found out that the cartel's director had an entrepreneurial mistress, and that this lady had sold some gold dust to the Georgian black marketeer. The militia rushed off to arrest the lady, but she had disappeared. The investigation had taken six months, during which the cartel had halted operations; everyone lost money. Although indeed they might occasionally be guilty of some infraction, the cartels are far more productive than State-run companies, which themselves are not free of corruption. State gold miners have been known to open the sealed pipes containing the refined gold and take some of it. This gold later resurfaces at Black Sea resorts, where miners try to sell it either to rich Georgians or to foreigners. Slag heaps are another source of private profit, because current gold mining technology is oriented toward catching gold dust and nuggets.

In the end, Tarakanovsky went to prison—whether guilty or a victim of anti-private cartel prejudice. Tarakanovsky was not the only one who suffered for supporting the cartels, or at least for giving the impression that he had. The head of the Department for Gold and Diamonds at the Ministry of Nonferrous Metallurgy, Peter Zshmurko, favored the cartels at the expense of his own career.

Zshmurko was a man of action, not a paper pusher. When I started a think-tank at SibAuto to study the economics of nonferrous metallurgy's future and to write forecasts, Zshmurko and his department, as I have mentioned, were the first to request our services and pay for them. When we found out that our gold mining dragas had been crippled by the workers because of the backward compensation system, he did all he could to correct the system.

Zshmurko was born in Krasnoyarsk and studied at the Lumber Industry Institute during the Stalin years. As a first-year student, he told a joke about Stalin, and was rewarded with a five-year prison sentence. He was fortunate enough to be put in a prison directly across the river from his house, where conditions were fairly good compared to other jails. But he was young and reckless. He escaped from the prison and went home, where the NKVD (the early KGB) guards captured him. They beat him savagely and then dragged him back to prison. He was sentenced to an additional ten years and sent to the Gulag in Norilsk.

After Stalin's death, Zshmurko was completely rehabilitated, although the experience had left him a marked man.

I met him when I started working at the same mine where, years earlier, his first job had been to open the doors to the ore-laden carts. It wasn't long before his managerial talents were discovered, or rather uncovered, however. The director of the Norilsk Combine, Vladimir Dolgih (a future associate Politburo member) literally unearthed Zshmurko, brought him up out of the pit and into the main offices, first appointing him a mine director, then head of the mining division, and finally deputy general director of the entire company. Zshmurko eventually went on to become a deputy Soviet minister. It was an absolutely remarkable career for a former Gulag prisoner.

He was no angel, though. I once heard him at the ministry yelling at a woman engineer for taking a sick day.

"Sick? How can you be sick?" he thundered. "You're a young woman. Are you married?"

She said she wasn't.

"Then you are sick. Take another day off and I'll check in on you myself."

Crudeness such as this is typical of Russian managers, who generally showed no compassion whatsoever for the feelings of an employee. What did the employees being married or not have to do with anything? (Sexual harrassment was not a concept for which Soviet managers had any sympathy. Things are only slightly better today.)

However, when it came to business, Zshmurko was living proof that not all Soviet officials were foot draggers. Any business would be lucky to have him on its team.

Zshmurko was a strong advocate of the gold mining cartels because he knew they made the lives of gold miners tolerable. The wealth of Russian mines contrasted terribly with the squalor in which miners lived. One of the scariest characters in Russian fairy tales (which abound in despicable types) is the terrible Grandma Yaga, who lives in the middle of the forest in a crooked wooden house, an izba, perched on stilts as thin as chicken legs. This is how most Russian gold and diamond miners still live today. Miner's houses, like Grandma Yaga's shack, aren't really even houses, but more like ramshackle piles of half-rotted logs and sticks.

During our expedition, we visited the town of Kular, the gold capital of Yakutia and the worst example of an industrial town. Ten thousand people live, or rather squat, there. The average living space per person in the region is thirty square feet, roughly the size of an open grave. Miners cannot even dream about moving out of the settlement and buying their own house because there is nowhere else to go; buying a house is still well beyond the average Russian's means.

The ministry does not want to build permanent, decent housing for miners because gold deposits are usually not very large and the assumption is that they will soon move to another location. Yet, what usually happens is that just at the moment the mine is depleted, geologists discover another gold field in the same region, and so the temporary villages often remain in existence for several decades. Television didn't make it to the northern regions until the 1970s, and up to then, mining communities were almost completely cut off from the rest of the world. In winter, miners suffer from the severe frost; during the short summer, from mosquitoes. They work in mud and permafrost.

Because of their isolation, families use reindeer as a means of transportation. If a child falls ill in winter, the only way he can be taken to a hospital in a neighboring village is by helicopter. It is painful to see children bundled in every article of clothing they own, trudging off in the morning to their shabby school, which operates in double shifts of six hundred students each. It was cold where I grew up in Norilsk, too, but there, at least, the school was brightly lit and warm, and had music rooms and gymnasiums. (It was housed in the

"Palace of Culture," built by Director Dolgih.) The children of gold miners have nothing.

Considering how much miners contribute to State coffers, they deserve far better. Their salaries are ridiculously low in comparison to the profits they earn for the government. Even when Party bosses did make one of their infrequent visits to these miserable places, they expected bribes. Miners would give the visiting official their last piece of meat or the last drop of their vodka, desperately hoping that would persuade the authorities to allocate more money for their living conditions. Usually the lump would drink their vodka, leave the next morning, and forget all about them. Foreign investors should take careful note of this melancholy story. Russian miners can be among the world's best—if you take proper care of them.

In the Yakutia region, most of the gold is mined in open pits 50 to 250 feet deep. Because geological research is so poorly funded (the mining company at Kular spends only $250,000 a year), proven reserves constantly diminish. In 1992, mining operations were able to produce only 85 percent that of the amount of gold mined in 1975. Every year, miners have to work more ore to maintain the same level of gold production. The work is also hampered by out-dated equipment. Excavators are so heavy that they can work only in winter, when the ground is frozen. In the summer, they sit unused, stuck in the deep mud. Because of ineptness in Gorbachev's government, for the first time in Soviet history gold reserves fell dramatically—from 983.5 tons in 1985 to 450 tons in 1990, according to my figures; at $350 an ounce, a difference of almost $6 billion. Very roughly, the former Soviet republics together produce about 15 percent of the world's gold, although the amount of gold they extract per ton of ore has been steadily decreasing.

Any foreign company that comes to mine gold should know that the region has all of the basic facilities. It has a port on a river, which is the main route of communications: 165,000 tons of cargo and 175,000 tons of oil a year arrive in Kular along the river. Kular is also served by a railroad and has three transportation companies, a repair facility, a geological survey center, two large farms, a communications center, and 30,000 native deer. Television and radio communication are also available. Now is the time to mine it, but it should be done carefully, so as to avoid damaging the fragile northern ecosystem: a track left by a vehicle in the tundra can take as long as fifteen years to disappear.

In May of 1991, the Japanese signed an agreement with Russia to run a ferry line between Sakhalin and Japan. When it goes into full operation, that ferry will act as a bridge between Yakutia's natural resources and the outside world. By the end of this century, foreign investment will bring new technologies; then, perhaps, workers in the region will finally begin to enjoy a decent standard of living.

The Northern (Arctic) zone occupies nearly 40 percent of what used to be the Soviet Union. It accounts for half of Russian oil production and supplies more than a third of Russia's natural gas and timber. It also contains a large percentage of the country's nonferrous, rare, and precious metal ores. A sizeable portion of these resources, in turn, can be found in the so-called Near North, where the habitat and climate are quite amenable. However, studies have already made it clear that there are greater treasures waiting in the far northern latitudes. The Arctic has sometimes been referred to as the Russian El Dorado, which flatters not the Arctic but El Dorado. The opportunities for investment there are unimaginable.

The farther north you go, the more you find. In ancient times, one northern people thought the earth rested on three whales. I believe the foundations of modern life are oil, gas, and coal—for without them, civilization would collapse. The Arctic has all three.

The mere mention of the word *Arctic* is enough to send a shiver down the spine of people who have had no first-hand experience of it. It can do the same for those who do. These are very severe lands. Every region's weather can be measured in terms of how difficult it is for human habitation on the index of climatic severity, which computes temperature and wind speed. In Moscow, for instance, it is 1.9; in Paris, about 1. On Dickson Island in the Kara Sea, it is 7. Ten is the maximum.

Organizing the academy's economic expedition to the Arctic took an enormous amount of time. We began by studying the basins of the Yenisey, Lower Tunguska, and Angara rivers. We next analyzed the Northern Seaway and the Pacific Coast. Then we studied the lower reaches of the other great Siberian rivers—the Lena and the Ob. The Arctic expedition lasted nearly two months, and at various stages we were joined by other scientists, officials of the Soviet Central Planning Committee, local economic executives, and State and regional bosses. Never had so exhaustive and detailed a study of so vast an area been undertaken. Our expedition had two missions; they were collecting data and focussing on two questions: 1) How beneficial would it be for the country to invest there? and 2) How much would it cost?

Development in that part of the world, we concluded, entails particular problems. The durability of machinery, for example, is always a critical issue throughout Russia, where difficult terrain—the northern regions, deserts, mountains, and swamps—constitute more than 60 percent of the total area. This is even more critical in the Arctic. But the one guiding principle firmly established by our expedition was that transportation would be key to developing that part of the world. Transportation expenditures will account for 60 to 70 percent of the total cost of doing business there. Despite these costs, we concluded, northern products can still prove highly profitable—provided their production is properly organized and carried out.

Shipping along the Arctic Seaway has already begun. Still, additional port facilities must be developed, because breaking through Arctic ice will never be something to take for granted. Even our own expedition ship, which was built in Finland and designed for use in Arctic research, occasionally got stuck in the ice. The transition from Europe to Asia proved to be particularly difficult. The Karsky Gate and Jugorsky Shar straits, situated between the mainland and the islands of New Land, were closed to us for two days because of the ice. While waiting for an icebreaker, we put the time to good use by going out on the ice and fishing for omul, a northern salmon that looks like a trout and has an indescribably delicious flavor. In just two hours, we caught about a hundred. The Arctic waters are an excellent place for sport fishing.

After our fishing break, the icebreaker had still not arrived, so we organized a small side trip. Our map showed that the small village Khabarovo, where the famous Norwegian explorer Fridtjof Nansen had once stopped, wasn't far off, so we went in search of it. When we got there we found it was deserted; nothing remained but an abandoned Stalin-era prison camp. Walking through the empty barracks, we saw abandoned tractors, and the narrow-gauge railway the prisoners had used to haul cargo to the shore. The site should be turned into a museum for people to see the real face of Soviet socialism.

Finally, the 26,000-horsepower modern icebreaker, *Captain Sorokin*, arrived. After cutting through the ice for several hours, the ship entered ice of force 8 (10 is maximum) and stuck fast—and that was at the end of June! We waited for six hours until the world's first nuclear 43,000-horsepower icebreaker, the *Lenin*, came to the rescue and escorted us through. (Most modern Russian icebreakers have a 75,000-horsepower capacity, which enables them to go directly to the North Pole. A 100,000-horsepower vessel is currently under construction.) We spent the entire night on the *Lenin*, talking with its legendary sea-wolf captain, Grigory Entin. The expedition members were so engrossed by his stories about life in the Arctic that they asked if we could stay one more day on the icebreaker. Our schedule was too tight, however, and we had to push on.

Other forms of transportation are also available to expedite economic development in the Arctic regions. For example, work is currently underway to increase the navigability of Siberian rivers, nearly twenty thousand of which flow into the Arctic ocean. Railway tracks and pipelines also extend into the Far North. There is, however, a pressing need for transport vehicles that can negotiate every type of terrain.

Because of the harsh climate, any kind of work in the Arctic costs at least three times as much as in more temperate regions. Sophisticated machinery often does not adapt to the harsh conditions. Breakdowns and losses exceed a machine's initial costs three- to sevenfold. Conversely, one ruble of added cost to adapt machines to northern conditions will later save seven or eight rubles.

But adapting Western equipment to Arctic conditions represents only half the battle. Maximum productivity in this part of the world requires using a minimum of workers, which is why prefabricated construction was widely and effectively used in developing oil and gas deposits in western Siberia. Factories outfitted the units with all of the necessary equipment, and on-site workers used them to assemble industrial installations. However, as always, demand is ahead of supply. Such climate-adjusted equipment probably accounts for only about 3.8 to 5 percent of the total cost of construction, mining, and transportation machinery produced. To meet the demand, the figure should be closer to 30 percent. The shortage of such equipment costs the country some $10 billion a year, using 1990 prices. Equipment suited for use in the frozen north will soon be in great demand, and those companies ready to meet this demand will make significant profits.

How will future industries and towns beyond the Arctic circle be supplied with the energy they require? Throughout the Arctic, there are highly promising oil and gas deposits; coal and hydroelectric reserves are also substantial. There are atomic, tidal, and geothermal power plants being built, as well as plans to use wind power.

Siberian economists have already developed major regional programs, among them the construction of the aforementioned Baikal-Amur Railway, the development of the brown coal deposits of the Kansk-Achins basin, the mining of the polymetallic ores of Norilsk Combine and Yakutia Diamond, and the super program called Siberia. The role these programs have started to play in the economic life of the entire country cannot be overstated. They have already exerted a powerful influence on the the world's energy balance—an influence that will continue to grow.

Siberian oil and gas fields, the riches of the Baikal and Amur regions, and the Arctic zone are now becoming major attractions for businesses in Europe, the United States, Japan, South Korea, and other industrialized nations. Because of its size and its influence on the world economy, the basis of the regional program called Arctic, which grew out of the reports of our economic expeditions, is a sign of things to come. The Arctic zone contains approximately half the world's forecasted oil reserves, and most of its natural gas. Major oil deposits stretch across the Russian Arctic, in places such as Lena-Tunguss, western Siberia, Anadir, the Eastern Arctic, and Chukotka. In the next century, various types of synthetic fuel, some made from bituminous coal, will become a main source of energy. Massive deposits of high-quality bituminous coal are located in Russia's far north, among them the Taimir, Tunguss, and Lensky coal basins.

I am a Siberian, so I understand and share my countrymen's enthusiasm about opening the region up to foreign investment. European Russians have always been somehow enslaved, either by czars or by Party bosses, but Siberia, despite being the home to the infamous prisons of the Gulag, has ironically never known either serfdom or slavery. Siberians have always been more independent and free-thinking than other Russians. The yoke of the Russian empire never extended to them. Siberia's potential, as the great explorer Nansen once said, extends beyond the horizon. The time will come when the Siberian giant will wake up and become an economic force to be reckoned with.

I should add that all of the regions I have discussed in this chapter are of great interest to Russians themselves—particularly now that they can be shareholders, and own brokerage firms, factories, or even newspapers. Stalin and his successors never managed to liquidate the Russian entrepreneurial drive; all they were able to do was put it in cold storage. Russians can be excellent businesspeople when given the chance. The entrepreneurial miracles Russian women pull off every day simply to feed their families are but one small example. The New York Stock Exchange operates at a leisurely pace compared to a Russian grocery store when the meat delivery arrives.

By the year 2000, foreign companies will have invested more than $10 billion in the Arctic regions. Russia itself, despite its current financial problems, nonetheless plans to invest $2 billion over the next decade—$1 billion before 1997. These sums will be used to develop communication networks, roads, tourist facilities, and other elements of the local infrastructure. Since the establishment of the European Economic Community, European countries are now more closely linked than the Soviet republics ever were. In any case, every nation in the world is beginning to think in terms of markets, rather than national identities. Free economic zones play a big part in this thinking.

CHAPTER 10

Look
Before You Venture

No foreign company should rush into the former Soviet Union, even into the free economic zones, without doing its homework first. Mistakes can be costly. ACC, the company I discussed in the early chapters made a few, as did Chevron, initially, and *Burda Moden Russia*, the fashion magazine. Chevron underestimated public opinion; ACC underestimated the bureaucracy; *Burda Moden Russia* had not planned for shortages. Everybody saw the huge resources and markets; few knew what they were in for. Their individual errors might have been very different, but they all had one mistake in common: they assumed that doing business in Russia would be like doing business in other countries, even other Eastern European countries, and that they could dive in on their own. Large ships navigating difficult waters often take on local pilots to guide them through. Large companies interested in investing in Russia should, figuratively, do the same. Although the success rate for joint ventures, once they are in operation, is high, the hard truth is that only 8 percent of potential foreign joint venturers succeed in setting up their businesses. This chapter will show why so many don't succeed the first time around.

Next to finding a partner for a joint venture—an issue I have already addressed in some detail and will talk about further—the main reason planned joint ventures fail to materialize has to do with financing. Lack of a partner accounts for 28 percent of the failures; problems in financing, 20 percent. Not all of these financial problems occur only at the Russian end, of course, but those that do, stem from a number of issues.

Commercial banking in Russia and the other republics is below standard and will need to be reformed before it can play its part in bringing about long-term economic expansion. Some independent commercial banks dealing in hard currencies have already been formed, but foreigners might themselves participate in the creation of new banks that can handle securities and insurance. (They must first obtain a license from the Ministry of Finance, but this should not be difficult). However, true banking reform will only occur when a new, independent national bank—subordinate solely to the Russian (or relevant republic's) Parliament and, of course, the law—is established.

This will happen when the government's fiscal policies stabilize. Today, in Russia, new currency is being printed as fast as new baseball cards are in America. The reasons Yeltsin has been printing one trillion rubles a month, by the latest estimates, are more complex than they might seem. Were he to stop, there would be widespread civil disobedience. Ninety-five percent of the Russian people are living below the poverty line. (Before price "liberalization," it was 60 percent.) If the Russian government suddenly halted printing rubles for a period of two months, deflation would be so strong that almost 70 percent of Russian industrial companies would be unable to meet their payroll. The lack of currency backing by any standard or commodity has inevitably led to inflation, and the billions of dollars the International Monetary Fund has ear-marked to help stabilize the ruble is, in my opinion, a colossal waste. The money would be better spent if dispensed directly to private enterprises and entrepreneurs.

Two other factors hamper attempts at economic reform in Russia. One is that banks pay interest that amounts to as little as one twentieth of the yearly rate of inflation (which, I mentioned, soared to an unbelievable 2,100 percent during 1992). Rather than putting rubles in the bank, people are keeping their money close at hand, so that they can spend it should the opportunity or need arise. The other factor is the scarcity of goods. When consumers have cash in hand but nothing to buy and no reason to save, prices of goods rise like two-minute popovers in an oven.

Until 1986, there were three Soviet banks, all State owned. In 1988, three more State banks were formed for specific financial purposes: construction (of housing, schools, and hospitals), agricultural investment, and savings. The first commercial banks opened their doors that year. These cooperative, publicly held banks are not State banks, although ministries were among their founders. Tehknobank, for instance, was created at the initiative of the Moscow city council. A modest amount of capital, 6.2 million rubles, was raised in shares valued at 100,000 rubles. Shareholders received a 5-percent return at the end of the first year. Tehknobank has already lent money to transportation cooperatives, and, to support the growth of consumer goods, it plans to lend to military factories converting to civilian production. Today, it is one of the largest private banks in Russia.

The other independent bank, Credobank, is licensed to open foreign currency accounts for companies doing business abroad. This means that hard currency on account in a Russian commercial bank can be given to bank customers in any country around the world or deposited in any foreign bank. Credobank can also pay dividends in foreign currency.

Another is the Mosbusinessbank, which, between June and September of 1992, organized a subscription for new shares amounting to 1 billion rubles, and increased its outstanding reserve to 1.8 billion rubles. The bank's reputation is solid. Yet another is Ukrsibbank, in the Ukraine. Since July of 1992, the Russian government, finally, has also been trying to create a hard currency market in the country, and has permitted the Russian Central Bank's foreign currency exchange to hold auctions twice a week. A minimum bid is $10,000.

The existence of banks such as these should no longer surprise foreigners. Today numbering about two thousand, they are fully commercial, autonomous institutions. Still, regulations constraining the banking industry as a whole are working very badly. Few can open hard currency accounts, and few can have corresponding relations with foreign banks. Obstacles such as these remain some of the largest on the road to a free-market economy in the former Soviet Union.

Another financial arena in which the republics have little experience is in commodities and stock exchanges. Before the breakup of the Soviet Union, enterprises dealt mostly with the State, rather than with each other. Companies in the same line of business had no way of communicating with each other, and hence no way of gauging their place in the market. Commodities and stock exchanges will enable them to compete, and hence to be more efficient; however, to set them up, cooperation with the West will be essential. The Chicago Board of Trade has offered to help train Russian brokers with this complex business, and the assistance is timely.

I have recounted how the mismanaged storage system and excess of unnecessary materials were among my main headaches at SibAuto. Directors at practically every other State company faced the same problem. What was needed was a channel for these directors to rid themselves of superfluous supplies and get the materials they required to do their jobs. The first board of trade, a commodities exchange, was created in May of 1990. In September of that year, it became operational. The exchange is a perfect example of successful business contacts between State enterprises, cooperatives, and, in this case, a Soviet-Yugoslavian-Italian joint venture. Creating it was like an errand in the wilderness: nothing like it had existed before. The board began with barter operations. Gradually, in spite of the scarcity of goods, it became the heart pumping blood into the new arteries of the market. Available goods started pouring in, not only from the country's officially sanctioned inventory levels, which are worth 500 billion rubles, but from enterprises that had been hoarding them (amounting to nearly 200 billion rubles-worth). One reason for the hoarding was that domestic bartering was a more effective, if also more awkward, way of obtaining production supplies. A company could more readily procure bricks by proffering, say, telephones, than it could by paying for the bricks with rubles.

The exchange provides enterprises with a civilized method of exchanging goods and information, as well as a way for foreign buyers to get access to valuable materials. Again, however, the system is far from perfect, and a lack of coordination between the enterprises makes for all sorts of inefficiencies.

Another hindrance to economic cooperation with Russia and the other republics is the accounting techniques in practice there. To interact freely with the rest of the world economy, Russians will need to learn Western accounting techniques. The current system does not allow for a realistic appraisal of products or assets. Concepts such as "depreciation" and "current market value" simply do not exist. These gaps lead to disparities between governmental and commercial numbers. The inaccuracies also make it difficult for managers and potential investors to make informed choices.

Until the summer of 1990, there was only one auditing body in the Soviet Union. Inaudit, as it was called, was created by the Ministry of Finance to oversee joint ventures with foreign companies only, not audit Soviet enterprises. In June of 1990, two foreign accounting firms, Arthur Andersen & Co. and Ernst & Young, were licensed to practice in the Soviet Union. In 1991, the New York accounting firm Weiner Associates established a relationship with the Russian and Daghestan governments, and later with the private firm Rufaudit, to audit both foreign and Russian companies. The last of the Big Six—Peat Marwick—opened an office in Russia in 1992. There are currently about three hundred private accounting and auditing firms in the former Soviet Union. More companies will follow.

From the point of view of foreign investment, the current accounting system is a hindrance. Foreigners often have trouble assessing the financial status of a potential partner. As long as Russian and international accounting practices differ, and there is no common language in which to share financial information, Russians and outsiders will have to be careful when they deal with each other. Foreign companies need to understand the domestic tax structure and the lack of a coherent accounting system. Russian enterprises will need the help of Western accounting firms to interpret financial information and to evaluate, in dollars, the assets of State companies undergoing privitization.

The chaos has undermined economic progress in all of the republics. One of Russia's biggest automobile plants, the Moscow-based firm AZLK, recently announced its plans for privatization based on a vote of its employees. The workers wanted to interest foreign companies in buying shares in the new shareholding company. The necessary authorization was obtained from the Soviet Cabinet of Ministers and Russia's Council of Ministers, but an unexpected snag appeared. The plant's accounting books were so radically unlike anything outsiders had ever seen that they looked like what Russians call a Chinese manuscript. Their illegibility very nearly killed the deal. In April of 1992, the plant hired Arthur Andersen to translate their accounts into a coherent Western balance sheet, which put the share-selling plan back on track.

In August of 1992, one of the largest companies in Russia, another automobile manufacturer called Zil, reorganized itself into an open shareholding company, with authorized capital amounting to about $3 billion. The plant employs 120,000 people, and among its products are the former government limousines (Chaika), and medium-duty trucks. The privatization of this company in particular is a real signal that privatization has taken hold. However, without thousands of auditors and CPAs familiar with the ways of Western balance sheets, depreciation schedules, first-in, first-out, and so on, the process could take as long as a decade to complete.

The presence of Western accounting firms will, albeit slowly, lead to the creation of a genuine accounting profession in the country. Accountants and bookkeepers currently enjoy little prestige and earn less than half that of an engineer. Properly trained (and self-respecting) accountants are essential if the country is to make the transition to a free-market economy. Accounting is the language of business. Russian accountants must both learn it and adapt it to a Russian dialect.

Like accounting practices, the legal system poses difficulties. My estimate is that that 10 percent of joint-venture failures are attributable to legal problems. Some former Soviet republics retain the vestiges of the old Soviet legal system, and others have all but scrapped them; still others are somewhere between the two. Dealing with the various legal codes is not easy for lawyers whose job it is to protect Western investment. Widespread involvement of foreign lawyers, however, should eventually help promote further reform and bring legal principles more in line with Western standards.

Investing in Russia and the other republics means assuming all of the risks of dealing with a developing economy—the glittering opportunities as well as the maddening inadequacies and paradoxes. Many concepts basic to Western capitalism are only now being introduced into the business consciousness of their Eastern neighbors.

Bankruptcy, for example, is now permitted in the former People's Paradise. The 1991 Law of Enterprise declares that all companies, whether State-owned or private, have equal rights; sets forth the legal and economic definition of a joint venture; and gives a proprietor the right to manage his own company. It also allows an enterprise to go into bankruptcy. The idea was that businesses suffering losses would no longer be propped up with subsidies from the State. Bankruptcy proceedings are essentially what they are in Western countries: a special committee is created to assess debts and to investigate creditors' claims. When all debts have been paid and all the claims satisfied, employees and foreign investors are given what remains of the assets in either currency or securities.

I should add that, in practice, some types of enterprises, such as the military, still receive substantial subsidies. This is part of an time-honored Russian tradition. With one hand, Yeltsin signed the Law on Bankruptcy, but with the other, he signed in June of 1992 a resolution called the Decree of Support to State Enterprises. The decree was an act of generosity and beneficence that makes no business sense particularly, but which stems from the system's ingrained paternalism. "Beneficence is the worst thief of all," runs a Russian proverb.

Last, this is a good time to mention taxation, the word that causes most good capitalists to shiver. First, the good news; the aforementioned Law of Enterprise contains a bonus for would-be joint venturers: a tax abatement lasting two years in most parts of the former Soviet Union, three years in the Far East, and even longer in the free ecomonic zones. Some foreign partners have managed to prolong this luxury by closing their joint ventures after two years and then creating new ones.

Taxation, like accounting and commercial banking, is a novel concept to Russians. The Soviet Union adopted its first tax law in May of 1990, which affects all joint ventures and organizations created between foreigners and citizens. The law gives official tax inspectors the right to check an enterprise's balance sheets, book-keeping records, and any other document relating to the payment of taxes; to fine companies; and, if necessary, to close down a company's operations. Initially, there was a chill on American-Russian joint ventures because of double taxation. In July of 1992, as I've mentioned, Russian and American officials eliminated it. Other republics have not yet followed suit. Similarly, it is important to know that in August of 1992, the Russian Customs Commission declared that forty-seven of the world's poorer countries would be allowed duty-free importation, and that almost every other country—currently 119, including the European Community—would enjoy Most Favored Nation status (calling into question the concept of "most favored," of course).

Getting into the market means knowing who to contact, what to say when you do, who to meet and who to avoid, how to calculate expenses and profits, and how to locate alternatives and new markets. A company, once it knows what it wants to achieve, needs to develop a strategy designed especially for its market, but not to the point of blindly pursuing only one strategy. Success will come by combining focus with flexibility—by learning from mistakes and adjusting quickly to changing circumstances.

The first steps are the most difficult. The Russian method of making managerial decisions is sometimes opaque. Authority frequently resides in places Westerners would never expect to find it. Foreign investors will inevitably knock on the wrong doors, overestimate the influence of this or that ministry, and underestimate the strength of this or that enterprise. The biggest challenge of all for a would-be joint venturer is finding the right Russian partner.

The Soviet-American joint venture Perestroika was one of the first success stories, illustrating that Russian business—for good or for ill—is catching up with business practices in the West. Founded by the Atlanta-based Worsham Group in conjunction with a State-owned Moscow construction and engineering unit called Mosinzhstroy, Perestroika was registered in June of 1988. A year later, it posted a profit of $1.6 million and an annual cash flow of $13 million. At that point, Western partners were able to repatriate their hard currency profits, and Worsham was turning a handsome profit.

Given that perestroika means "reconstruction" in Russian, the company was appropriately named: the joint venture renovates abandoned buildings of historical and architectural value and then rents them out as office space, mostly to foreign companies. This means it generates dollars. The American founder, Earl Worsham, and the American director, John S. Reuther, couldn't have done better in their choice of a Soviet partner. Mosinzhstroy is strong and well positioned in the market, and has all of the necessary facilities, expertise, and contacts in Moscow. Its energetic and entrepreneurial chairman, Andrey Stroev, speaks English fluently and is unburdened by communist prejudices. He started the business using foreign workers, but by the time the company began work on the fifth building, they were employing an entirely Russian work force.

What Stroev and Perestroika are doing is not only profitable, but is a service to the city. This is worth pointing out because too many other joint ventures have all but ignored the needs of the locality in which they are doing business. An example is the former Hotel Berlin, located directly across from the Kremlin, which was renovated by Finnair and some Russian partners and turned into a first-class establishment housing an excessively chic restaurant called the Savoy. The hotel quickly gained recognition and wealthy foreign business-people began staying there, paying probably the highest prices anywhere in Russia.

Wealthy foreign businesspeople might be welcome at the Savoy restaurant, but Moscovites, with their poor, mostly inconvertible rubles, get the cold shoulder. A table can be had only for foreign currency. The owners thus deprive the locals use of a good hotel and a gourmet restaurant. Given the scarcity of hotels and entertainment facilities in Russia, this exclusionary policy seems unfair, and has triggered a fair amount of grumbling.

With Perestroika's success, however, came problems. Before long, the company was swept up in the growing competition within the Russian market: head-hunting rivalry, cut-throat competition, and, finally, competition from a new type of joint venture founded by the Communist Party for the sole purpose of securing its holdings.

In the middle of 1991, Perestroika stunned the Russian business community with a scandal implicating top-level management. It became public that Reuther had secretly been investing private funds in a joint venture called Putnik, which was Perestroika's main competitor in the Moscow market. Money to start Putnik had come in large part from a Communist Party-backed cooperative and non-State bank.

Earlier that year, the deputy general director of Perestroika, Victor Shtil, found out that Reuther, his boss, was representing in the Moscow market the interests of a company, based in Cyprus, called Kapora Holdings Company, Ltd. (Like Ireland, Panama, Luxembourg, and other small countries, Cyprus attracts offshore companies by providing them with a tax shelter. Even Soviet businesspeople, supposedly so new to the ways of capitalism, can see the advantages and have started establishing companies there. What they value most is the anonymity it affords.) In an interview with the Russian business newspaper *Commercant*, Shtil said that he had not paid serious attention to Reuther's outside involvement at the time, because it did not conflict with the the conditions established in the agreement between Reuther and Perestroika. Soon, however, Worsham found out that the Kapora Holdings Company was the foreign parent company of Putnik. He also discovered that Reuther and the financial deputy director of Perestroika, Michael Morgenstern, were the owners of Kapora. To make the situation even more complicated, Perestroika's founding Soviet organization, Mosinshstroy, was performing work for Putnik at the time. It stopped the moment Reuther's double-dealing became known.

Andrey Stroev and Earl Warsham did not want a scandal. They offered Reuther and Morgenstern a deal: to stay on, but transfer 70 percent of their share in Kapora to Perestroika. They refused, so Perestroika terminated its contracts with them.

Reuther sent a letter to *Commercant* that attempted to convince potential clients he was not guilty of any wrongdoing, claiming that his contract with Perestroika had not dictated in specific terms what he could or could not do with his personal investments, particularly in that he did not have any interest in Perestroika's profits. Reuther's switch to Putnik made it an even stronger competitor to Perestroika. Because Mosinzhstroy would no longer fill Putnik's orders, Reuther founded another construction organization and supplier, both of which charge higher prices for their services.

Why Reuther, a leading member of a successful management team, would make such a switch remains unclear. His justification was that Perestroika was too focused on the immediate demands of the marketplace and lacked a long-term strategy. This might be true. By switching to the shadowy Kapora, however, Reuther was fishing not only for a long-term business strategy but for big money.

The Perestroika scandal points to three elements of the current Russian market. First, it is becoming highly competitive in certain industries. Second, even if internal problems arise, a strong venture can cope with them. (Perestroika was the first Russian-American joint venture to declare a profit—1.6 million dollars in January of 1990; in 1992, total assets reached 158 million dollars.) Third, the Party has been trying to preserve its ill-gotten gains by using front companies as vehicles. These front companies are now under investigation by the Russian government, which has hired foreign companies (such as Kroll Associates, the well-known private investigation firm) to look into matters.

With the advent of glasnost and the dissolution of the communist empire, the top leadership in the Soviet Communist Party made a strenuous effort to protect the wealth they had accumulated during their years of power. The connection between these efforts and the Perestroika scandal made this clear. It should come as no surprise that the Communists would scramble to save their enormous wealth. The Nazis did the same with their stolen treasures when Hitler's Reich was crumbling. So, more recently, did the East German Communist Party, which was able to benefit from German chancellor Kohl's support of Gorbachev, and had started sending money abroad. Putnik was one of the first businesses in which this hidden money was invested.

In 1991, another American company was contacted by a Russian who claimed to be the chairman of a large new business, and who wanted to meet with the American company's chairman to discuss a partnership. He brought with him a letter of reference from Arcady Volsky, Gorbachev's closest friend and his right-hand man in the Soviet Scientific-Industrial Union, which is one of many new organizations created by Gorbachev's circle to operate outside the bureaucratic structure. Because they are ostensibly independent of the Communist Party, these organizations never received much scrutiny from the democratic elements in the Russian Parliament.

The American company hired me to investigate matters. After checking with banks and Russian economic and financial organizations, I found out that this newly created company lacked the legal authorization to engage in foreign economic activity. On the other hand, the letter from Volsky gave it some viability, for it meant that the Central Committee of the Communist Party was interested in the company's success. In the end, the American company decided against working with the front organization for the Party. I agreed with their decision. Collaborating with ventures such as these is like dealing with the devil. Former Party bosses might prove instrumental in the early stages of starting a joint venture in the former Soviet Union because their connections can expedite things, but democratization is moving quickly. Party bosses are gradually losing influence and their support will become more a burden than an advantage to foreign businesses.

Some consultants are advising foreign companies to move slowly. Such advice reflects fear of the unknown more than it does sound business sense. Once a foreign company has made the initial decision to start a joint venture, I believe it should get things moving swiftly—before it gets bogged down in a swamp of bureaucratic trouble. Moving things along doesn't mean doing it all in one leap. The initial capitalization of a joint venture called Sterkh, founded by Honeywell and several Soviet partners in 1988, was small—only $300,000. Over the next three years, Sterkh, an engineering service company for foreign companies, generated $40 million in sales. Today, Sterkh is in a strong enough position to invest some of its hard currency profit (about $5 million) in the production of industrial equipment. To help them with that production, Honeywell sold it some of its technology.

Another joint venture that began with modest foreign investment and grew rapidly is a company called Dialogue. The American founder, G. Richi, had invested initially because he wanted to promote the cause of peace between the Soviet Union and the United States. He was put in touch with Peter Zrelov—the future Soviet director general of Dialogue—who worked at the Kamaz plant on the Volga River, which manufactured quality trucks.

Zrelov was excited at the prospect of participating in a joint venture with a foreign company. With his wife, he invited several groups and institutions to join in, and their joint venture was registered on December 31, 1987. Dialogue's initial capitalization was 15 million rubles. The American partner, Management Partnerships International, owned a 21.8-percent interest, if you evaluate its share in dollars. Its investment consisted mostly of equipment, technology, and expertise. Four years later, Dialogue founders had increased their initial capital investment to 100 million rubles.

At the beginning of the new era of joint ventures, there were several Lilliputian joint ventures, but also a few giants ("giants" means working capital of anywhere between $160 million and $250 million). Today, the average amount of initial capitalization is actually smaller than it was in the early days. What has changed is the distribution of shares. At first, foreign partners were limited to owning no more than 49 percent of shares—a restriction that no longer applies. Lower levels of investment by foreign partners are discouraged not through prohibition, but through taxation. If the hard currency share in the initial capitalization is less than 30 percent, the rate of taxation is higher.

Dialogue's Peter Zrelov could not have chosen a better partner. The basis of the joint venture (the twenty-first joint venture started in the Soviet Union) consisted of capital from the Kamaz truck plant, whose initial investment was 32.6 percent of the total capitalization. The data processing center of the Soviet Exhibition of National Economic Achievements also contributed a 32.6-percent share, and Moscow University 13 percent. The university's involvement, though smaller, turned out to be key, not only because of the scientists and researchers it could put at the joint venture's disposal, but because in the first days of operation it gave the company nearly free use of space. The right choice of partners allowed the company to survive the difficult start-up period.

I have mentioned that about 28 percent of joint-venture projects failed either because the wrong partner was chosen or no suitable partner could be found in the first place. Dialogue is an example of a successful partnership, right timing, and a product filling a real need. Assembling computers from American parts and selling them to Soviet companies for dollars, the company made its move at the right moment. Soviet enterprises and ministries had very little hard currency with which to satisfy their growing technological appetite, but they could still afford to buy a few computers. If they didn't purchase them from Dialogue, they would be forced to purchase them abroad using Soviet foreign trade agencies, which would be a tedious, expensive process. Most Soviet organizations couldn't even afford to send their employees abroad.

Dialogue was the third American joint venture. With his feel for the market, Zrelov began to actively create sister companies, and his efforts, in spite of some early mistakes, have paid off. One of these sister companies was a joint venture with a Danish company called Time Manager International A/S, which offered courses on time management and other aspects of Western-style managerial practices to Soviet businesspeople.

For a foreign company, choosing a partner should mean insisting on due diligence during the process of preliminary negotiations. The desire to do business with foreigners is so overpowering to Russians that even a traffic cop would sign a joint-venture agreement if the opportunity arose. Too often, foreign companies squander their time and money signing contracts or joint-venture agreements with organizations that are not legitimate entities, and which have no legal right to enter into such agreements. Foreigners often assume that everything Russian is backed by the State. Not so. The first stage of due diligence is finding out if the Russian company is legitimate.

The second stage is to find out whether the company is licensed by the Russian government for the particular type of business in which it plans to engage. When foreigners ask a prospective partner to show its documents, the documents should include registration numbers. There are more than 1,153,000 legal businesses throughout the republics, but only about thirty thousand of these companies have the right to deal internationally, and only about seven thousand are actually engaged in international transactions. *All* of them have the right to develop foreign economic ties. But for any Russian company proposing to do business with outsiders involving the use of natural resources or advanced technology, it is still imperative that it obtain operating and export licenses. These are the businesses in which finding the right partner is vital.

The same licensing requirements apply to all joint ventures, regardless of their line of business. In addition to being registered with the Ministry of Finance, joint ventures must also obtain certification from the Russian Ministry of Foreign Economic Ties. Some joint ventures might have trouble obtaining this license; however, keep in mind that although trying to circumvent the cumbersome bureaucratic procedure is tempting, it could lead to grave business consequences, as the following example eloquently demonstrates.

The second largest Soviet publishing house, Molodaya Gvardia, decided to acquire modern computer equipment for its printing facilities. Because the publishing house had almost no hard currency, it planned to pay for the computers in wastepaper, which it had in quantity. An Austrian computer company agreed to supply Molodaya Gvardia with computers and take the waste as barter. A contract was signed by the publisher and the chairman of the Austrian company. A third company, a trading company, contracted to buy the computers.

The chairman of the Austrian company had neglected to check on one critical detail: finding out whether the publishing house had been granted permission by the Supplies Committee to sell its waste. The committee regulates all waste produced by State enterprises. Each enterprise has a certain quota of waste it must submit for verification to this committee every year, whether the waste is paper, metal, or food products. The publishing house hadn't been granted permission and the whole deal was off.

The Austrian businessman's mistake was largely the result of a different mindset. It is difficult for a Western executive to understand that a State-owned firm cannot simply dispose of its waste as it chooses. Even had the Ministry of Supplies allowed the publishing house to dispose of its waste, it would still have needed a license from the Ministry of Foreign Economic Ties to sell abroad.

Sometimes a strong Russian partner will know all of the ins and outs of the labyrinthine bureaucratic system; sometimes it won't. It might not yet have all of the required documents, but still open negotiations with foreign companies, hoping to get the documents along the way. In that authorization is difficult to obtain, the Russian partner might stretch things out by stalling for time—finding excuses not to hold a certain meeting, or pleading illness, or even disappearing temporarily. Lenin's favorite adage was "trust but verify." The proviso is as applicable to Russian capitalism as it was to Russian socialism.

Following Lenin's advice, I like to advise foreign companies not to sit and wait until a Russian partner obtains the papers. Keep the relationship alive, but don't overinvest time or money. Until a deal is signed, foreign companies should keep looking for a partner with all of the necessary documents.

Finally, it is also critically important for a foreigner to make sure that a given enterprise in which he would like to invest is willing to participate in a joint venture; meaning that the enterprise has sought or welcomed investment free of government interference. The Ministry of Foreign Economic Ties, which used to dictate everything in a command economy, is now supposed to act in only a regulatory capacity. Its job is to make sure that whatever agreement is signed between a Russian business and a foreign company follows protocol, and that the new entity doesn't overstep its legal bounds. Using government connections to strongarm a Russian business into a partnership is the wrong approach. If an enterprise doesn't want the partnership, no one should force it on them. From 1992 onwards, by law, joint ventures organized by the State have had to sell 50 percent of their hard currency revenues to the Russian government. Given the inflation rate for rubles, this is hardly an attractive prospect.

Foreigners must also understand that many of the Russians who put together joint ventures invest an enormous amount of their spare time and personal capital. They sacrifice weekends to pore over the texts of agreements and other documents. Meetings often take place at their apartments, with children exiled to the kitchen. What inspires these men and women is an idea, the fascinating prospect of doing something really new and useful with their lives. From the Russian perspective, the motivation to work in a joint venture remains personal satisfaction more than financial reward.

Foreign businesspeople often find it difficult to understand why their Russian partners sometimes lose interest in a deal even after an agreement has been reached, as sometimes happens. To an American, for example, a joint venture might represent only financial profit; to the Russian director, a joint venture might be just one more headache. Often, the director's only incentive is the remote chance he might get to travel abroad and buy a pair of Levis for his kids.

There is a difference in quality of investment for outsiders and Russians. Westerners sometimes invest money they can afford to risk losing. Russians, on the other hand, always have to invest their lives—all of the knowledge and experience they have gained over the years. Sometimes they get nothing for it, paticularly in those joint ventures created by the State, which snatches up nearly all of the profits.

Foreign investors, in other words, ought not take their Russian partners' efforts for granted. Russians need motivation. Incentive is, after all, the heart and soul of the capitalist system. Sometimes such motivation needs to be other than cash, because in many situations unless there is some type of back-room agreement by which the foreign partner secretly hands over part of his share of the profits, the Russian partner never shares in the wealth. He therefore needs to know that the time and effort he is putting in will lead to a better life for his children, and that his partner's view is as long as his.

It would be accurate to say that Russian business is going through a phase of "wild capitalism," a Klondike-like feverishness in which everyone smells money in the air and is testing the limits of new-found freedom. There are plenty of competent and even visionary Russian managers, such as Tzar, who would make ideal partners for joint ventures. Sharing the stage with them, however, and sometimes stealing the show, is a new breed of Russian manager: black marketeers—"sharks,"as we call them—who have managed to swim free of government regulations and are the first to head out into international waters (some even finding their way to the shores of the Hudson). There have always been black marketeers in the former Soviet Union, but what is new is that because they have working capital to do business with foreigners they are aggressively seeking out foreign partners in crime. Eventually, honest Russian managers will also make it into the mainstream of international business as enterprises become more and more independent. However, in the meantime, black market trade is a problem of considerable proportions.

The largest illegal Soviet fortunes were made in the *levak* trade. Levak means "left" and refers to the practice of selling goods from the back door. Stealing became rampant, and remains so. Everything, and especially consumer goods, is in short supply, and anyone with access to food products, goods, or services helps himself to an illegal commission.

Nobody knows exactly how rich Russian black marketeers are. Their profits are, shall we say, tax deductible, in that they are unreported. It is almost impossible for those who work for the State in some trading capacity, domestic or foreign, to remain honest.

Under Stalin, the State was so vigilant there was almost no organized crime. By contrast, the Brezhnev period was marked by near-total governmental paralysis and blindness. The top political leaders (especially those in the Ministry of the Interior) reminded one of the saying "A fish begins to rot from the head." The Minister of the

Interior himself, Comrade Schelokov, and his deputy, Comrade Churbanov, who also happened to be the beloved son-in-law of Brezhnev, actively engaged in illegal transactions. Minister Schelokov's wife, a leading light of high society, regularly "bought" confiscated jewelry, antiques, and art for her own collection from the ministry's treasury. Actually, anything that caught her eye would get confiscated and later find its way into her collection. Churbanov corrupted whatever good was left in the Ministry of the Interior. At one point, a general named Krilov started a crusade against crime and corruption in government. Churbanov fabricated a case against this honest man, who was so shamed by the dishonor that he committed suicide.

After Brezhnev's death, a case was opened against the Schelokovs and they, too, committed suicide. Churbanov was convicted of his crimes and is now doing time in a prison in the Urals, where he works as a sauna attendant. Others in the Brezhnev family have managed to keep their wealth and position. Brezhnev's granddaughter's husband, a man named Varakuta, has become active in several joint ventures.

The big-time thieves often formed strategic alliances with the Party bosses in creating a Soviet mafia. The republics of Azerbaijan and Uzbekistan provided the most fertile soil. The heads of the republics were themselves mob bosses. Like primitive conquerors, these criminal Party bosses surround themselves with their booty. Their residences look like warehouses of refrigerators, carpets, and TV sets.

Shiraf Rashidov, the Uzbekh leader, made a small fortune by cutting back-room deals on cotton. The First Party Secretary of Azerbaijan, Geidar Aliev, was one of Brezhnev's pals and a mob boss who would have made Al Capone shake in his shoes. Tall, handsome, irresistibly charming, smart, and as tough as an angry bull, Aliev was Azerbaijan's KGB boss before he became head of the republic; he therefore knows all, sees all, and has everyone under his callused thumb.

Aliev's private militia punished his enemies without mercy. No one will ever know the exact number or names of all of his victims. Under his malignant influence, corruption in the republic reached an unimaginable level. Everything has a price. The managers of State-owned stores routinely hike up prices and pocket the profits. Although Aliev had officially retired as a public official, he remained a national hero in Azerbaijan. In 1991, Aliev became president of the Republic of Nahichivan, which has autonomous status in Azerbaijan.

He has forged strong ties with Turkey (one of the keys to stability in this troubled region), and it seems unlikely, as long as everyone wants to keep the peace, that his power will in any way be threatened.

In 1990, when I asked the Minister of the Interior, Vadim Bakatin (who later became head of the KGB)—one of Yeltsin's competitors for the presidency—about the scale of the country's "shadow economy," he said it was worth half a trillion rubles. That was the figure being circulated by reactionary forces, who were urging a return to centralized power, and it is absurdly inflated. Were it accurate, the amount would almost equal the total national income of the former Soviet Union. A more realistic estimate of the black market's size is 100 billion rubles. (By point of comparison, the entire cash flow of the country at the time held at about 120 billion rubles.)

New openings for legitimate enterprise have also provided new opportunities for swindlers. When progressive Soviet economists launched an attack against the monopoly on State property, the result was those cooperatives I mentioned earlier, cooperatives in which citizens were permitted to invest their own money (although initially only retirees could work full time in these enterprises). The cooperatives might have solved some of the country's economic woes early on, but they were quickly infected by black marketeers and adventurers. It wasn't long before underground businesspeople established contacts with international criminal organizations, or with Western companies that although technically legitimate were not above doing a little business on the side with the black market.

Most of the activity in these cooperatives centered on barter deals, because they offered the easiest way to turn substantial profits. Outmoded industrial technologies meant that industrial waste was poorly processed and therefore very rich—and very profitable to recycle. Cooperative dealers were continually on the lookout for industrial waste and raw materials that could be exported for dollars. Goods legal in Russia but prohibited in other countries were in particular demand. For a time, urea fertilizer was queen of the market. Everyone became a specialist in urea. China started to buy it in huge quantities and prices skyrocketed. As a result, urea was overproduced and the prices dropped as dramatically.

Russian producers still have little chance to sell on world markets, which is why they continue to deal with shady foreign companies. These organizations bribe the new generation of bureaucrats, who are not very much different from the older generation, given that there are no democratic traditions in the country. A new kind of mafia has grown up around the barter market. Mafias are arguably a natural outgrowth of economic development, especially during the "wild" phase. Russia has no monopoly on corruption.

The obvious remedy for corruption is to give these businesses unlimited access to world markets. The cooperatives would then have to compete to survive. Understand, I'm not suggesting that the only prominent business figures in Russia are corrupt. In spite of their controversial qualities, those early Soviet cooperatives also spawned entrepreneurial talent. Armen Kazarian, one of the first brokers at the Moscow Commodity Exchange, has concluded contracts worth 300 million rubles. In 1991, twenty-two millionaires founded a club, their version of the communist ideal of solidarity among equals.

These Russian businesspeople have gotten bolder and bolder. Artem Tarasov, a successful young entrepreneur, was among the first businessmen to throw down the gauntlet before the socialist ethic. There was an uproar in 1988 when his monthly Party membership fee, 3 percent of total income, amounted to a million rubles. The Ministry of Finance immediately froze his bank account and launched an investigation. Tarasov explained that he had made his money merely by collecting unused industrial waste and selling it abroad (as I have suggested, a very lucrative short-term option). With the proceeds, he imported badly needed computers for Soviet enterprises. He then turned the tables on the ministry, suing them and winning. The State arbiter has ordered the ministry to return to him millions of rubles in compensation.

The famous Russian eye surgeon Svetoslav Fedorov has also proven how freedom can work to the people's benefit. He leased a hospital and research center from the State and turned it into a medical empire with centers across the country, ten joint ventures, and hospital ships touring Europe. He has not only helped thousands of patients, but created thousands of well-paying jobs.

How do common citizens feel about entrepreneurs such as Fedorov? They elected him to the Russian Parliament. Tarasov was elected as well.

The number of millionaires in the former Soviet Union is growing even though the purchasing power of the ruble is falling. To locate and name them, _Forbes_ magazine would have to hire the first private investigation agency in Russia, Alex, headquartered in St. Petersburg, to do considerable digging.

The establishment of normal, civilized, legitimate business will take time. Before 1987, when joint ventures were first legalized, business exchange in Russia was limited to primitive forms of barter and trade. Its true potential had not even begun to be realized. Russian business resembled the popular Russian folk hero, the giant Ilya Muromets. He slept in an oven (of the Russian variety—slightly more spacious than what you find in America) until he was thirty-three before beginning his epic adventures. Today, he is wide awake.

CHAPTER 11

The Beginning of a Beautiful Friendship

The ongoing political and economic struggles that chain millions of Russians, and, thanks to cable, a substantial number of foreigners worldwide, to their television sets every night are finally beginning to yield dividends. The concept of private property, once anathema to the very soul of the communist agenda, has taken hold.

I have argued that Russia is prepared for capitalism, and that the laws are in place for joint ventures. In January of 1987, when the Soviet Council of Ministers passed the Resolution on Joint Ventures, permitting their establishment and allowing Russians to go into business for themselves, a new era began. It started, symbolically, on New Year's Eve (according to the old Russian calendar), seventy years after the Revolution. The hard-liners, of course, were outraged. One of their leaders, Alexey Sergeev, one of Yeltsin's chief rivals for the Russian presidency, believes to this day that all of the economists from the Academy of Sciences should be sent to prison for "selling Russia." Fortunately, he is part of a dwindling minority.

Since then, in Russia, further legislation has opened the floodgates of private enterprise. In June of 1991, the Soviet Parliament passed the Law on Privatization, which in practical terms put nearly all State property up for sale, and from a foreign business perspective signaled tremendous new opportunities, since it meant that foreigners could purchase factories and stores in the former Soviet Union. (Only the purchase of military plants was prohibited.) On July 4, 1991, the Russian Parliament passed a law permitting foreigners to engage in practically any type of business activity in the republic and—this is key—to take all of their profits home. The other republics soon followed Russia's example and adopted their own laws on foreign investments. Today, foreign companies enjoy virtually the same rights domestic companies do. In some respects, foreigners have even more rights, particularly in the area of money management.

For the first time since the Soviets took power, legislation was ahead of reality, instead of lamely catching up with it. This is why although Russian businesses were eager to immediately begin working with foreign investors, they moved very cautiously. They simply couldn't believe they were finally free to do so. Initially, foreign investors were caught unprepared as well. They knew almost nothing about the new legislation and were extremely hesitant about risking their money.

Today, however, stock exchanges, commodity exchanges, wholly owned foreign companies, private banks, and private companies are now sprouting like flowers in springtime. German, American, Italian, Finnish, British, South Korean, Canadian, and Japanese companies are all jockeying for position. In 1992, some twenty-five ex-Soviet-American (including twelve Russian-American) joint ventures were being created every month, a testament to the feeling of kinship between Americans and Russians. It had taken the American community three years to gear up their joint-venture activity, in part because before 1992 the United States and other NATO countries, as well as Japan, couldn't export high technology and know-how to the Soviet Union. The Coordinating Committee for Multilateral Export Controls has now lifted some of its restrictions, which has helped speed up the pace of Western investment. IBM has established a wholly-owned company; General Electric created a joint venture; and Ford, Hewlett Packard, Eastman Kodak, Salomon Brothers, Goldstar, Sealand, AT&T, and EI DuPont de Nemours have all found their way to Russia.

When Russia's parliament adopted that resolution to begin privatization, it began an irreversible process. The government is convinced that technological backwardness is the main cause of the currency crisis, and in 1992 began an ambitious program to privatize

4.285 trillion rubles worth of State property by 1993. One and a half trillion rubles, or a little more than a third of the total, will be distributed among Russian workers (although I believe that only a portion of that reallotment will be available to them in 1992 and 1993). Russia had planned to privatize 96,000 companies in 1992. Only 42,000 were actually privatized; none were industrial giants. For 1993, the plan is to privatize 88,000 companies, including industial giants and, for the first time, military plants. Yeltsin and the Russian Parliament deserve credit for tying privatization and foreign investments to industrial reconstruction. Any foreign company interested in doing business should also find a way to tie these issues together.

Byelarus, the Ukraine, and the Baltic states have also developed an economic program, aimed at attracting foreign capital that defines priorities, directions, and key industries—as well as incentives and guarantees—for foreign investors. In 1993 and 1994, special attention will be given to attracting foreign investments in the hotel business, the medical industry, computers and software, waste recycling (food waste, lumber waste, and metal waste), the food industry, gas station construction, and automotive repair. In some republics, such as Russia, Armenia, Georgia, and Latvia, privatization of housing is the top priority. Significant attention will also be given to reconstruction, technical advancement, and the privatization of big industrial enterprises on the basis of competition. Outright private ownership of natural resources—mineral, timber, hydro, geological, seaport, and electric and gas supply enterprise—is prohibited, which is not likely to change.

Anyone looking for easy money—dividends in under two years—should not look to invest in the former Soviet Union. There can be short-term capital gains for trading companies, particularly those dealing in industrial waste, as I've said, but those who can make long-term commitments, with more than simply an infusion of cash, will achieve even more gratifying returns on their investments. Real estate prices are at rock bottom at the moment. If you pay ten thousand rubles for a percentage piece of property today, and wait a few years, inflation will mean that the value of the property in rubles will soar, particularly as the real estate market begins to boom—and everything indicates that it will, now that joint-venture activity is heating up. Inflation is also one of the reasons short-term, joint-venture investment makes little sense. Profits in rubles, when they are converted to dollars, will diminish. The dollar continues to rise against the Russian ruble, and the exchange rate might even reach about two thousand rubles to the dollar. In my view, it will go no higher than that. If and when it hits about 2,000, several years down the road, the dollar will begin to decline. At that point, the ruble will have the support it needs to stand more firmly in international exchange, and the newly privatized economy will be generating income.

This is why it makes far more sense for foreigners participating in a joint venture to leave their profits in the new company for reinvestment. State companies proposing joint ventures with outsiders are offering very generous percentages as incentives to foreign business, purposely underestimating the value of their own contribution. Such terms are critical. When the moment comes to remove such generous percentages, foreign joint-venture partners will earn profits according to the assessment of their initial investment—whether that investment be in know-how, technology, equipment, or capital. A foreign investor's patience will pay off.

The current "wild" phase the Russian economy is going through will eventually calm down; speculating wildly is the wrong response. Foreign investors should be cautious. State enterprises, or joint-stock companies formerly owned by the State, usually make for the safest partners, especially if you can offer them incentives. Anyone dealing with a cooperative, as I suggested in the last chapter, ought to be particularly careful and should make an extra effort to obtain very specific information about a partner's revenues and personnel. Legitimate cooperatives and private companies, particularly if they are linked to a large enterprise of good standing, should prove excellent partners for a joint venture.

Potential investors often wonder which is potentially more profitable: a joint venture or a wholly-owned company. Should they buy all of a Russian company or part of it? There are a number reasons investors might prefer one over the other. For example, if the foreign company or investment group is family owned, the preference might be to buy the Russian company outright. The problems and challenges associated with either choice are essentially the same, and their advantages even out. A wholly-owned company is less vulnerable to Soviet laws than a joint venture, and has more of a free hand to provide incentives to its workers. A joint venture, on the other hand, is initially more profitable, in that it can be partially capitalized in rubles. I would say that the best investment package is a joint venture

in a free economic zone, as that combines the best of both worlds—
managerial freedom and ruble capitalization.

There are nearly 350 wholly foreign-owned companies in Russia
alone, and the number will continue to grow. This raises a thorny
issue. I strongly believe that if a State company is for sale, it should
first be offered to its employees. If they can't buy the company, then,
and only then, should it be placed on the block. Employees ought to
have first right of refusal, despite the fact that their chances of finding
the money are slim. Most can barely make ends meet.

Employee ownership was one of the many points of contention
between Yeltsin and Gorbachev. Yeltsin thought that at least 25
percent of every factory's shares should go to the workers for free, so
that they could share in the bounty. They had earned this right, he
felt, by virtue of having toiled at the factory for years and getting
practically nothing in return. Yeltsin's line of thinking resembles Japanese corporate capitalism, which motivates workers to work harder
by giving them a real stake in the company. Gorbachev, on the other
hand, saw no reason why workers should be given any percentage of
a company's shares for nothing. Yeltsin won, and State employees
were given shares in the companies in which they worked—the 1.5
trillion rubles-worth I mentioned previously—beginning in January
of 1993, when auctions to sell off State companies got underway.

In addition to wholly-owned and joint ventures, a third configu-
ration for foreigners to consider is a trading business that can act as
an intermediary between Russian companies and foreign markets.
These companies, so essential for a market economy to work, were
legalized in November of 1991, when the Russian Parliament abolished the quotas that had been strangling exports and keeping trading companies from getting in the game. The quotas were imposed by
government hard-liners who wanted to maintain a monopoly on all
foreign trade. Today, only some exports are restricted: natural resources, chemicals, high technology, and military hardware. Some
experts claim that Russian-foreign joint ventures are not really creating industry inside Russia, but simply importing foreign equipment. In fact, total exports by Russian-American joint ventures, for
example (which are allowed to export only what they produce), are
twice their imports.

A trading company, created with the assistance of Karen J. Hedlund, a lawyer, is a good example of how well they can work. (That
the Russian business world even today is predominantly a male world

doesn't mean that foreign businesswomen will not be accepted. Russian businessmen often prefer negotiating with foreign businesswomen.) Born in Chicago, Hedlund spent a considerable amount of time in Alaska and, like me, loves the harsh beauty of the north. She carved out a niche for herself by negotiating for Western clients in the beauty and cosmetics industry. Thousands of State companies have hard currency, and many of the larger ōnes have gift and cosmetic stores for their employees. However, these stores' shelves are nearly empty. Hedlund's very shrewd reasoning was that by joining forces with these enterprises she could give foreign cosmetic companies the best chances for national distribution.

Many foreign companies are taking advantage of the distribution potential in Russia and have opened stores selling products for both hard currency as well as rubles. These companies include Estée Lauder, Nina Ricci, Polaroid Europe BW, Phillips, and Alan Manukian. Ruble sales are usually limited because store owners have to be assured they will be able to convert them into hard currency. Local authorities limit by means of rationing cards the amount of certain types of goods Russians can buy. Factory workers get these cards as a reward for good work.

A wholesale showroom of American products has been created in Moscow to sell goods to both individuals and to the twenty thousand Soviet enterprises that have hard currency. This project was put together by a Boston company, Bomosko. Companies with products on display include a number of well-known American names. A spokesman for the company estimated first-year sales at $200 million.

Polaroid conducts business through a combination trade and a joint-venture company. Polaroid's William J. McCune first got it going in 1985. In July of 1989, Svetozor, a joint venture manufacturing electronics blocks and other items marketable in the West for dollars, was founded. The dollars it generates go toward purchasing film and spare parts for Polaroid cameras assembled in Russia. These are then sold for rubles, which are reinvested, bartered, or auctioned off for hard currency.

In 1990, Japan's Minolta Corporation established a joint venture, Minolta Trading Ukraine, with a hard currency distribution trade company. MTU sells imported consumer goods for dollars inside the Ukraine, and markets Ukrainian-made goods abroad. Minolta underestimated the competitiveness of the market in the former Soviet Union, and MTU has been struggling; however, the trading company-joint venture hybrid is being used by a number of other companies.

Baskin-Robbins and J. Lyons & Company have opened an ice-cream joint venture in Moscow and plan to build an ice-cream production facility.

Foreign companies can also take advantage of existing trade agreements between the former Soviet Union and other countries to develop business. Politics and business have always been closely connected. For example, India's trade deficit with the former Soviet Union runs at about $15 billion. Indian companies sell their goods to Russian companies for rubles, which Indian banks convert into rupees. Rupees are easily convertible into dollars. The actual governmental agreement is more complex, but it boils down to hard currency for goods for rubles for hard currency. One of my clients has done very well selling Indian companies products that they then send to Russia and the other republics, getting rupees, not rubles, in exchange.

When a Russian partner proposes a location for a joint venture to a foreign investor, the first thing the investor usually wants to know is how close that location is to the Kremlin. The only thing the Kremlin produces is bureaucrats. Westerners in particular are still too anchored to Moscow.

Moscow-based joint ventures run into plenty of problems and get very little attention. Moscow's communication system might be the best the country has to offer, but successful joint ventures need more than efficient communications systems. They need powerful allies, inexpensive production facilities, and, most of all, individual attention. In Moscow, joint ventures get lost in the crowd. A good location outside Moscow, on the other hand, will make a foreign business the center of attention of regional bosses. This is one of the many reasons I have been promoting the Russian Far East so enthusiastically.

Currently, of the seven thousand two hundred total joint ventures in the former Soviet Union, about 34 percent of all Western joint ventures (and 61 percent of all Russian-American joint ventures) are located in Moscow (see appendix). The Russian Federation is home to more than four-fifths of all joint ventures. Estonia, the smallest of the former Soviet republics, has more joint ventures than either of the other two Baltic republics, Lithuania and Latvia. Turkmenia, Tadzhikistan, and Azerbaijan lag far behind the others. Azerbaijan provides probably the least desirable location for a joint venture because the political and financial risks are still so high. The other high-risk locations are Armenia, Tadzhikistan, Moldova, and Georgia. Between 1989 and 1992, I recommended to my Western clients that they not invest there. There are plenty of far more stable parts of the country.

As the independent republics struggle to get economically and politically on track, a certain amount of unrest is unavoidable. Civil war of any consequence is highly unlikely, however, although small-scale fighting between Armenia and Azerbaijan will continue, as will ethnic clashes in Georgia, Central Asia, and Moldova. On the whole, the leaders of the republics have proven that they can face most political and economic problems directly.

What's the timetable for the new order? The entities forming in the wake of the Soviet Union's breakup will develop nontraditional economic ties with one another. Until these ties become regularized, there are risks—risks toward which the new nations will develop protectionist stances as they come to understand their potential, and that political leaders on whom foreign investors bet will simply prove to be the wrong horses to back. But countries with common histories as former Soviet republics, or as traditional allies, will integrate into loose economic blocs of fully sovereign countries in the next few years. This will happen, I think, so that economies can be linked and strengthened. These new alliances offer rare opportunities for foreign business.

Every historical epoch creates its markets out of a blend of politics and economics, and this one will be no different. There was the Hanseatic League in the thirteenth to seventeenth centuries. There were the trade routes of the Age of Discovery. Now, America, Canada, and Mexico are uniting in one market, as are the European countries (albeit both instances with a few glitches).

The Soviet Union has already broken apart. Because of ethnic divisions, economic and social problems, and territorial disputes over rich natural resources, something similar is likely to happen in the Russian Federation. At least three republics—Tatar, Bashkir, and Checheno—will break away from Russia. For some of the same reasons, Georgia will probably lose the Republic of Abkhasia and the autonomous territory of South Ossetia.

This is not to diminish Russia's importance—and potential. It will still produce more oil each day than Saudi Arabia, Iraq, and Kuwait together, and more natural gas, steel, cement, and tractors than any other country in the world. Boris Yeltsin and other leaders know foreign, and particularly Western, participation offers the only path to economic revival. Foreigners will find it worth the effort, despite all of the problems, to join in. This book has talked about the former Soviet Union's absurdly low real estate prices, inexpensive skilled labor, and industrial waste crying out for recycling. The truth is that the former Soviet Union, and Russia in particular, still does not know its own worth.

Nor does the United States. The figures show the United States invested with more caution than other countries. Germany, Austria, Finland, Switzerland, Italy and, recently, Great Britain, have all surpassed the United States in the intensity of their joint venturing (see appendix). Austria alone, with a population smaller than that of Moscow, invested two billion Austrian shillings, which is, proportional to its size, much more than the United States.

Still, American companies are generally much more receptive to the possibilities now than they were even a year ago. They lead the field in heavy industry joint ventures, with 35 percent of the total. American joint ventures account for 12 percent of the total number of joint ventures in the former Soviet Union, and American capital represents 15 percent of the total capital ($3 billion as of January of 1993). In only 8 percent of all American joint ventures is the American partner's share of ownership higher than 70 percent; yet, in only 5 percent is it less than 30. Investment is growing quickly, and by the end of 1993, the total amount of American money invested in the republics might reach as high as $5 billion, putting the United States in first place in terms of authorized capital.

Some American consultants writing about business ventures in the republics focus only on the negative, citing reports indicating that 15 to 17 percent of the established joint ventures are actually in operation. In fact, as of July 1, 1992, at least a third of the registered joint ventures were active, already manufacturing goods, providing services, and generating profits. If that percentage still seems low, one must take into account the dynamics of the process. Because of bureaucratic problems during the transitional period, it took longer for new companies to go into operation. Since 1990, the number of industrial joint ventures has been growing faster than other types of joint ventures, and now amounts to nearly half the total amount. The rate of growth in terms of production volume is double that of the growth in terms of numbers of new businesses.

What about the quality of production? A glance at those countries that have become the largest consumers of Russian goods says a great deal. Japan is the largest consumer of joint-venture products, with Germany and Austria right behind. The United States seems to be an outsider to this group, which might account for the American perception that Russian joint ventures are less than optimally productive. Conversely, these joint ventures import most of their goods from Germany, Poland, Norway, and Denmark, rather than from the United States.

By January of 1993, the net worth of all joint ventures and wholly-owned foreign businesses in Russia reached $2 billion. Again, about 34 percent are located in Moscow—a drop of 5 percent from the previous year, which means that joint ventures are being created more rapidly in the provinces than in the capital. By August of 1992, there were ninety-five joint ventures in operation in Siberia, or about 9.3 percent of all operational joint ventures in all of Russia.

I have talked about how difficult it was to get reliable information from the Soviets, and that official information is *still* not reliable; not because the government is unwilling to release the facts, but because Russian companies have been trying to hide their true income, especially in hard currency, from the government. They know the government will open accounts, for whatever amount these companies make, in the Russian Vnesheconombank, the State bank for foreign trade—whose interest rates are lower than those of foreign banks. Also, Vnesheconombank can freeze accounts at any moment without justification. This is why the official dollar amount of foreign joint-venture export activity in 1992 was $1.387 billion. By my own estimate, the figure should have been closer to $3.8 billion. Similarly, the official number for import was $1.725 billion, and my estimate was about $1.9 billion. Russian companies are trying to conceal their money in foreign banks.

Until 1861, when serfdom was abolished, Russian serfs were allowed by their owners to leave their village to start their own businesses, provided they paid monthly fees to their owners. Some of these serfs went on to become outstanding actors, scientists, and merchants. Still, they had to pay a"quit rent" because they physically belonged to someone else. Stalin revived serfdom under a different name. Even today, Russian engineers, workers, and managers working in State enterprises, or in joint ventures established by these enterprises, largely remain just peasants forced to fork over their quit rent. I am certain the current process of privatization and internationalization of State businesses, now that it is beginning to accelerate, will change this relationship between the individual and the State, thereby changing not only the way Russians do business, but the way they live.

Paving the way to economic freedom and a free-market system has not been easy. My country's people have had to start from scratch. Joint ventures and free economic zones came as the result of bitter battles against those hard-liners who think that doing business with foreigners corrupts the soul. The majority of Russians know that it frees the spirit.

Ever since my Arctic expedition, when I stood on the deck of our expedition boat and gazed at the dark shore of America, I have devoted my professional life to helping bring the East and the West together economically. Yet, I am well aware that success will not come cheaply. Many attempts at establishing joint ventures have failed—some even before they got started. I began this book with the example of ACC, which never did succeed in getting the approval it sought. I knew when I was invited to partipate in the proceedings that ACC had made mistakes, and that those mistakes would be repeated by other foreign companies trying to forge links with Russian companies. I know now that the biggest mistake ACC made was in stepping out of the ring. The only losers are quitters. Even with all of the uncertainties and miscommunications, there was then, as there is now, everything necessary for the beginning of a beautiful and mutually profitable friendship.

Appendix

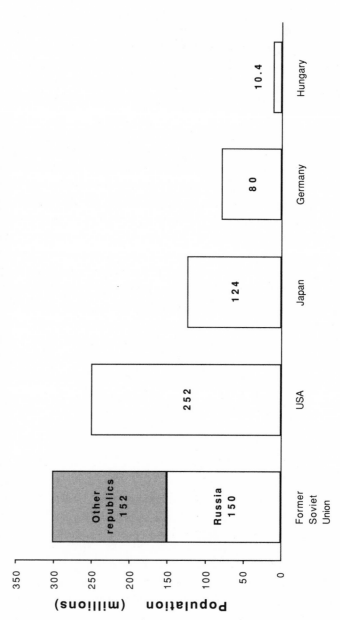

Population Comparison of
Selected Industrialized Nations

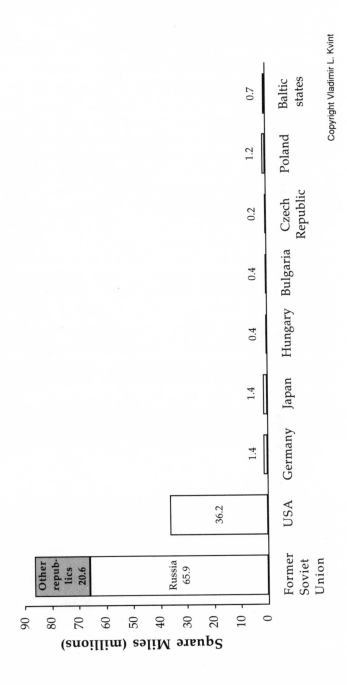

Total Area Comparison of
Selected Industrialized Nations

Square Miles (millions)

Copyright Vladimir L. Kvint

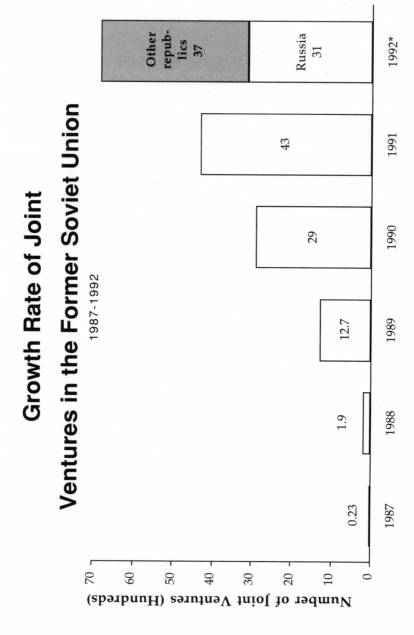

Growth Rate of Joint Ventures in the Former Soviet Union
1987-1992

*Projected as of July of 1992

Location of Joint Ventures
As of July of 1992
(percentage)

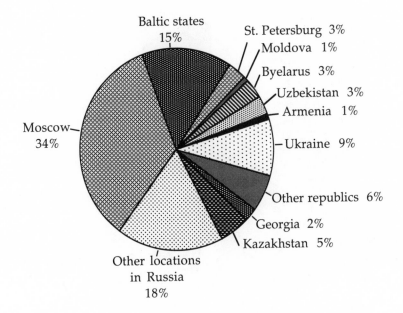

Baltic states 15%

St. Petersburg 3%

Moldova 1%

Byelarus 3%

Uzbekistan 3%

Armenia 1%

Moscow 34%

Ukraine 9%

Other republics 6%

Georgia 2%

Kazakhstan 5%

Other locations in Russia 18%

Nations Engaging in
Joint Ventures

(percentage)

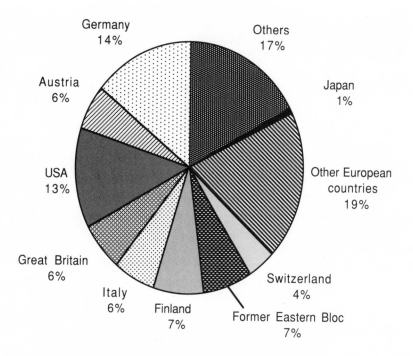

Germany 14%

Others 17%

Japan 1%

Austria 6%

Other European countries 19%

USA 13%

Switzerland 4%

Great Britain 6%

Italy 6%

Finland 7%

Former Eastern Bloc 7%

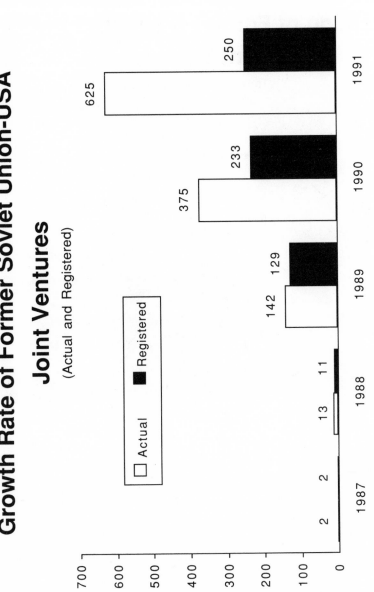

Growth Rate of Former Soviet Union-USA Joint Ventures (Actual and Registered)

Location of Former Soviet Union-USA Joint Ventures

Through January of 1992

(percentage)

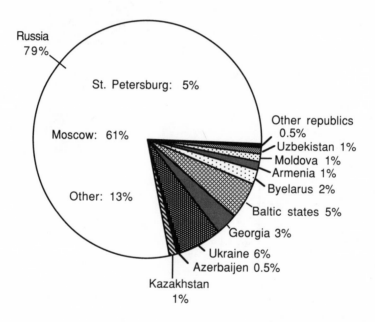

Reasons for Joint-Venture Failure

(percentage)

Established joint
ventures
8%

Unfavorable
feasibility/market study
5%

Other problems
3%

Unfavorable negotiations
10%

Legal problems
10%

No partner found
28%

Bureaucratic problems
16%

Financing
20%

Index

Abalkin, Leonid, 141, 145
Abkhasia Republic, 208
Academy of Sciences, 114, 116, 139, 201
  Institute of Economy, 16, 116, 141, 145
  Russian, 34
  Siberian branch, 128, 129–131
  Soviet, 29, 33
accounting and auditing, 4, 184–186
Aenne Burda GmbH, 68
Aganbegian, Abel, 47, 115–116
agriculture, 54
Alan Manukian company, 206
Alaska, 36, 37, 157–158, 164, 169
alcoholism and drinking, 60, 110
Aliev, Geidar, 197–198
aluminum, 28, 60, 67, 135
American International Group, 138
Amur River/Region, 169, 179
Andropov, Yuri V., 7, 19, 70

Angara River, 124, 136
anonymka (anonymous letter), 69–70, 107, 108, 109, 111, 172
Arctic, 29, 33, 34, 35, 146, 168–169, 176
  investment opportunities, 176–177, 179, 180
  natural resources, 176, 178, 179
Arctica complex, 28
Arctic Ocean, 168
Arctic Seaway, 28, 29, 33
  shipping, 36, 160, 168, 177
Arkhangelsk, European Russia, 150
Armenia, 142, 143, 203, 208
Arthur Andersen & Co., 185
Astrakhan oil fields, Kaspian region, 34
AT&T, 169, 202
Australia, 150, 157
Austria, 209, 210
automation, 71, 97, 103, 115

automobile production and repair, 2, 203
Azerbaijan, 34, 51, 197, 207, 208
AZLK automobile plant, 185

Baikal, Lake, 150
Baikal-Amur Railway, 36, 57, 160, 167, 179
Baikal-Amur Region, 167
Bakatin, Vadim, 198
Baku oil fields, 34
Baltic republics, 59, 142, 144, 203, 207. *See also* Estonia; Latvia; Lithuania
Bandera, Stepan, 44
bankruptcy, 73, 78, 186, 187
banks, 4, 8, 90, 182, 183, 210
  foreign-owned, 138–139
  interest rates, 4, 22, 122, 182, 210
  private, 3, 202
Barclays Bank, 17
barter system, 22, 23, 128, 184, 200
  in cooperatives, 198–199
  in joint ventures, 107, 122
Bartram, David, 11
Bashkir Republic, 208
Baskin-Robbins, 207
"bearded" (unfinished) sites, 85, 122
Belgium, 141
Bering Strait, 36, 40–41
Bismarck, Otto von, 9
blacks, 148–149
blat ("connections"), 14, 49
bonuses. *See* labor force
Bosmosko joint venture, 206
Boys of the North juvenile camp, 93–94
Brezhnev, Leonid, 70, 129, 196, 197
bribery, 24, 25, 26–27, 38, 50, 54–55, 105, 106, 126, 175
Britain, 147, 202, 209
British Petroleum, 35
Brodsky, Joseph, 51
brokerage houses, 3

Brynner, Yul, 142
Burda Moden Russia magazine, 68–69, 181
Bush, George, 13, 61, 157
business practices, 3, 10
  bureaucracy and, 65–66, 67, 78
  misreporting of figures, 89
  negotiations, 4, 9, 11–12, 24, 38, 86, 139–140, 157, 194
  personal relationships, 64–65, 69, 105–106, 153
Byelarus, 59, 138, 142, 143, 203

C. Itoh, 169
Canada, 57, 152, 202, 208
cartels, 171–172, 174
Case of the 140 Billion, 12, 15–17
Caspian Sea, 34
Castro, Fidel, 57
Catherine the Great, 123
censorship, 7
Central Asia, 34, 51, 116, 208
Central Statistical Bureau, 10
Chase Manhattan Bank, 9
Checheno Republic, 208
chemical industry, 131
Chernenko, Konstantin, 7
Chernobyl disaster, 101
Chevron-Tengiz joint venture, 12, 13, 14–15, 19–20, 181
Chicago Board of Trade, 184
China, 43, 57–58, 135, 141, 158, 164
  investment in Russia, 157, 198
Chukotka province, Siberia, 59, 169, 170
CitiBank, 144
coal, 7, 28, 131, 162, 164, 167, 176, 179
cobalt, 6, 28
Commercant newspaper, 18, 19, 189
Committee for Precious Metals and Stones, 169, 170
commodity exchanges, 3, 144, 183–184, 199, 202

Communar gold mine, 172
communes, 45
Communism, 1, 7, 41–42, 57, 113, 190
labor and management under, 44, 51, 63
Communist Party, 7, 21, 27, 69, 120
Central Committee, 103, 115, 120, 191
continuing influence of, 120–121
joint ventures and front companies, 189, 190, 191
computer equipment, 192–193, 194, 199, 203
concession law, 117
condoms, 52
Constitution, 137
construction industry, 48–50, 97, 126, 167
joint ventures, 2, 128
unfinished sites, 85, 122
consulting groups, 8, 11–12, 139
consumer products, 3, 40, 106, 152, 161
joint ventures, 209–210
legislation, 91–92
shortages, 92–93, 182–183, 196, 206
transfer deals, 16–17
cooperatives, 52, 62, 90, 184, 198, 204
barter system in, 198–199
recycling by, 93, 198
regional authority and, 121
Coordinating Committee for Multilateral Export Controls, 202
copper, 6, 28, 71, 143
corporations, multinational, 128. See also enterprises; joint ventures
cosmetics industry, 205–206
Cossacks, 60, 109, 110
Council of Ministers, 17, 114, 115, 116, 126, 137
countertrade system, 22
Credobank, 183

crime, organized, 196–198, 199
currency/money, 16, 20
auctions, 22, 142
clearing, 90–91
exchange rate, 17
hard, 16, 22–23, 62, 67, 78, 158, 182, 206
See also ruble
Customs Commission, 187
Cyprus, 189
Czechiya, 144

Dagestan Republic, 51
Daimler Benz, 169
"dead souls" (unnecessary workers), 50–51, 62
De Beers Centenerary (de Beers), 22, 170
debt, 22–23
Decree of Support to State Enterprises, 187
Denmark, 210
Department for International Cooperation, 26
Department for Marine Expeditions, 29
Deutsche Aerospace, 169
Dialogue joint venture, 191–192
diamond(s), 67, 101, 169
mining operations, 169–170, 171
reserves, 22, 23
Siberian, 6, 71, 104
state fund, 22
disclosure, 10. See also secrecy
Documents of Unseen Works, 58–59
Dolgih, Vladimir, 129, 132–133, 173, 175
Dove Trading International, 18
DuPont, 65, 202

Eastern Europe, 8
East Germany, 51–52, 118, 190
Eastman Kodak, 202
East Prussia, 144
ECO magazine, 47, 141

economic programs, 116
  joint ventures and, 114
  regional, 117, 121–122, 123, 139
  State, 126, 128, 136, 139
economy, 65, 117, 182, 204
  command, 4, 63, 195
  decline and collapse, 7, 23, 100
  market, 2, 8, 145
  reforms, 7, 145, 182
  semicapitalist, 62
ELF Aquitaine, 15, 20
emigration and travel laws, 13, 21
energy, 128, 178
  geothermal, 165
  hydroelectric, 28, 125–126, 128,
    132, 134, 135, 161
  synthetic fuel, 179
enterprises
  foreign-owned, 202, 204
  individual, 116, 121
  privatized, 185–186, 202–203, 210
  regional, 116
  See also State enterprises
Entin, Grigory, 178
environmental concerns, 35, 36–37,
  135, 150–151, 164, 175
Estee Lauder cosmetics, 206
Estonia, 143, 207
Eurofin, Ltd., 17
Europe, 8, 179, 180, 208
European Economic Community, 22,
  180, 187
European Russia, 143
expeditions by Kvint
  Arctic, 29–33, 40–41, 176–178
  Far East, 29
  Mongolia, 16
  Russian ports, 159, 160–163
  Siberia, 29, 124
export(s), 12, 16, 103–104, 169
  joint ventures and, 122
  quotas, 11, 205
  restrictions, 104, 205
Exxon, 35, 128

Far North, 143
Fata company, 122
Fedorov, Svetoslav, 199
Ferrostaal AG, 68
File 2, 73. *See also* bankruptcy
Filshin, Gennady, 16, 18
Finland, 119, 146, 147, 159, 202, 209
Finnair, 188
First Department, 10
fishing industry, 162, 163–164, 177
food industry, 2, 8, 203
Forbes magazine, 8, 199
Ford, 65, 202
France, 15
fraud, 58–59
free economic zones, 141, 142–143,
  146, 152, 156, 158, 171, 180,
  181, 211
  currency policy and, 22
  defined, 141–142
  joint ventures in, 204–205
  locations of, 142–143, 145, 161
furniture industry, 146, 147

Gaidar, Yegor, 104
gas, 34, 39, 40, 203
  Arctic, 176
  Far East, 156, 164
  investment opportunities, 146
  Russian, 23, 36, 39, 40, 208
  Siberian, 6, 28, 34–36, 37, 71, 131
General Electric, 8, 65, 202
Georgia, 203, 208
geothermal power plants, 165
Germany, 135, 144, 202, 209, 210
Gibbins, Colin S., 15, 17, 18
Gidan Peninsula, 35
glasnost, 7, 15, 68, 190
Global Air Transportation Systems and
  Services, 169
Gogol, Nikolai, 51, 107
gold, 28, 67, 71, 103, 104, 164, 169,
  172, 175
  cartels, 171–172, 174

gold (*cont.*)
  mining operations, 170–171, 173, 174–175
  reserves, 22, 175
  Siberian, 170, 172, 174–175
Goldstar company, 202
Gorbachev, Mikhail, 7, 13, 103, 133, 137, 157, 175, 190, 191
  economic policy, 152
  fiscal and monetary policy, 4, 21
  labor policy, 47, 51–52
  Lithuania and, 7–8, 17
  loss of power, 12–13, 14, 17, 40, 68
  Yeltsin and, 8, 12, 15–16, 17, 181, 205
Gorbachev, Raisa, 68, 156
Gorbachev Foundation, 153
Gorevka lead deposit, 124–127, 128–129, 130, 131, 132, 134, 136
Gosplan, 125, 126, 129, 137
Grandma Yaga folk character, 174
Guangz Hou free economic zone, China, 158
Gubkin oil field, Siberia, 131
Gulag prison system, 43, 179
Gurtovoy, Mikhail, 19

Hakassia Republic, Siberia, 29, 60, 172
Hedlund, Karen J., 205–206
Hewlett Packard, 202
Hint, Dr., 70
Honeywell, 191
hotel industry, 203
Hotel Savoy (formerly Berlin), Moscow, 188–189
housing, 46, 97–98, 152, 174, 203
Hudenko, Ivan, 70
Hussein, Saddam, 39
hydroelectric power plants, 28, 125–126, 128, 132, 134, 135, 161
Hyposwiss Bank, 17

IBM, 169, 202
Igarka, Siberia, 148, 150

Ilya Muromets folk character, 200
Importers and Exporters Association of Taiwan, 157
Inaudit, auditing company, 185
incentives, 100, 152
  financial, 56, 62, 100, 103, 105
  for joint ventures, 105–196, 201–202
Incombank, 183
India, 207
Indigirka River, 36, 169
Industrial Robots: An Introduction (Kvint), 115
industry, 8, 52, 139
  heavy, 3, 59, 209
inflation, 4, 23, 46, 182, 203
information, unreliability of, 10, 22, 123, 210
infrastructure, 3, 59, 131, 180
inspection, annual financial, 107
insurance companies, 138
interest rates, 4, 22, 122, 182, 210
intermediary companies, 12
International Monetary Fund, 3, 22, 152, 182
international organizations, 198
Iraq, 39, 40, 208
Irkutsk, Siberia, 37
iron, 164
Italy, 122–123, 184, 202, 209

J. Lyons & Company, 207
Japan, 115, 150, 151, 152, 160, 179, 210
  investment in Russia, 8, 34, 152–153, 156, 157, 160, 202, 265
  investment in the Ukraine, 206
  labor force, 43, 205
  oil and gas investments, 36, 40
  trade with Russia, 156, 162, 167, 176
Japanese Union of Entrepreneurs, 152
Jewish Autonomous Region, 143, 151, 164
Jews, 57, 94–95

joint stock companies, 52, 204
joint ventures, 2, 63, 75, 90, 201–202, 209, 211
  barter system and, 107, 122
  capitalization of, 192, 195, 204, 209
  certification of, 11–12, 136, 193, 194
  Communist Party, 189, 190, 191
  economic programs and, 114, 117
  failure of, 66, 68–69, 181–182, 186, 192, 209, 211
  industrial, 209
  laws, 137, 201, 204
  leased companies and, 62
  length of investment, 203–204
  location choices, 207, 210
  partners for, 181–182, 188, 192, 195, 204
  profits from, 195–196
  vs. purchase of company, 204
  quality of production, 209–210
  U.S./Russian, 2, 8, 156, 158, 202, 205, 209

Kaliningrad Region, 143–144
Kamchatka Peninsula, 36, 151, 162, 164, 165
Kamchatka Petfield joint venture, 158
Kamchatka Shipping company, 162
Kansk-Achinsk Fuel and Energy Complex, 131
Kapora Holdings Company, Ltd., 189, 190
Kara Sea, 176–177
Kask, Richard, 161
Kazakhstan Republic, 51, 116
  oil, 14, 15, 20, 34
Kazarian, Armen, 199
KGB, 18, 70, 79, 86
Khabarovsk Region, 119, 146, 150, 151, 156, 171
Khantaiskaya HPP, 28
Khazars, 60
Khrushchev, Nikita, 130, 145, 157

Kiev, Ukraine, 60, 145
Kievan Russia, 60
Kirgizia, 3, 57–58
Koenigsberg, 144
Kohl, Helmut, 190
Kolargon prison, Norilsk, Siberia, 61
Komsomol, 148, 149, 150
Koncrin, Yegor, 57
Korea, 157, 164
Kosygin, Aleksei, 130, 132
Krasniy Mountain, Siberia, 109–110
Krasnoyarsk Region, 27, 28, 37, 43, 48, 109–110, 134, 135
  aluminum industry, 59–60
  natural resources, 71, 116–117, 147
Krasov, Lev, 106, 171
Kremlin, 63, 114, 115, 116, 121, 137
  joint ventures in Moscow and, 207
Kruchkov, Vladimir, 18
Kular, Siberia, 170, 174, 175
Kureiskaya HPP, 28
Kuril Islands, 151, 163, 165
Kuwait, 39, 208

labor force, 43–44, 52, 57, 61–62, 205
  bonuses, 91
  cost of, 142, 208
  foreign, 47, 61
  housing for, 46, 97–98, 152, 174
  investment considerations, 44–45
  living standard, 45–47, 58, 91, 174, 176
  relocation of workers, 56–57
  shortages, 4
  unemployment, 4, 51–52, 165
  unnecessary workers, 50–51, 62
  wages, 45–46, 48, 50, 54, 55–56, 75, 91
  women in, 71
Lake Svatikovo, Siberia, 85–86
land. See property
Land Codex, 138
Latvia, 203, 207

Law of Enterprise, 107, 186, 187
Law of the State Enterprise, 137
Law on Bankruptcy, 187
Law on Privatization, 201–202
Law on Property, 142
Law on Sale of State Property and
    Privatization, 138, 139
laws and acts, 137, 139, 186
    concession, 117
    consumer product, 91–92
    emigration, 13
    foreign investment, 122, 137–138,
        139, 171, 202
    joint venture, 201, 204
    land and property ownership, 3, 6,
        138–139, 142
    privatization, 3, 122, 138, 201
lead, 124, 127, 130–131, 135, 136
leasing of companies, 62, 138
Legislative Basis for Leasing, 138
Lena River, 34, 36
Lenin, Vladimir, 43, 91, 115, 194
Lesosibirsk, 148
Levsha folk character, 54
licenses, 16, 193–194
liquid fuel, 131
Lithuania, 8, 17, 60, 143, 144, 207
living standards, 45–46, 58, 91, 174,
    176
lumber. *See* timber
"lumps" (bosses), 12

McCune, William J., 206
McDermott International, 36, 156
McDonald's, 8, 67
mafia, Soviet, 197, 199
Magadan, Far East, 156, 158, 160,
    162, 164
management, 9, 11, 66, 74, 108, 188,
    202
    American system, 58, 62
    Communist, 63
    employee relations, 173
    restrictions on, 74–75, 76

    spending power, 89–90
    wages, 46
Management Partnerships Interna-
    tional, 192
Marathon Oil Corporation, 35, 36,
    156
Mari El Republic, 122–123
market(s), 66–67, 130–131, 187–189,
    208
    black, 106, 172, 196–197, 198
    economy, 2, 8, 145
    free, 8, 11, 14, 74, 138, 158, 211
    real estate, 98, 203, 208
    world, 198, 199
Marxism, 23, 153
mat (obscenities), 32, 33, 55, 82, 96,
    115
media/press, 7, 19–20, 47, 140
medical industry, 203
Medveshie gas field, Siberia, 131
mentality, 3, 64–65, 109–110
Merchant Marine, 29, 33
Messoiaha, Siberia, 28
metals/metallurgy, 23, 164, 176
    nonferrous, 23, 44, 67, 71, 164,
        173, 176
    See also specific metals and ores
Mexico, 208
Middle East, 2, 36, 39, 40
military production, 106, 146
mineral fertilizer, 23
mining industry and technology, 94,
    101
    bucket dredge (*draga*) system, 94,
        103–105, 173
ministries (general discussion), 11–12,
    26, 75, 78, 79, 85
    economic programs and, 117
    joint ventures and, 116, 128–129,
        133
    research institutes, 139
Ministries
    Civil Aviation, 169
    Economic Forecasting, 125

Ministries (*cont.*)
  Economics, 125, 139
  Energy, 125–126
  Finance, 16, 52, 182, 193, 199
  Foreign Economic Ties, 18, 193–194, 195
  Geology, 6, 10, 11, 27
  Interior, 197
  Justice, 16
  Nonferrous Metallurgy, 94, 101–102, 172, 174
  Oil and Gas, 14
  Radio Industry, 122
Minolta Corporation, 206
Minolta Trading Ukraine (MUT), 206
Minusinsk, Siberia, 161
Mitsubishi Corporation, 156, 159
Mitsui and Company, 36, 156
MMM Consortium, 36
Mobil, 35
Moldova, 59, 208
Molodaya Gvardia publishing company, 194
molybdenum, 85, 111
money. *See* currency/money; ruble
Mongols, 60
Morgenstern, Michael, 189–190
Mosbusinessbank, 183
Moscow, 34, 145, 207, 210
Moscow Commodity Exchange, 199
Moscow News, 19
Moscow University, 192
Moshaiskov, Oleg, 17
Mosinzhstroy unit, 188
Most Favored Nation status, 13, 187
Motorola, 11
Muscovy principality, 60
Muslims, 59

Nadeshda copper works, 126
Nakhodka, Russia, 145, 156, 159, 160
Nansen, Fridtjof, 27, 29, 177, 199
NATO, 202

natural resources (general discussion), 3, 11, 23, 29, 36, 203
negotiations. *See* business practices
nesuni (thieves, "carriers"), 52
Nicholas I, Czar of Russia, 57, 170
nickel, 6, 28, 71
Nina Ricci cosmetics, 206
NKVD, 173
nomads, 59, 60
Norilsk, Siberia, 28, 37, 43, 47–48, 53, 56, 135, 174–175
  labor and prison camps, 44, 61
Norilsk Concern, 28, 43, 48, 69, 173, 179
North Pole, 29
North Sea, 37
Norway, 210
Novgorod Region, 143, 145–146

Ob-Yenisey Region, 2, 161
Ohio River, 161
oil resources and production, 2, 19, 34, 39, 40
  Arctic, 176, 179
  exports, 20, 39, 40, 128
  Far East, 3, 34, 36, 40, 164
  investment opportunities, 146
  Kazakhstan, 39
  Russian, 23, 34, 35, 36, 38, 39, 40, 208
  Siberian, 10–11, 27–28, 34–36, 37, 38, 39–40, 71, 131–132
OPEC, 34, 39

Pacific Rim, 36, 40, 146, 156, 157, 159, 167
Papanin, Ivan, 29–33
Paramushir Island, Far East, 163
Parliament, Russian, 2, 8, 12, 27, 139, 152, 191
  investment legislation, 202, 203
  private property legislation, 6, 138, 142, 201–202
Parliament, Soviet, 138

partnerships, 52, 62, 63, 66
Pavlov, Valentin, 16, 17, 104
Peat Marwick, 185
People's Control Board, 108–109
Pepsico, 8, 65
perestroika, 7, 65, 145, 152
Perestroika joint venture, 188–190
Perry, Robert, 29
Peter the Great, 145
petrochemical industry, 38, 131
Petropavlovsk-Kamchatsky, Far East,
    152, 156, 162
Phillips, 206
platinum, 28
Plekhanov Institute of National Econ-
    omy, 74
Pochinok, Alexander, 17–18
Poland, 23, 60, 144, 210
Polaroid Europe BW, 206
Politburo, 63, 129
pood (measure of weight), 66
Primorsky Region, 142, 146
Primorzoloto Company, 171
pripiska (inflation of figures), 89
private sector, 3, 62, 93
Privatization Program, 2–3, 142
production system, Soviet, 63
productivity rates, 50–51, 54, 90,
    178
    foreign workers and, 57–58
profits, 93–94, 105, 119, 190, 203–
    204
propaganda, 57, 95, 101, 123, 148–
    149
property
    laws, 3, 138–139, 142
    privatization of, 6, 138, 201, 202–
        203
    State, 90, 101, 137–138, 198
prostoy (idle waiting), 49
Putnik joint venture, 189, 190

Questions of Economy journal,
    137

Rashidov, Shiraf, 197
real estate market, 98, 203, 208
recycling, 92–93, 198
regional authority, 116–121, 133
regional programs, 117, 121–122,
    123, 139
research, 91, 115, 116, 139
Resolution of Joint Ventures, 201
Reuther, John S., 188, 189–190
Richi, G., 191
Rizshkov, Nicolai, 38, 104, 112
robotization program, 101–103,
    115
Rose, Hazel, 153–156
Rotterdam, 160
Royal Dutch/Shell, 35
ruble, 182, 206
    inconvertibility of, 20, 21–22, 23,
        46, 89–90, 142, 206–207
Rufaudit, 185
Russia, 2, 8, 16, 28, 60, 180, 203
    currency laws, 142
    European, 143–146
    free economic zones in, 145
    unemployment, 51
"Russia: Capitalism Now!" (Kvint),
    45
Russian Far East, 29, 57, 119, 156,
    164, 165–167, 169
    free economic zones, 145, 161
    gas deposits, 40
    investment opportunities, 143, 146,
        152, 156, 158–159, 163, 164,
        165, 207
    metals and precious stones, 164,
        169, 170
    natural resources, 3, 151–152, 156
    oil fields, 34, 36, 40, 164
    timber, 146–148
Russian Federation, 207, 208
Russian Oil and Gas Sourcebook, 10
Russian Republic, 51
Russian State Property foundation,
    138

"Russia Should Quit the Soviet Union" (Kvint), 8
Rutskoy, Alexandr, 151

St. Petersburg, 34, 118, 119, 142, 159
Sakhalin Island/Region, 36, 40, 142, 146, 151, 160, 162, 165
   gas and oil fields, 156, 164
Salomon Brothers, 202
Saudi Arabia, 2, 39, 208
saunas, 109, 110, 111
Sayano-Shushenskaya HPP, 126, 132, 161
Scandinavia, 60
School for Young Managers, 74
schools, 174–175
Scientific-Industrial Union, 191
scientific-technical corporations (STCs), 91, 94, 95, 105
Sealand, 202
secrecy, 58, 64, 79
Semper Bio-Technology, 20–21
Sergeev, Alexy, 201
sexual harassment, 173
shareholding companies, 63, 138, 158
Shell Development, 156
Shevchenko oil fields, 34
Shikotan Island, Far East, 165
shipping and ports, 159–160, 162
   icebreakers, 168, 177–178
ship repair, 158–159, 162
shito-krito (buried and gone), 59
shortages, 67–69, 75, 89, 164, 169, 181
   consumer products, 92–93, 182–183, 196
   housing, 97
Shtil, Victor, 189
SibAuto (Siberian Nonferrous Metallurgy Automation Company), 66–67, 91
   Bazooka project, 83–84, 95
   bucket dredge (*draga*) automation system, 94, 103–105, 173

chandelier production, 92–93, 105–107
diamond mining operations, 169–170
Geophysica division, 79, 80
housing project, 97–98
robotization program, 101–103
Siberia, 36–37, 54, 57, 116–117
   aluminum industry, 60
   gas, 6, 28, 34–36, 37, 71, 131
   gold, 103, 170, 172, 174–175
   investment/joint ventures in, 28, 36–37, 179, 210
   labor camps, 43, 44
   natural resources, 3, 6, 10, 33–34, 71, 124, 161, 179
   oil, 10–11, 27–28, 34–36, 37, 38, 39–40, 71, 131–132
   timber, 147, 150
   weather, 35, 47–48
Siemens company, 118–119, 128
Silaev, Ivan, 16
silver, 124
Slavianka, 158, 159
Slovakia, 144
Solioninskoye, Siberia, 28
South Africa, 18, 22
South Korea, 150, 151, 156, 157, 162, 179, 202
South Ossetia, 208
Sovetskaya-Gavan, 151, 158, 162
Soviet Economic-Mathematical School, 129
Soviet Exhibition of National Economic Achievements, 192
Soviet Exporters Association, 157
Soviet Union, 13, 51, 60–61, 170
SovItalprodmash joint venture, 122
Stalin, Joseph, 7, 22, 43, 59, 132, 144, 173, 179, 196, 210
state committees, 26
state enterprises, 62, 78, 79, 90, 93, 121, 137, 138
   as joint venture partners, 204
   privatization of, 210

state enterprises (*cont.*)
  productivity, 171, 172
  wages, 91
  worker-owned, 205
steel industry, 23, 100, 164, 208
Sterkh joint venture, 191
stock exchanges, 3, 183–184, 202
Stenkard, Frank, 9
Strauss, Robert, 136
Stroev, Andrey, 188
subsidies, 3, 186–187
Supplies Committee, 194
Svetozor joint venture, 206
Sweden, 54, 145
Switzerland, 209

Tadzhikistan, 59–60, 207, 208
Taimir Peninsula, 34, 179
Taiwan, 157
Talleyrand, Charles, 35
Tarasov, Artem, 199
Tataria, 59
Tatar Republic, 208
tax(ation), 3, 4, 139, 143, 185, 187
  double, 62, 139, 187
  shelters, 189
Tazov Peninsula, 35
technology, 11, 202
Tehknobank, 183
telephones, 105
television, 8, 106, 174, 201
Tengiz Region, 12, 13
Terney national preserve, Far East,
  150–151
theft, 52, 196–198
timber, 23, 132, 146–148, 150, 162,
  176
Time Manager International A/S, 193
tourism, 165
trade, 8, 22
  agreements, 2, 13–14, 206–207
  boards, 8, 184
  unions, 56, 91
  See also barter system

trading companies, 205
transportation, 2, 144, 167, 177, 178
  air, 169
  rail, 36, 57, 160, 164, 167–168,
    178, 179
  shipping, 159–160, 161, 168, 169,
    176
Trans-Siberian Railway, 167, 168
travel restrictions, 13, 21, 88–89
Trishka folk character, 72
Trudeau, Pierre, 57
Tumanov, Vadim, 171
tuneyadets (goof-off), 51
Turkey, 60
Turkmenia, 207
Tuva, Siberia, 60, 85

Udakan copper mine, 143
Ukraine, 28, 44, 59, 60–61, 142, 183,
  203
Ukrsibbank, 183
unemployment, 4, 51–52, 165
United States, 115, 157–158, 210
  free trade zones, 141
  joint ventures in Russia, 2, 8, 156,
    158, 202, 209
  oil and gas investments, 2, 36, 40,
    179
Uralmash plant, Urals, 137
Urengoy gas field, Siberia, 131
U.S. Commercial Office, 123
Uzbekistan, 197

Vancouver, 168
Vanino, Russia, 151, 160, 161–162
Varangians, 60
Veblen, Thorsten, 23
Vietnam, 162
viezdnoy (travel permission), 88–89
Vladivostok, Far East, 148, 151, 156,
  157
Vnesheconombank, 210
Vneshtorgizdat trade publication, 68
volcanoes, 162–163

Volsky, Arcady, 191
Vostochniy, Russia, 158–160

wages. *See* labor force: wages
waste recycling, 92–93, 198, 199, 203, 208
Weiner, Ronald, 11
Welch, John F., 8
West Germany, 118, 135
Westinghouse, 45, 169
wholly-owned company. *See* joint venture
women, 71–72, 205–206
workers. *See* labor force
Worsham, Earl, 188, 189–190
Wrangel Island, Arctic and Far East, 168

Xerox Corporation, 65

Yakovlev, Alexander, 152, 153
Yakutia Diamond, 72, 100, 101, 103, 104, 179

Yakutia Region, 22, 169, 170, 174, 175–176
Yamal, Siberia, 35
Yeltsin, Boris, 8, 12, 19, 26, 38, 46, 201
    economic policy, 8, 208
    fiscal and monetary policy, 4, 8, 16, 21, 78, 90, 182, 187
    free market and, 16, 27, 104, 138, 139, 144, 152
    Gorbachev and, 8, 12, 15–16, 17, 205
    investment policy, 2, 3, 139, 203
Yenisey Mountains, Siberia, 124
Yenisey River, 27, 28, 34, 36, 37, 109, 124, 135, 170

zeks (prisoners), 55, 56
Zentsov, Vassiliy, 124, 132, 133, 134, 136
Zil automobile plant, 185
Zrelov, Peter, 191–192, 193
Zshmurko, Peter, 94, 172–174

kill